Inverne's Stage & Screen Trivia

The Greatest Entertainment Trivia Book Ever...

Printed and bound in Great Britain by MPG Books Ltd, Bodmin

Arcane is an imprint of Sanctuary Publishing Limited
Sanctuary House, 45–53 Sinclair Road
London W14 0NS, United Kingdom

www.sanctuarypublishing.com

ISBN: 1-86074-592-X

Inverne's Stage & Screen Trivia

The Greatest Entertainment Trivia Book Ever...

State Library OF Ohio

James Inverne

arcane

— ACKNOWLEDGEMENTS AND DEDICATION —

While I was writing this book, few people visited my house or had a conversation with me without being quizzed for ideas and more helped than I will probably remember (if I forget anyone, I hereby offer to make amends with a – quiz-free – dinner). Those I can remember and whose contributions I deeply appreciate include:

Joel Branch, Michael Brunton, Daniel Cohen, Jodie Cohen, Tim Cole, Jamie Gatoff, Sarah Halter, David Herz, Michal Herz, Richard Inverne, Michael Kessler, Zoe Kessler, John Nathan, Benedict Nightingale, Scott Robbie, Toby Stephens, Matt Wolf, David and Paula Ward.

Thanks also to the extremely helpful staff of the Theatre Museum, Covent Garden, whose archive was invaluable, as usual. Also thanks to the staff at the British Film Institute, and to Rosie Runciman at Cameron Mackintosh Ltd.

The team at Sanctuary have been as professional and supportive as ever – thanks especially on the editorial side to Iain MacGregor and Albert DePetrillo.

Raphael Guedj was a terrific fountain of original ideas (I seem to recall that the idea for an entry about prominent spanking scenes came from him).

And my most grateful thanks go to Kareen Cartier, untiring advisor and (as it happens) my wife to be – to whom this book is dedicated.

James Inverne, London 2004

— ABOUT THE AUTHOR —

James Inverne is performing arts correspondent for *Time* magazine. He also works as London theatre correspondent for *Playbill On-Line*, and regularly writes about the arts for various publications including *The Times* and the *Financial Times*. He is a frequent guest-commentator for CNN, BBC Radio and others. He is the author of *Jack Tinker: A Life In Review*, *The Impresarios* and, also published by Sanctuary, *Wrestling With Elephants: The Authorised Biography Of Don Black*.

— WOODY ALLEN ONE-LINERS #1 —

'We fell in love. Well, I fell in love, she just stood there.'
– Fielding, *Bananas* (1971)

'I wonder if she actually had an orgasm in the two years we
were married, or did she fake it that night?'
– Allan, *Play It Again, Sam* (1972)

— THE CURSE OF SUPERMAN —

The curious thing about the man of steel is that many people associated with his screen persona have encountered tragic fates. It's a mystery that would leave even Superman baffled!

The so-called 'Superman curse' first made its mark on Kirk Alyn, who played the cape twirling Kryptonian in the 1948 TV series. Afterwards, his career crumpled and he disappeared into anonymity. Alyn blamed Superman for the demise of his career and has now developed Alzheimer's disease. More dramatically, the curse hit George Reeves, who took Superman from TV to the cinema in the 1950s – he turned up dead in 1959, with a gunshot wound in his head. The inquest ruled that Reeves took his own life, though suspiciously his fingerprints were never found on the gun.

Bud Colyer, who voiced Superman in the 1941 cartoon series, thought he'd escaped when he resigned the role in 1943 and proceeded to a distinguished small-screen career. You might dodge the curse once, but twice? Colyer signed on for more Superman cartoon duties in 1966 for CBS. In 1969, he died from a circulatory disease.

Then came the much loved Christopher Reeve films. For the first time, not only Superman, but some of his fellow cast members were struck down. Margot Kidder, Reeve's Lois Lane, suffered a nervous breakdown and was found naked and babbling in a bush in LA. Richard Pryor, who had a turn as a villain in *Superman III*, found himself up against far more than the superhero. He developed multiple sclerosis. And, famously, Christopher Reeve himself fell off his horse, resulting in paralysis from the neck down.

Some have attributed Hollywood's difficulties in casting the lead in a new *Superman* film to actors being scared of the curse. W-why would anyone be s-scared?

— ALMOST-CAST ALTERNATIVES IN FAMOUS FILM ROLES —

Role	Almost cast	Actually cast
Indiana Jones *Raiders Of The Lost Ark*	Tom Selleck	Harrison Ford
Han Solo, *Star Wars*	Christopher Walken	Harrison Ford
Princess Leia, *Star Wars*	Sissy Spacek*	Carrie Fisher
Vito Corleone, *The Godfather*	Frank Sinatra Laurence Olivier Anthony Quinn	Marlon Brando
Michael Corleone *The Godfather*	James Caan† Robert Redford	Al Pacino
Lawrence *Lawrence Of Arabia*	Albert Finney	Peter O'Toole
Deckard, *Blade Runner*	Dustin Hoffman	Harrison Ford
Velma Kelly, *Chicago*	Madonna	Catherine Zeta-Jones
Rocky	Ryan O'Neal	Sylvester Stallone
The Terminator	OJ Simpson Lance Henriksen	Arnold Schwarzenegger
James Bond, *The Living Daylights*	Pierce Brosnan	Timothy Dalton

* *Spacek was cast as Leia, while Carrie Fisher had landed Brian De Palma's* Carrie. *Fisher refused to do nude scenes and so swapped roles with Spacek.*
† *Caan ended up playing Sonny Corleone, Michael's brother.*

— MOVIE STARS IN THE DOCK —

Sometimes, even a movie star has to face the judge.

OJ Simpson – One of America's most celebrated footballers, Simpson achieved international fame through his fall-guy role of Nordberg in the *Naked Gun* movies. In 1994 he was accused of murdering his wife, Nicole Brown Simpson, and her companion Ronald Goldman. The police chase to catch the fleeing OJ (around 95 million television viewers tuned in worldwide) and the resultant court proceedings dominated the news for months. It was the longest trial ever held in California and arguably the most famous court case in recent history. The world was gripped, with the verdict on 3 October 1995 reportedly watched by 91 per cent of the viewing public and listened to by 142 million over their radio sets. OJ was acquitted. He hasn't made a film since.

Robert Downey Jr – After his stunning turn as Richard Attenborough's *Chaplin* (1992), Downey widely was credited as one of the best actors of his generation. Then he ran foul of the police. June 1996 saw the 31-year-old arrested for possessing heroin, driving while drunk and possessing an unloaded gun in his truck. Found guilty, he received a suspended three-year prison sentence. Probation was awarded, but a month later he was found in a neighbour's garden, under the influence. The police took him away for drug rehabilitation treatment. The next year found Downey in the dock again for violating probation and he was imprisoned for 180 days. In March 1998 he was allowed to move to a drug rehab centre and created controversy when he was allowed out to film a movie. Come August 1999, he was back in court and this time slammed with a three-year prison term for continued parole-violations. Throughout his continued problems with drugs and the law, Hollywood seems to have supported him, offering him a steady stream of parts.

Winona Ryder – On 12 December 2001 the popular elfin movie star was arrested after being accused of shoplifting $5,570-worth of goods from a Beverly Hills Saks Fifth Avenue store. Ryder protested that she was carrying out a director's instructions in preparation for a film role. 'Free Winona' T-shirts became popular around Hollywood. However, Ryder was found guilty of grand theft and vandalism (she tore off the labels) and received three years supervised probation, 480 hours of community service and an $8,700 fine plus payments. 'She came, she stole, she left,' pronounced prosecutor Ann Rundle. Odd when you consider that Ryder's 1997 film, *Alien Resurrection*, gave her a reported $2.8 million payday.

— SOME ACTORS WHO HAVE PLAYED JESUS —

Philip Van Loan, *Jesus Of Nazareth* (1928)
Robert Powell, *Jesus Of Nazareth* (1977)
Roy Magnano, *Barabbas* (1962)
Max von Sydow, *The Greatest Story Ever Told* (1965)
Ted Neeley, *Jesus Christ Superstar* film (1973)
Kenneth Colley, *The Life Of Brian* (1979)
Willem Dafoe, *The Last Temptation Of Christ* (1988)
Matt Stone, *South Park* TV series (1997)
Mr Burns (in a self-produced movie epic for TV's *The Simpsons*)
Jeremy Sisto, *Jesus* (1999)
James Caviezel, *The Passion Of The Christ* (2004)

— JAMES BOND'S DOUBLE-ENTENDRES —

Honey Ryder: 'Are you looking for shells too?'
James Bond: 'No, I'm just looking.'
Dr No (1962)

Pussy Galore: 'My name is Pussy Galore.'
James Bond: 'I must be dreaming.'
Goldfinger (1964)

Aki: 'I think I will very much enjoy serving under you.'
You Only Live Twice (1967)

James Bond (remarking that Chinese girls taste different from all other girls): 'Like Peking Duck is different from Russian caviar.'
Chinese Girl: 'Darling, I give you very best duck.'
You Only Live Twice (1967)

Plenty O'Toole: 'Hi, I'm Plenty...Plenty O'Toole.'
James Bond: 'Named after your father, perhaps?'
Diamonds Are Forever (1971)

Solitaire: 'Is there time before we leave for Lovers' Lesson number three?'
James Bond: 'Absolutely. No sense is going out half-cocked.'
Live And Let Die (1973)

James Bond: 'I am now aiming precisely at your groin. So speak now or forever hold your piece.'
The Man With The Golden Gun (1974)

James Bond: 'When one is in Egypt, one should delve deeply into its treasures.'
The Spy Who Loved Me (1977)

M: 'Miss Moneypenny, where is 007 now?'
Moneypenny: 'He's on a mission, sir. In Austria.'
M: 'Well tell him to pull out. Immediately!'
The Spy Who Loved Me (1977)

M: 'My God, what's Bond doing?'
Q: 'I think he's attempting re-entry, sir.'
Moonraker (1979)

James Bond: 'I take it you spend quite a lot of time in the saddle.'
Jenny Flex: 'Yes, I love an early morning ride.'
James Bond: 'Well, I'm an early riser myself.'
A View To A Kill (1985)

Max Zorin: 'You slept well?'
James Bond: 'A little restless, but I got off eventually.'
A View To A Kill (1985)

James Bond (making love to his language teacher): 'I always enjoyed learning a new tongue.'
Tomorrow Never Dies (1997)

Moneypenny: 'You always were a cunning linguist, James.'
Tomorrow Never Dies (1997)

James Bond (speaking to Christmas Jones): 'I thought Christmas only comes once a year.'
The World Is Not Enough (1999)

Verity (fencing instructor): 'I see you handle your weapon well.'
James Bond: 'I have been known to keep my tip up.'
Die Another Day (2002)

Jinx (looking at Bond's crotch): 'Ornithologist, huh? Now there's a mouthful.'
Die Another Day (2002)

— THE GREAT GATSBY ON STAGE AND SCREEN —

In 1925 F Scott Fitzgerald published his novel, *The Great Gatsby*, an American parable about the dangers of pursuing dreams too intensely. Such was its popularity that it has been stage and screen-fodder ever since. A theatrical adaptation and a silent film (with Warner Baxter and Lois Wilson) came along in 1926. Another movie followed, starring Alan Ladd, in 1949, and then another screen version starring Robert Redford and Mia Farrow in 1974. The Metropolitan Opera, New York, in 1999 mounted an operatic retread, by John Harbison and starring Jerry Hadley. A TV version with Mira Sorvino and Toby Stephens arrived in 2001.

— GRADUATING —

In Mike Nichols's film *The Graduate* (1967), there is one shot where Benjamin (Dustin Hoffman) holds Mrs Robinson's breast. She ignores him, rubbing at a spot on her clothes. He turns and bangs his head against the wall. This was because breast touching was Hoffman's spur-of-the-moment idea and he was laughing so much he banged his head against the wall, convinced the shot would be cut. It stayed in.

— SCREEN STARS' BIRTH NAMES —

Not everyone's born with such a billboard-friendly name as Clint, Rock or Chuck. Here are some examples of less wieldy birth names and their famous owners.

Birth name	Changed to
Winona Horowitz	Winona Ryder
David Kaminski	Danny Kaye
Archibald Leach	Cary Grant
Marion Morrison	John Wayne
Thomas Cruise Mapother IV	Tom Cruise
Roy Harold Scherer Jr	Rock Hudson
John Charlton Carter	Charlton Heston
Greta Gustafson	Greta Garbo
Margaret Hyra	Meg Ryan
Maurice Micklewhite	Michael Caine
Ilyena Lydia Mironoff	Helen Mirren

— SPRINGING *THE MOUSETRAP* —

When Agatha Christie was retiring to her hotel bedroom on the eve of her new play's opening night in Nottingham, she called back down the stairs to members of her worried company who were discussing drastic rewrites. 'Go to sleep,' she urged, 'I'm quite sure we'll get a nice little run out of it.' Her leading man, Richard Attenborough, remembers that by 'a nice little run' she meant around four months, but for once the queen of sleuthing was wrong. *The Mousetrap* yielded an enormous, record-breaking run that has yet to reach its end.

When the play opened (with Attenborough and his wife, Sheila Sim, in the cast), a film producer bought the movie rights on the condition that it could not be filmed until the theatrical production had closed. He never lived to see that day. *The Mousetrap* reached London on 25 November 1952, at London's Ambassador's Theatre. It moved next door to the St Martin's Theatre in 1974 where, more than 50 years after its premiere, it's still going strong.

In 2002 the production celebrated its 20,000th performance. By the end of January 2004 it had played more than 21,300 performances and employed 344 actors. The production staff had also ironed some 103 miles of shirt and sold 398 tonnes of ice cream.

— DOMINGO VERSUS PAVAROTTI —

Opera-fans have long enjoyed the friendly rivalry between the two most famous tenors of the 1980s, 1990s and beyond – Placido Domingo and Luciano Pavarotti. As Pavarotti is due to retire in 2005, whom will future generations judge to have 'won?'

It's hard to tell. Although both are known for the core Italian repertoire of Verdi, Puccini and Donizetti, Domingo has a far broader range of roles. While lucky Luciano has mainly kept to his native Italians, his rival (who is Spanish) has sung a dizzying catalogue of parts – including operas by Wagner (German), Bizet (French) and Tchaikovsky (Russian). Some sources put the number of roles he has sung at 118.

But Domingo always had a heavier type of voice, suited to many different styles, and as ever it's about quality, not quantity. The best judges are their public, but there too it's hard to tell. Pavarotti holds the official record for the most curtain calls – when, on 24 February 1988 after singing in Donizetti's *L'Elisir D'Amore* at Berlin's Deutsche Oper, he was applauded for 1 hour and 7 minutes and took 165 curtain-calls. However, it's Domingo who holds the record for the longest applause – after a performance of Verdi's *Otello* at the Vienna Staatsoper in 1991, he was clapped for an amazing 1 hour and 20 minutes (during which he took 101 curtain-calls). That, incidentally, is well over half the length of the opera itself!

Verdict? Call it a draw.

— THE TEN HIGHEST GROSSING FILMS OF ALL TIME —

Box-office grosses and ratings correct as of 15/03/2004

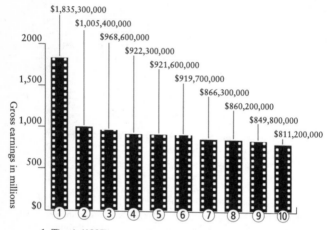

1 *Titanic* (1997)
2 *The Lord Of The Rings: The Return Of The King* (2003)
3 *Harry Potter And The Philosopher's Stone* (2001)
4 *Star Wars Episode One: The Phantom Menace* (1999)
5 *The Lord Of The Rings: The Two Towers* (2002)
6 *Jurassic Park* (1993)
7 *Harry Potter And The Chamber Of Secrets* (2002)
8 *Lord Of The Rings: The Fellowship Of The Ring* (2001)
9 *Finding Nemo* (2003)
10 *Independence Day* (1996)

— WHO WANTS TO BE A MILLIONAIRE? —

Legendary English actor Henry Irving was not only the first actor ever to be knighted, he left £20,527 when he died in 1905. Which equates to over £2 million today.

— MOVIE MISTAKES —

Given the number of people it takes to make a major movie, it's amazing how many mistakes make it through to the final print.

Jaws – Robert Shaw as the shark-hunter Quint made up his speech about the sinking of the USS *Indianapolis* and the subsequent devouring of his fellow crewmembers by sharks. Despite being much admired for his work in the scene, Shaw actually gets the date of the ship's sinking wrong, saying it was 29 June 1945. It happened on 30 June 1945. You'd think Quint would remember!

Ben-Hur – Judah (Charlton Heston) takes the ladle full of water from Jesus and then in the next shot takes it again. Some miracle! Another miracle – during the chariot race, one rider is wearing a watch.

The Shining – At a climactic moment, Wendy (Shelley Duvall) hits Jack (Jack Nicholson) with a baseball bat. But perhaps it's not the best weapon. Close observers will note that the bat bends.

The Shawshank Redemption – Crucially, Andy wears a suit belonging to the warden. And despite the fact that the inmate (Tim Robbins) is much taller than Warden Norton (Bob Gunton), the clothes fit. Well, what do you know?

The Empire Strikes Back – This well-loved movie is chock-a-block with mistakes. Two examples: when Luke (Mark Hamill) has his hand cut off, you can see the knuckles of the 'absent' hand holding the 'stump' under his shirt. And Han Solo (Harrison Ford) is mysteriously frozen in a different shirt to the one he was wearing (he's later unfrozen with the first shirt on in *Return Of The Jedi*).

Top Gun – The 'MiGs' enemy planes are in fact F5 American aircraft. There is also no MiG 28 in existence because Soviet fighter planes are given odd numbers, with other categories of aircraft given even numbers.

— THE BIRTH OF BROADWAY #1 —

The first play to be produced in New York was
Farquhar's *The Recruiting Officer* in 1732.

— 'ALWAYS LOOK ON THE BRIGHT SIDE OF LIFE' —

The unforgettable ending to Monty Python's *The Life Of Brian* features Brian and the assembled prisoners being crucified, all tunefully deciding to 'Look on the Bright Side'. The song, written and led by Pythonian Eric Idle, became an instant classic.

Some things in life are bad.
They can really make you mad.
Others just make you swear and curse.

When you're chewing on life's gristle,
Don't grumble, give a whistle,
And this'll help things turn out for the best. And...

Always look on the bright side of life (whistles).
Always look on the bright side of life (whistles).

If life seems pretty rotten,
There's something you've forgotten,
And that's to laugh and smile and dance and sing.
When you're feeling in the dumps,
Don't be silly chumps,
Just purse your lips and whistle,
That's the thing. And...

Always look on the bright side of life (whistles).
Always look on the bright side of life (whistles).

For life is quite absurd,
And death's the final word.
You must always face the curtain with a bow.
Forget about your sin,
Give the audience a grin.
Enjoy it, it's your last chance anyhow. So...

Always look on the bright side of death (whistles).
Just before you draw your terminal breath (whistles).

Life's a piece of shit,
When you look at it.
Life's a laugh and death's a joke it's true.

You'll see it's all a show,
Keep 'em laughing as you go.
Just remember 'that the last laugh is on you. And...

Always look on the bright side of life (whistles)...*continue and fade.*

— BRICKBATS —

An inevitable part of being a performer is facing the critics and sometimes wittily written bad reviews can be wickedly good fun to read. Here are some of the nastiest ever reviews.

Laurence Olivier as Shylock in *The Merchant Of Venice* (1974) for Associated Television (ATV). Reviewed by Clive James in *The Observer*: '...any fan of Walt Disney comics could turn on the TV and see that he had modelled his appearance on Scrooge McDuck.'

Peter O'Toole as Macbeth at the Old Vic Theatre, London (1980). Reviewed by Robert Cushman in *The Observer*: 'His performance suggests that he is taking some kind of personal revenge on the play.'

A revival of the musical *Godspell*, at the Old Vic Theatre, London (1981). Reviewed by Michael Billington in *The Guardian*: '*Godspell* is back in London...for those who missed it the first time, this is your golden opportunity: you can miss it again.'

Jackie Mason's first Broadway show, a play entitled *A Teaspoon Every Four Hours*, New York (1969). Reviewed by Clive Barnes in *The New York Times*: 'I realised it was not a particularly distinguished play when at the intermission I found myself rushing up the aisle for a cigarette outside. It was not until I got there that I remembered that I don't smoke.' (The play's opening night was also its last.)

— WATER-WORRIES —

Films involving water have always been a worry for financiers, prone as they are to a tidal wave of extra costs. When Lew Grade made his ill-advised sequel to the *Titanic* story, 1980s *Raise The Titanic*, he reportedly grumbled that 'It would have been cheaper to drain the ocean.'

At $36 million it became known as one of the most expensive films ever made. A $350,000 model of the *Titanic* was constructed, and then found to be too big for the water tank. So Grade then had to fork out another $6 million for a new tank.

If anything, even greater problems beset the 1995 Kevin Costner vehicle *Waterworld*. Set in a world almost completely underwater, tales of sets sinking (a storm submerged the vital Slave Colony set) and the huge expense of details such as artificial gills for Costner's character were rife. It rapidly became the most expensive film ever made, costing $175 million!

At the time it seemed wildly excessive for a film (though it defied expectations by eventually turning a profit), but another tide took costs higher for *Titanic* in 1997. Water again took its toll when the required 120,000 gallons pumped into a corridor made the set collapse, necessitating rebuilding. The sets were so massive and so many that after filming wrapped, they were sold off as scrap metal. It was estimated that the $200 million *Titanic* cost around $50 million more than the actual ship itself would have taken to build in 1997! Nevertheless, like *Waterworld* before it (though unlike *Raise The Titanic*), it made money.

— WOODY ALLEN ONE-LINERS #2 —

'No, my parents never got divorced, although I begged them to.'
– Allan, *Play It Again, Sam* (1972)

'If it turns out that there *is* a God, I don't think that he's evil. I think that the worst you can say about him is that basically he's an under-achiever.'
– Boris, *Love And Death* (1975)

— THE *MONKEY MAGIC* THEME SONG —

Born from an egg on a mountain top,
The funkiest monkey that ever popped.
He knew every magic trick under the sun,
To tease the gods,
And everyone and have some fun.

CHORUS:
Monkey magic,
Monkey magic.
Monkey magic,
Monkey magic.

What a cocky saucy monkey this one is.
All the gods were angered,
And they punished him.
Until he was saved by a kindly priest,
And that was the start
Of their pilgrimage west.

CHORUS

With a little bit of monkey magic,
There'll be fireworks tonight.
With a little bit of monkey magic,
Everything will be all right.

Born from an egg on a mountain top,
The funkiest monkey that ever popped.
He knew every magic trick under the sun,
To tease the gods,
And everyone and have some fun.

by Micky Yoshino

— THE REAL SHERLOCK HOLMES —

Almost since its inception, Sherlock Holmes has been a mainstay of the large and small screen, not to mention the stage, with notable actors to don the deerstalker including John Barrymore, Basil Rathbone, Frank Langella, Peter O'Toole, Christopher Plummer, Michael Caine, Jeremy Brett, Christopher Lee and Roger Moore. In fact, more than 70 actors have played him in over 211 films since 1900. Yet no one has been able to definitively solve the detective's most profound and mysterious riddle. Just who was Holmes?

Are we to trust the character's creator Arthur Conan Doyle, who credited his famous Baker Street resident to one Dr Joseph Bell, a surgeon born in 1837, who practised the distinctly Holmesian trick of looking at a patient to deduce, not only his illness, but also where he lived and what he did for a living? For a time Doyle worked as Bell's outpatient clerk and greatly admired his powers of observation. There are, however, other suspects.

Holmes scholar Owen Dudley Edwards has written of Professor Robert Christison (born 1797), a Scottish toxicologist who worked on the famous trial of Edinburgh body snatchers Burke and Hare and whose methods of experimental science included hitting a dead body to see whether it bruised. That's very Sherlock, as was the Bayswater professional detective Wendel Scherer who became famous for murder investigations around four years before Doyle created his sleuth. Also, there was American anatomy professor and author Oliver Wendell Holmes (spot the surname!), whose writing was eagerly devoured by an admiring Doyle. As for Sherlock's appearance, Walter Paget, the brother of Sidney Paget, the stories' original illustrator in *The Illustrated London News*, is credited with providing the Holmes features and his deerstalker, which Doyle never refers to. As for the distinctive pipe, it came from the imagination of an American illustrator, Frederick Dorr.

So then, what is the verdict in the search for the real Sherlock Holmes? As with all the best murders, it seems there are a number of accomplices.

— THE ROCKY HORROR PICTURE SHOW NEED-TO-KNOWS —

Since its 1973 London stage debut, and then its 1975 screen bow, Richard O Brien's *The Rocky Horror Picture Show* has been a cult hit unlike any other. Faithful devotees, who turn up to live performances and screenings appropriately dressed as the characters (with Transylvania's 'sweet transvestite' a favourite), have evolved their own audience participation rituals for each performance and screening. It can be nerve-wracking trying to keep up for those new to the experience, so here are a few pointers.

• Whenever the character of Brad is mentioned, the audience should shout 'Arsehole.'
• His girlfriend Janet is in the same way labelled a 'slut'. Rice should be thrown during both wedding scenes. Confetti is also fine.
• For the movie, toast should be thrown during the dinner scene. In the play, party poppers can be popped during the 'Happy Birthday' scene.
• During the storm, audience members should fire water pistols and hold newspapers over their heads.
• During the line 'cards for sorrow, cards for pain', playing cards should be thrown.
• In the song 'There's a light (over at the Frankenstein place)', torches should be waved.
• Rubber gloves should be snapped during the creation scene.

— REAL-LIFE FILM LOCATIONS —

There are a tribe of film fans who like to spend their holidays scouring the world for the real-life locations of their favourite film scenes. Many of the settings are pretty easy to find – you just need to know where to look! Here are ten of the best.

Back To The Future – Marty's school, in which the early scenes are set, is actually Whittier High School in Whittier, California. The Twin Pines Mall is the Puente Hills Mall in the City Of Industry, California.

Talking of school and 1980s movies, the Glenbrook North High School in Northbrook, Illinois, is the school setting for two seminal teen flicks – *The Breakfast Club* and *Ferris Beuller's Day Off*. This is hardly surprising since John Hughes, the director of both films, is a Glenbrook North old boy!

Jaws – The fictional Amity Island, which a famous great white decides to make his personal canteen, is in fact Martha's Vineyard, Massachusetts. Most of the locations are largely unchanged.

The Sound Of Music – Salzburg, Austria, was Julie Andrews's stomping ground and there are many recognisable landmarks still there, including the horse fountain and the Mozart footbridge. One of the score's most famous numbers, 'Do-Re-Mi', was mainly filmed in the Mirabell Gardens.

Ghostbusters – The monumental apartment building where Sigourney Weaver found demons in her fridge is 55 Central Park West, New York.

Lawrence Of Arabia – Many of the sweeping desert vistas in David Lean's epic are found in Ait Benhaddou, Morocco. The same location was used for the desert in the Michael Douglas feature, *Jewel Of The Nile*.

Out Of Africa – There were equally spectacular views in this Robert Redford vehicle, which was shot mainly around Kenya – especially Kenya's National Game Reserve.

Withnail And I – Richard E Grant and Paul McGann's boozy holiday is taken in Penrith, in England's Lake District.

Jurassic Park – The gorgeous yet lethal island of the dinosaurs was principally filmed around Hawaii, with notable locations in the Olokele Valley, Kualoa Ranch, Lawai and Kauai.

— SOME ACTORS WHO HAVE PLAYED US PRESIDENTS —

George A Billings, *The Dramatic Life Of Abraham Lincoln* (1924)
Walter Huston, *Abraham Lincoln* (1930)
Henry Fonda, *Fail Safe* (1964)
Peter Sellers, *Dr Strangelove* (1964)
Charlton Heston, *F.D.R.* (1965)
Hal Holbrook, *Lincoln* (1975)
EG Marshall, *Superman II* (1980)
Edward Herrmann, *Annie* (1982)
Martin Sheen, *Kennedy* (1983)
Barry Bostwick, *George Washington* (1984)
Sam Waterston, *Lincoln* (1988)
Jason Robards, *Lincoln* (1992)
Kevin Kline, *Dave* (1993)
Donald Moffat, *Clear And Present Danger* (1994)
Anthony Hopkins, *Nixon* (1995)
Michael Douglas, *The American President* (1995)
Jack Nicholson, *Mars Attacks* (1996)
Harrison Ford, *Air Force One* (1997)
Morgan Freeman, *Deep Impact* (1998)
Martin Sheen, *The West Wing* TV series (from 1999)
John Goodman, *The West Wing* TV series (from 1999)
Bruce Greenwood, *Thirteen Days* (2000)
Richard Dreyfuss, *Fail Safe* (2000)
Jon Voight, *Pearl Harbor* (2001)
James Brolin, *The Reagans* (2003)

— 'GREED IS GOOD' —

The most famous quote from the 1987 film *Wall Street*, spoken by Michael Douglas, has passed into folklore:

> 'The point is ladies and gentlemen that greed, for lack of a better word, is good. Greed is right. Greed works. Greed clarifies, cuts through and captures the essence of the evolutionary spirit. Greed, in all its forms – greed for life, money, knowledge – has marked the upward surge of mankind and greed, you mark my words, will not only save Teldar Paper but that other malfunctioning corporation called the USA.'

— SIMPSONS CELEBRITIES —

The Simpsons has been a mainstay of worldwide television schedules since it broke free of its progenitor, the *Tracy Ullman Show*, in 1989. It is now the longest-running comedy series in the history of American TV. A key ingredient of its success has been the gimmick of matching the voices of real-life celebrities to their lookalike, Springfield-yellow counterparts. Here are some classic examples.

• Elton John plays himself in the episode 'I'm With Cupid'. Key line: 'When I was dubbed Sir Elton the Queen paddled me silly!'

• Aerosmith play themselves in the episode 'Flaming Moe's'. Key line: 'Mrs Krabappel, I really need my drumsticks.'

• Meryl Streep plays Jessica Lovejoy, Bart's mean girlfriend in the episode 'Bart's Girlfriend'. Key line: 'You're just yellow trash.'

• Bette Midler plays herself in the episode 'Krusty Gets Cancelled'. Key line: 'It's time to take out the trash.'

• The Red Hot Chilli Peppers play themselves in the episode 'Krusty Gets Cancelled'. Key line: 'Our lyrics are like our children, man!'

• Dustin Hoffman plays Mr Bergstrom in the episode 'Lisa's Substitute'. Key line: 'You're trying to seduce me, Mrs Krabappel.'

• Gillian Anderson and David Duchovny play agents Mulder and Scully in the episode 'The Springfield Files'. Key line: Mulder: '(Homer's) jiggling is almost hypnotic.' Scully: 'Yes. It's like a lava lamp.'

• Elizabeth Taylor plays Maggie in the episode 'Krusty Gets Cancelled'. Key line: 'Daddy.'

• Mel Brooks plays himself in the episode 'Homer vs. Patty And Selma'. Key line: 'I hate Rob Reiner!'

• Mel Gibson plays himself in the episode 'Beyond Blunderdome'. Key line: 'It's hell being Mel.'

• Jackie Mason plays Rabbi Hyman Krustofski, Krusty's father, in 'Like Father, Like Clown'. Key line: 'Pies are for noshing, not for throwing.'

• Danny DeVito plays Herb Powell, Homer's long-lost half-brother, in the episodes 'Oh Brother, Where Art Thou?' and 'Brother, Can You Spare Two Dimes?' Key line: 'So many conflicting emotions. How to express them?' (He punches Homer in the face.)

• Michelle Pfeiffer plays Mindy Simmons, the new worker at the nuclear factory who tempts Homer in 'The Last Temptation Of Homer'. Key line: 'Let's do it – let's call room service!'

• Jerry Springer plays himself in the episode 'Treehouse Of Horror 9'. Key line: 'Homer, how did it feel to learn your baby was fathered by a drooling space octopus?'

• Tony Blair plays himself in the episode 'The Regina Monologues'. Key line: TB: 'Hello. Welcome To England.' Homer: 'Wow. I can't believe we just met Mr Bean!'

— INDIAN THEATRE —

The earliest Indian theatre evolved from religious ceremonies, with wandering players visiting temples and palaces – where the stages were consecrated before the performance. It was the British who built the first permanent theatre in India, in Calcutta in 1776.

The first plays came from Bhasa in the south and were written in Sanskrit. They ranged from small-scale stories like *The Little Clay Cart*, to vast epics like the *Ramayana* and the *Mahabharata*. Kalidsa, the best-known Sanskrit playwright, was born towards the end of the 4th century. His play *Shakuntala*, about a hermit's daughter who marries a king, influenced the 18th century trend for romanticism in European drama, chief among which was Shakespeare's *Cymbeline*. Other great Sanskrit playwrights include the great writer of the north, Sri Harsha (born in 590 or thereabouts). About 160 years later came Bhavabhuti, whose *Rama's Later History* is considered one of the true masterpieces of Indian drama.

— THE GOODFELLAS HELICOPTER SCENE —

Martin Scorsese's headrush of a 1990 gangster classic culminates in the great scene where lowish-grade Mafioso Henry Hill (Ray Liotta) is finally caught. As his last day of freedom spirals out of control, a helicopter that he thinks is an FBI surveillance unit, hovering ominously above him, increasingly maddens Henry. Worse, he has to rush all over the place, between cooking a family meal, preparing drugs and visiting his invalid brother in hospital. More and more frenetic, the day becomes a drugs and anxiety-fuelled blur. To clarify matters, here are the details.

Sunday 11 May 1980, 6:55am – Henry snorts cocaine, packs some guns into a cardboard bag and, noticing a helicopter in the sky, drives to his associate Jimmy's (Robert De Niro) to deliver the guns. As he drives, he nervously looks up at the helicopter, which appears to be following him. Jimmy angrily rejects the guns, which don't fit his silencers.

8:05am – Henry is on the way to the hospital to see his brother Michael. He's so busy looking up at the helicopter that he nearly drives into the car in front of him. Collecting his thoughts, he makes it to the hospital for 8:45am. Michael's doctor insists on examining him, administering 10mg of Valium. Driving Michael back to his house, Henry points out the helicopter, but his brother isn't convinced that it's on his trail.

11:30am – Henry starts preparing that night's family dinner. He has to braise the meat, for his meal – Michael's favourite – zilli with meat gravy, flame-roasted peppers, string beans with olive oil and, as an appetiser, garlic with cutlets. He checks outside the door to check if the helicopter is gone. Leaving Michael to watch the sauce, he takes his wife Karen in the car. They plan to sell the guns Jimmy has rejected and pick up drugs for a shipment to Atlanta that night. On the way Karen spots the helicopter's return and they decide to divert to her mother's, where they hide the bag of guns in a dustbin. Once the sky is clear they drive to a shopping mall where Henry telephones an unnamed gangster to report the helicopter (he's told that he is paranoid).

1:30pm – They leave the mall, return to Karen's mother's house and pick up the guns.

3:30pm – They reach Henry's Pittsburgh associates, offload the guns and Karen takes some drugs ('I'll show you helicopters!' jokes the dealer). Henry phones his home-helper and drugs delivery girl Lois to remind her to use a public phone to call about the imminent deal. After she hangs up with him, she uses the house phone for the call, supplying the listening FBI agents with the shipment details.

6:30pm – Henry reaches home and begins cooking in earnest. By 8:30pm he is at his mistress's flat to pick up the drugs she has been mixing for him.

10:45pm – Henry and family eat dinner. After the meal, just as Henry is about to leave to take Lois to the airport to deliver the drugs, she declares that she has to go to her home in Rockway to pick up her 'lucky hat'. Irritatedly, he hides the drugs package in a kitchen cupboard and gets in the car to drive Lois home. He is still in the drive when an FBI agent points a gun at him and orders him to freeze. In the house, Karen runs wildly upstairs and pours the drugs into the toilet. Hammering is heard on the door. Next stop, the police station.

— LONDON'S LOST THEATRES —

All of the following were once major London theatres, now redeveloped or demolished.

- Daly's Theatre – Now the Warner Village cinema complex in Leicester Square.
- The Alhambra Theatre – Now the main Odeon cinema in Leicester Square.
- The Opera Comique – Demolished, was on the Strand.
- The Pantheon – Oxford Street, now a branch of Marks & Spencer.
- The Queen's Theatre – Long Acre. The site, between Endell Street and Charles Street, redeveloped.
- The St James's Theatre – King's Street, St James. Turned into offices.
- Terry's Theatre – Demolished. Stood between 105 and 109, The Strand.
- The Tivoli Theatre – The Strand. The site, between Durham House Street and Adam Street, was redeveloped as shops.
- The Trocadero Palace Of Varieties – Great Windmill Street, Soho, has been redeveloped.

— KILLING DRACULA —

According to Bram Stoker, it was all very simple – to kill Dracula, king of the bloodsuckers, you just had to chop off his head and fill it with garlic, then finish him off by driving a stake through his unholy heart. Assuming, of course, you had the bottle to get that close. In the movies, though, it doesn't always work the way the author intends and the demands of sequels and audiences have kept an inventive stream of new ideas for killing the undead!

The Hammer Horror films starred Christopher Lee as Dracula in a series that required the prince of darkness to be killed in a dazzling array of crowd-pleasing ends (he was, of course, always revived in the next film). In *Dracula* (1957), Lee was foiled by daylight streaming through the windows of his dining room. *Dracula, Prince Of Darkness* (1965) sees the rule that fresh flowing water kills him, as he falls into an ice-covered river. In 1968, *Dracula Has Risen From The Grave* has him impaled on a giant cross. *Taste The Blood Of Dracula* in 1969 had poor Drac overcome by the religious imagery in an abandoned church (death by religion-rage), while *Scars Of Dracula* (1970) sees him set on fire by a bolt of lightning and then, just in case, he falls into a ravine. *Dracula A.D. 1972* has Dracula, who must have been getting a bit depressed by this point, falling into a grave lined with stakes. Oh, and as if that weren't enough, Van Helsing drives another stake into his heart. Finally for Lee, *The Satanic Rites Of Dracula* (1972) has Van Helsing lure his old enemy into a hawthorn bush – apparently hawthorn branches were used to make the crown that Christ wore when crucified. Another stake through the heart and Lee's Dracula hung up his cape. Well, wouldn't you?

Other vamp-killing fun from Hammer saw Van Helsing (again) take on long-toothed Baron Meinster in *Brides Of Dracula* (1960), blind him with holy water then trap him in the shadow of a cross which he makes from the blades of a windmill. And in a 'kill one bird with two stones' moment, Carmilla Karnstein is left in a burning castle and then impaled by a burning beam in *Lust For A Vampire* (1970).

Joel Schumacher's 1987 cult classic *The Lost Boys* features one particularly nasty teen-vamp getting electrocuted by a sound-system. 'Death by stereo!' says his young opponent in awe.

In Quentin Tarantino's 1996 fang-fest, *From Dusk Till Dawn*, Harvey Keitel and friends came up with some novel spins on the old methods. A crossbow became a stake-shooting automatic weapon. While condoms filled with water became, once Keitel had blessed them, holy hand grenades.

Wesley Snipes has several interesting new methods in the *Blade* films. The day-walker kills vamps with everything to hand, from a samurai sword, to deadly injections, to a frankly harmless looking blue torch. Who says the life of the undead is fun?

— SOME ACTORS WHO HAVE PLAYED GOD —

Charlton Heston, *The Ten Commandments* (1956)
Graham Chapman, *Monty Python And The Holy Grail* (1975)
George Burns, *Oh, God!* (1977)
George Burns, *Oh, God! Book II* (1980)
Ralph Richardson, *Time Bandits* (1981)
George Burns, *Oh, God! You Devil* (1984)
Val Kilmer, *Prince Of Egypt* (1998)
Alanis Morissette, *Dogma* (1999)
Morgan Freeman, *Bruce Almighty* (2003)

— SOME ACTORS WHO HAVE PLAYED THE DEVIL —

Emil Jannings, *Faust* (1926)
Walter Huston, *The Devil And Daniel Webster* (1941)
David Warner, *Time Bandits* (1981)
George Burns, *Oh, God! You Devil* (1984)
Billy Zane, *The Demon Knight* (1995)
Viggo Mortensen, *The Prophecy* (1995)
Billy Crystal, *Deconstructing Harry* (1997)
Al Pacino, *The Devil's Advocate* (1997)
Stan Marsh, *South Park: Bigger, Longer And Uncut* (1999)
Jennifer Love Hewitt, *The Devil And Daniel Webster* (2001)
Rosalinda Celentano, *The Passion Of The Christ* (2004)

— COPPOLA'S GODFATHER FAMILY TREE —

Francis Ford Coppola may be known as one of the great film directors, but he's equally well known for including members of his family in his movies. In *The Godfather* trilogy, this penchant reached mafia-like proportions.

Coppola's father Carmine Coppola had been first flautist in Arturo Toscanini's NBC Symphony Orchestra. He was also a talented composer, so Francis gave him joint composing credit with Nino Rota. Rota came up with the grand themes, Coppola senior with the peasant or generic Italian music (such as the famous tarantella at Connie's wedding). Coppola eventually won an Oscar jointly with Rota for his work and when Coppola himself collected an award he thanked the Academy 'for giving an Oscar to my Dad'. Carmine also conducted the score, Rota giving way as a favour to his director. There was a further tribute to Daddy Coppola in a scene from *The Godfather, Part II* where a boy plays a flute. Eventually cut, it resurfaced in the 30th anniversary DVD edition.

The important role of Connie Corleone was given to Talia Shire, Francis's sister. She made a notable success in the role, and in *The Godfather, Part III* Connie became an even more key character. She won an Oscar nomination for her performance in *The Godfather, Part II*.

Far more controversial was the casting of Sofia Coppola, Francis's daughter. She was born during the filming of the first *The Godfather* and in that film plays Connie's baby boy in the christening scene. However, when it came to the second sequel, Winona Ryder withdrew from the role of Michael Corleone's daughter Mary and Coppola cast 18-year-old Sofia in the part (meaning, of course, that her aunt Talia Shire was playing her aunt in the movie). The critics didn't like her performance and accusations of nepotism resounded. Perhaps alienated from a career in front of the camera, she is now a successful director (*The Virgin Suicides, Lost In Translation*).

The little girl who runs to dance with Sofia Coppola and Al Pacino in the party scene of *The Godfather, Part III* is Francis's granddaughter Gia who, seeing her aunt dancing, couldn't resist joining in! Sophia's brother Gio died in a boating accident in 1986, but a picture he drew of Francis in a limousine features in both the first and third movies of the trilogy. Her other brother Roman appears in *The Godfather, Part II* as the young Sonny Corleone. Sophia is also in that film as a child on a ship coming into New York. And one Vincent Coppola, who can be seen as a street vendor, also sounds suspiciously like a relative.

A front-runner for the role of Mary's cousin and lover in *The Godfather, Part III*, Vincent Corleone, was Nicolas Cage, though he lost out to Andy Garcia. Cage is Francis Ford Coppola's nephew.

In *The Godfather, Part III* the uncredited orchestra conductor in Michael's party scene is in fact Anton Coppola, Carmine's brother and Francis's uncle. He did indeed conduct the film's score, act as opera adviser, and his son Bruno Coppola came on board as financial technical adviser. Which is all rather apt for a story about 'the family!'

— *CATS* FACTS —

Andrew Lloyd Webber's moggie mega-hit was based on 14 poems from TS Eliot's *Old Possum's Book Of Practical Cats*, and was widely credited with proving that stage musicals could do far bigger business than previously thought possible.

• Since its 11 May 1981 opening, *Cats* has been seen in 32 countries and over 340 cities.

• It has been translated into 12 languages: Japanese, Korean, German, Hungarian, Norwegian, Finnish, Dutch, Swedish, French, Spanish, Italian and Danish. The title, however, has never been translated.

• There have been over 100 different versions and recordings of the show's hit song, 'Memory'.

• On 29 January 1996 *Cats* overtook *A Chorus Line* to become the longest-running musical in the history of the West End and Broadway, with its 6,141st performance. When the New York production closed in September 2000, over 10 million people at 7,485 performances had seen it.

• The London production closed on its 21st birthday, 11 May 2002, having taken over £136 million at the box-office.

• Worldwide the show has been seen by over 50 million people and grossed over $2 billion.

— THE ZANNI —

Zanni is the Italian collective name for the stock characters of the Commedia Dell'Arte Italian theatre tradition that flourished in the 16th and 17th centuries (Zanni referred specifically to the servant characters such as Arlecchino). In England the word moved into common usage as zani (zany), meaning a clown.

There were seven original zanni:

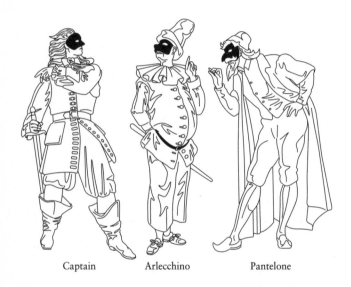

Captain   Arlecchino   Pantelone

Arlecchino – A servant to the Doctor, Pantelone or the Captain. Clever, he spends his time trying to outwit his employers, though he almost always fails. He wears a belt with a stick made out of two strips of wood that slapped against each other when they hit something (or somebody!). This is called a slapstick, which is where the modern word comes from. So Arlecchino, an acrobat who tumbles his way through the show, was the first slapstick character!

Captain – A young, adventurous soldier, usually extremely pompous and also secretly a coward.

Columbino – He is the main servant.

The Innamorati – Lovers, who appear with various names including Flavio and Vittoria, or Isabella and Lelio. They are noble, but caused by their love to act below the grace that their station demands.

Pantelone – An old man, he is usually a miserly Viennese merchant, who traditionally is deceived by his wife, servant, or son.

Pulcinella – The hunchback, traditionally equipped with long red nose, three-cornered cap and dark cape; he is a nasty bachelor always scheming to win the pretty girls.

La Ruffiana – An old woman who tries to come between Harlequin and Harlequine.

— BOMBING THE PIER THEATRE —

The 820-seater Pier Theatre at the end of Bournemouth's most famous landmark is a quaint throwback to the south coast town's tourist-happy 1960s heyday. Now it's a regular hotspot for Ray Cooney sex farces or murder mysteries, but it nearly became famous in 1993 for quite a different reason.

That summer the Conservative government were holding their annual party conference in the town, and the IRA began a steady bombing campaign in the town. A prominent furniture shop was blown up, other bombs were found and rumours began flying that the terrorists had planted a major bomb for the campaign's final, tragic flourish. That evening the Pier Theatre was due to play a farce starring the one-time dancer turned TV celebrity, Lionel Blair. An hour before curtain-up the town's police found enough explosives planted underneath the pier to utterly destroy it, including the theatregoers. The bomb was removed and the performance went ahead safely.

— DILWALE DULHANIA LE JAYENGE —

Dilwale Dulhania Le Jayenge (The Brave-Hearted Will Take The Bride) is a Bollywood classic. When it opened in India in 1995, it was an instant smash-hit, winning ten Filmfare Awards and enjoying huge amounts of repeat business.

Not bad for first-time film director Aditya Chopra, with music by Jatin Lalit and lyrics by Anand Bakshi. It starred Kajol and Shah Rukh Khan, propelling Khan to superstardom and making the two of them one of Bollywood's best-loved screen couples.

One of the most interesting aspects of the story was that it concerns young Indians living in London, yet reinforces traditional Indian values like respect for the older generations while also – of course – spinning a yarn about true love conquering all.

Kajol plays Simran, whose father has arranged for her to marry the son of his best friend. She asks for one last taste of liberty before she marries and her father (played by Amrish Puri) allows her to go travelling around Europe. Khan is a rich playboy, Raj Malhotra, who also goes travelling and predictably meets Simran. They spend a great deal of time together, begin by hating each other and eventually fall in love. They return to London and regretfully part.

The story shifts to India where Simran is to marry. Raj's father advises him that, if he truly loves Simran, he must go to Punjab to claim her. In Punjab, Simran and her family prepare for the wedding. Raj turns up and makes friends with the idiotic groom, who brings him into the wedding household. However, Simran's family think that he's interested in her sister and he finally has to reveal all. It ends happily, but not after an unexpected kung-fu fight at a railway station!

— WOODY ALLEN ONE-LINERS #3 —

'I don't wanna badmouth the kid, but he's a horrible, dishonest, immoral louse. And I say that with all due respect.'
– Danny Rose, *Broadway Danny Rose* (1984)

'For me, love is very deep, but sex only has to go a few inches.'
– Rita, *Bullets Over Broadway* (1994)

— KNIGHT-RIDING: KIT'S KIT —

Everyone who watched the cult 1980s TV series *Knight Rider* dreamed, with varying degrees of desperation, of driving super-car KITT (Knight Industry Two Thousand) for themselves. Those fans that weren't dreaming of its sleek-haired driver David Hasselhoff, that is. Anyway, here are some of KITT's mouth-watering special features.

- Voice Synthesiser
- Anti-Theft System
- ATX Surveillance Equipment
- Audio/Video Record, Playback and Transmit
- Auto Currency Dispenser
- Auto Cruise
- Blood Analyser
- Chemical Scan
- Composite Identification Mode
- Computer Override
- Hydraulic Ejector Seats
- Grappling Hook/Winch
- Ground-To-Air Surveillance
- Heat Sensors
- Homing Device
- Infrared Tracking Scanner
- Laser
- Medical Scan
- Oil Slick
- Phone Tap
- Pursuit Mode
- Radar
- Retro Rockets
- Silent Mode
- Ski Mode
- Tear Gas
- Telephone Trace
- Traffic Control System
- Turbo Boost
- X-Ray Mode

— THE SHAKESPEARE PLAYS —

Comedies

All's Well That Ends Well
As You Like It
The Comedy Of Errors
Cymbeline
Love's Labour's Lost
Measure For Measure
The Merry Wives Of Windsor
The Merchant Of Venice
A Midsummer Night's Dream
Much Ado About Nothing
Pericles, Prince Of Tyre
The Taming Of The Shrew
The Tempest
Troilus And Cressida
Twelfth Night
Two Gentlemen Of Verona
The Winter's Tale

Histories

King John
King Richard II
King Henry IV, Part One
King Henry IV, Part Two
King Henry V
King Henry VI, Part One
King Henry VI, Part Two
King Henry VI, Part Three
King Richard III
King Henry VIII

Tragedies

Antony And Cleopatra
Coriolanus
Hamlet, Prince Of Denmark
Julius Caesar
King Lear

Macbeth
Othello, Moor Of Venice
Romeo And Juliet
Timon Of Athens
Titus Andronicus

Possibly written or co-written by Shakespeare

Edward III
The Two Noble Kinsmen
Sir Thomas Moore
Cardenio*
Love's Labours Won†

* *Rumoured to be written by Shakespeare, but no text has survived*
† *As above, though scholars believe this may just have been a contemporary nickname for another of his plays*

— 'TOO DARN HOT' AND THE KINSEY REPORT —

One of the big show-stopping songs in Cole Porter's 1948 musical *Kiss Me Kate* is the steaming dance number, 'Too Darn Hot'. The song quotes 'the Kinsey report' as evidence that when the weather is hot there is less sexual activity.

'According to the Kinsey report every average man you know,
Much prefers his lover-dovey to court when the temperature is low.
But when the thermometer goes way up and the weather is sizzling hot,
Mister Pants, for romance, is not.
'Cause it's too, too, too darn hot!'

Alfred Kinsey's report *Sexual Behaviour In The Human Male*, also from 1948, was a study based on Kinsey's observation of a variety of people over several years (each subject was questioned on up to 521 items). Many of Kinsey's findings were shocking at the time, for instance that most sex was solo. America's National Research Council hired the American Statistical Association to examine Kinsey's report (and its sequel, about females). The checks revealed the report to be groundbreaking, but took six years to finish, by which time Kinsey had been effectively smeared, and most of his financial backers scared away. He died soon afterwards.

— THE SCOTTISH PLAY —

Why are actors obsessed with Shakespeare's chiller, *Macbeth* (or, as it could be called, *The Bard's Witch Project*)? If an actor says the play's name backstage, tradition dictates that he should leave the room, spin round three times, spit, knock thrice and beg to be allowed back in. Alternatively, he could recite the 'lucky' Shakespeare line, 'Fair thoughts and happy hours attend on you' (from *The Merchant Of Venice*). As someone who once appeared in an amateur production of *The Winter's Tale* in which there were two major late withdrawals and one suicide, I've never believed in the curse of *Macbeth*. But, there have been some startling accidents surrounding the play.

• A 1721 production ended with actors attacking an unruly audience; the army was called in.

• In 1937 Laurence Olivier played Macbeth at London's Old Vic; an audience member suffered a fatal heart attack when a fragment of Olivier's sword hit her.

• In 1947 Harold Norman, as Macbeth, was killed in the battle-scene.

• Cape Town, date unknown – a bystander watched some scenery being winched into a theatre. When he asked which play it was for, and was given the answer, 'Macbeth', a spear fell out of the load on the winch and skewered the bystander, killing him outright.

The most likely reason, scholars agree, for the superstition surrounding *Macbeth* is, ironically, the play's popularity in the 19th century. A surefire hit, theatre companies in financial trouble always presented it. So actors came to associate it with the threat of unemployment.

— *THE MAGNIFICENT SEVEN* —

Chris Adams, played by Yul Brynner
Vin, played by Steve McQueen
Bernardo O'Reilly, played by Charles Bronson
Britt, played by James Coburn
Lee, played by Robert Vaughn
Chico, played by Horst Buchholz
Harry Luck, played by Brad Dexter

— HOW UNIVERSAL STUDIOS GOT ITS NAME —

Universal, one of Hollywood's mightiest and best-known film studios, got its name in a very mundane manner. No flash of inspiration, no great marketing strategy. One day in 1912, the studio's founder Carl Laemmle (a German immigrant who landed in the US in 1884 with $40 in his pocket) looked out of his New York office window and saw a van drive past with the name 'Universal Pipe Fitting' emblazoned on the side. Aha, he thought, Universal – a very good name for his new film production company. And that was that!

— *DEAD POETS' SOCIETY* GRADUATES —

So what happened to all those promising young lads Robin Williams nurtured in the 1989 film, *Dead Poets' Society*? While some of them 'seized the day' (or carpe diem, as Williams's Mr Keating would say), others have been less successful.

Robert Sean Leonard – played Neil Perry, went on to star in *Much Ado About Nothing* (1993) and *The Last Days Of Disco* (1998). Is a Broadway regular, with hits including *The Iceman Cometh* opposite Kevin Spacey.

Ethan Hawke – played Todd Anderson. Went on to film stardom in *Alive* (1993), *Reality Bites* (1994) and *Before Sunrise* (1995). Was paid a reported $12 million for 2002's *Training Day*.

Gale Hansen – played Charlie Dalton, has been less high profile than some of his colleagues, mostly active in theatre.

Dylan Kussman – played Richard Cameron, has stayed active in TV and film, but not always in starring roles. (He played Stryker Soldier Wilkins 2003's *X2*.)

Allelon Ruggiero – played Steven Meeks, has done some directing and acting, but hasn't reached stardom. In 2002 took the lead in a horror flick about a country club's slasher gardener called *The Greenskeeper*.

James Waterston – played Gerard Pitts. Son of film star Sam Waterston, James has stayed in regular employment, appearing in 2002 with Dick Van Dyke in TV movie *Without Warning*, and alongside Michael Keaton and Helena Bonham Carter in TV movie *Live From Baghdad*.

— TOP THEATRE RESTAURANTS —

While you're splashing out on West End theatre tickets, you might as well treat yourself to a good dinner after the show! Finding a decent restaurant amidst London's tourist traps can be tricky, which is why we've compiled a brief list of some of the places the stars like to eat. After all, if it's good enough for Madonna and Gwyneth Paltrow…

Top Theatre Restaurants

THE IVY

The elegant Queen of Litchfield Street, opposite both the St. Martin's and New Ambassadors theatres, attracts a top-class clientele. Not just acting stars, either. It's quite common to see, say, Andrew Lloyd Webber sitting near prominent politician Gerald Kauffman, with the Pet Shop Boys or a national newspaper editor at a nearby table. Despite its fame, the stained glass windows have the joint effect of keeping prying eyes away and giving the place the air of a private club. One tip: it's not the 'done' thing to autograph-hunt here

JOE ALLEN

Theatre posters line the stairs to this buzzing underground Exeter Street bolt-hole, near the Royal Opera House and the Strand Theatre and just behind the Lyceum. A pianist plays songs from the shows as customers munch the much-admired hamburgers. (They're not on the menu, but regulars know to ask.) Popular for casts of nearby shows to drop in after performances, get there around 10pm if you want to see some big names.

Top Theatre Restaurants

SARASTRO

Not a place much frequented by the theatre cognoscenti, perhaps, but the Drury Lane Turkish restaurant is, as it boasts, 'the show after the show'. The entire place is decked out like the set of a lavish production of Mozart's opera The Magic Flute. You can actually sit in an opera box to eat while serenaded with your operatic favourites. Something to see, and conveniently located behind Drury Lane's Theatre Royal, near the Fortune Theatre.

ORSO

Round the corner from Joe Allen is another cavern-like refuge, specialising in Italian food. Wellington Street's Orso is a beloved haunt of showbiz power-players, producers and the like.

SAVOY GRILL

One of London's best-known restaurants, situated in the Savoy Hotel, set back from the Strand and within trotting distance of the Adelphi and Vaudeville Theatres. Not cheap, and smart dress is recommended, but the great and good go there.

— THE BIRTH OF BROADWAY #2 —

The first proper cabaret on Broadway was the *Folies Bergere*, established by Jesse Lasky in 1911.

— THE ORIGINAL CAST OF *EASTENDERS* —

Characters come and go in this popular BBC soap opera, but it was the original cast who first made it work. Here they are, as they appeared in series one, which first began broadcasting in the UK on Tuesday 19 February 1985.

Leslie Grantham – Den Watts, landlord of the Queen Vic
Anita Dobson – Angie Watts, his wife
Letitia Dean – Sharon Watts, their daughter
Anna Wing – Lou Beale, Pauline's mother
Bill Treacher – Arthur Fowler
Wendy Richard – Pauline Fowler
David Scarboro – Mark Fowler, Pauline and Arthur's son
Susan Tully – Michelle Fowler, Pauline and Arthur's daughter
Peter Dean – Pete Beale, Pauline's brother, fruit and veg vendor
Gillian Taylforth – Kathy Beale, Pete's wife
Adam Woodyatt – Ian Beale, Pete and Kathy's son
Nick Berry – Simon Wicks, one of Pete's two sons from his first wife
Nejdet Salih – Ali Osman, ran the Bridge Street cafe
Sandy Ratcliffe – Sue Osman, Ali's wife
Michael Evangelou – Hasan Osman, Ali and Sue's young child
Haluk Bilginer – Mehmet Osman, Ali's brother and partner in their minicab company
Andrew Johnson – Saeed Jeffrey, ran a convenience store
Shreela Ghosh – Naima Jeffrey, Saeed's wife (by arranged marriage)
June Brown – Dot Cotton
John Altman – Nick Cotton, Dot's no-good son
Leonard Fenton – Dr Harold Legg
Gretchen Franklin – Ethel Skinner, Dr Legg's receptionist
Tom Watt – George Holloway, also known as Lofty
Gary Whelan – Detective Sergeant Terry Rich
Oscar James – Tony Carpenter
Paul J Medford – Kelvin Carpenter, Tony's son
Sally Sagoe – Hannah Carpenter, Tony's ex-wife and Kelvin's mother
Linda Davidson – Mary Smith, a single mother who dresses as a punk
Samantha Crown – Annie Smith, Mary's baby girl
Ross Davidson – Andy O'Brien, a Scottish male nurse
Shirley Cheriton – Debbie Wilkins, Andy's partner, worked in a bank
Derek Quirke – Detective Sergeant Roy Quick

— STELLAR CAMEOS —

After too many years without a hit, auteur director Robert Altman hit paydirt again with his 1992 satire on Hollywood, *The Player*. Somewhat unexpectedly, Tinsel Town – depicted as a seedy, ruthless town devoid of feeling or morals – enjoyed the joke and the film became one of the hits of the year.

But Altman knows the rules of Hollywood, and with apt cynicism roped in dozens of stars hanging around the filming locations for walk-on cameos. The result was a cast list with perhaps more stars than any other feature film in history. Aside from the leads, taken by the likes of Tim Robbins, Whoopi Goldberg, Peter Gallagher and Greta Scacchi, the film included many stars playing themselves.

Steve Allen, Richard Anderson, Rene Auberjonois, Harry Belafonte, Shari Belafonte, Karen Black, Michael Bowen, Gary Busey, Robert Carradine, Charles Champlin, Cher, James Coburn, Cathy Lee Crosby, John Cusack, Brad Davis, Paul Dooley, Thereza Ellis, Peter Falk, Felicia Farr, Katarzyna Figura, Louise Fletcher, Dennis Franz, Teri Garr, Leeza Gibbons, Scott Glenn, Jeff Goldblum, Elliott Gould, Joel Grey, David Alan Grier, Buck Henry, Anjelica Huston, Kathy Ireland, Steve James, Maxine John-James, Sally Kellerman, Sally Kirkland, Jack Lemmon, Marlee Matlin, Andie MacDowell, Malcolm McDowell, Jayne Meadows, Martin Mull, Jennifer Nash, Nick Nolte, Alexandra Powers, Bert Remsen, Guy Remsen, Patricia Resnick, Burt Reynolds, Jack Riley, Julia Roberts, Mimi Rogers, Annie Ross, Alan Rudolph, Jill St John, Susan Sarandon, Scott Shaw, Adam Simon, Rod Steiger, Patrick Swayze, Joan Tewkesbury, Brian Tochi, Lily Tomlin, Robert Wagner, Ray Walston, Bruce Willis, Marvin Young.

— THE BIRTH OF BROADWAY #3 —

Broadway is often referred to as 'The Great White Way'. OJ Gude first coined the phrase in 1901 to describe the effect of all the outdoor electric lighting.

— SHAKESPEARE ON FILM —

The Bard has been well served on the big screen, with somewhere around 300 Shakespeare movies. *Hamlet* alone has had over 40 screen interpretations. Plenty of major stars have been traditionally eager to show their 'serious' acting credentials to the cinema-going audience (and less cynically, others like Laurence Olivier and Kenneth Branagh have been crusaders for getting Shakespeare talked about in the popcorn queue). Here are some examples.

Film	Cast includes
Richard III (1912)	Frederick Warde
	James Keane
	Violet Stuart
The Taming Of The Shrew (1929)	Douglas Fairbanks
	Mary Pickford
A Midsummer Night's Dream (1935)	James Cagney
	Mickey Rooney
	Olivia de Havilland
Romeo And Juliet (1936)	Leslie Howard
	Norma Shearer
	John Barrymore
	Basil Rathbone
Henry V (1944)	Laurence Olivier
	Leslie Banks
	Robert Newton
Hamlet (1948)	Laurence Olivier
	Jean Simmons
	John Gielgud
Macbeth (1948)	Orson Welles
	Jeanette Nolan
Othello (1952)	Orson Welles
	Michael MacLiammoir
	Suzanne Cloutier
Julius Caesar (1953)	Marlon Brando
	James Mason
	John Gielgud (uncredited)
Richard III (1955)	Laurence Olivier
	John Gielgud
	Ralph Richardson
	Claire Bloom

Hamlet (1964)	Richard Burton
	Alfred Drake
	John Gielgud
Othello (1965)	Laurence Olivier
	Maggie Smith
	Derek Jacobi
The Taming Of The Shrew (1967)	Richard Burton
	Elizabeth Taylor
Romeo And Juliet (1968)	Leonard Whiting
	Olivia Hussey
	Michael York
Hamlet (1969)	Nicole Williamson
	Anthony Hopkins
	Marianne Faithfull
Julius Caesar (1970)	Charlton Heston
	Jason Robards
	John Gielgud
	Richard Chamberlain
	Diana Rigg
Antony And Cleopatra (1973)	Charlton Heston
	Hildegarde Neil
Henry V (1989)	Kenneth Branagh
	Paul Scofield
	Emma Thompson
Hamlet (1990)	Mel Gibson
	Glenn Close
	Alan Bates
	Helena Bonham Carter
Much Ado About Nothing (1993)	Kenneth Branagh
	Emma Thompson
	Kate Beckinsale
	Denzel Washington
Richard III (1995)	Ian McKellen
	Jim Broadbent
	Annette Bening
	Nigel Hawthorne
	Kristin Scott Thomas
	Maggie Smith
	Robert Downey Jr
Othello (1995)	Laurence Fishburne
	Kenneth Branagh
	Irene Jacob

Hamlet (1996)	Kenneth Branagh
	Kate Winslet
	Derek Jacobi
	Julie Christie
	Billy Crystal
	Charlton Heston
	Jack Lemmon
	Ken Dodd
	John Gielgud
	Judi Dench
Romeo + Juliet (1996)	Leonardo DiCaprio
	Claire Danes
A Midsummer Night's Dream (1999)	Kevin Kline
	Michelle Pfeiffer
	Stanley Tucci
	Calista Flockhart
	Rupert Everett
	Anna Friel
	Christian Bale
Love's Labour's Lost (2000)	Kenneth Branagh
	Alicia Silverstone
	Timothy Spall
	Emily Mortimer
Hamlet (2000)	Ethan Hawke
	Kyle MacLachlan
	Bill Murray
	Julia Stiles

— SID CAESAR'S WRITERS —

One of the most celebrated groups of writers ever to argue around a table began their careers working on American comic Sid Caesar's TV hit *Your Show of Shows*. Sketch-writers for the legendary Caesar included the young Woody Allen, Mel Brooks, Neil Simon and his brother Danny Simon, Carl Reiner, Larry Gelbart, Mel Tolkin, Sheldon Keller and Aaron Ruben. In 1993 Neil Simon wrote a play about the experience, *Laughter On The 23rd Floor*. The Broadway production starred Nathan Lane as the Caesar character, as did the 2001 TV film version, while Gene Wilder did it in London's West End.

— THE REAL FAWLTY TOWERS —

Basil Fawlty, the definitive bad-tempered hotel owner in John Cleese's classic BBC TV series, was based on a real hotel owner. In 1970, when Cleese was a member of Monty Python's Flying Circus, the comedy gang stayed at the Gleneagles Hotel in Torquay's Asheldon Road. Cleese found the owner, Donald Sinclair, to be so rude that it inspired him to write *Fawlty Towers*. In 2002, when the series was released on DVD, Sinclair's widow broke her silence to give an interview to the *Daily Telegraph*. '[Cleese] has held my family up to ridicule and made a lot of money doing it,' she complained. 'My husband…was a gentleman and a very brave man.'

A documentary on the DVD finds plenty of witnesses who give evidence to the contrary, with tales including Sinclair locking customers out at night if they came home too late for his liking. None of which impressed Mrs Sinclair, who calls Cleese 'a complete and utter fool'. There is a reference to the real Fawlty Towers in the series (in the episode 'Gourmet Night'), when Basil tells Mrs Gatsby and Mrs Tibbs to 'go to Gleneagles for your din-dins'.

— BOBBY'S ALIVE?!! —

In perhaps the most unlikely soap opera development ever, the producers of *Dallas* brought Bobby Ewing (the character played by Patrick Duffy) back to life by declaring the whole of series seven a dream. In spring 1986 Bobby strode out of the shower to his shocked widow, Pam (Victoria Principal), to reassure her that she'd only dreamed his death. It was a grand cliffhanger to end the series, but Principal wasn't told. She filmed the scene with the character John Beck dead in her shower. The producers cut in Duffy's appearance later and Principal was shocked when she saw the episode on her TV at home!

Also not told were the producers of Dallas spin-off *Knot's Landing*. Several major plot developments depended on Bobby being dead and reportedly they were furious at not being informed. According to *Knot's Landing*, Bobby always stayed dead!

— THE PRINCE AND THE SHOWGIRL —

It was the theatrical scandal of the century – the 18th century. Prince William, the then Duke of Clarence and third son of George III , moved into a house on the river at Richmond. One of his neighbours was Richard Ford – whose father co-owned the Theatre Royal, Drury Lane – and his famous 'wife' Dora Jordan. Jordan was in fact the most celebrated and highest-paid actress in the country, the leading lady of Drury Lane. In the 1780s London was reported in the press to have succumbed to 'Jordan-mania'. William was infatuated.

Infuriated by Ford's refusal to actually get round to marrying her, despite their three children, she finally gave in to the prince's advances and moved into his house in 1791. The country was outraged. As far as they were concerned, the prince was behaving disgracefully by cavorting with an actress and breaking up her family at that! The satirists had a field day, with the great cartoonist James Gillray depicting Jordan as a chamber pot (for which her surname was a slang term) and the prince with his head up a crack in the middle.

On 10 December 1791 Dora took to the stage, where the audience booed and hissed her. She stopped acting and made an emotional appeal to her beloved audience. Such was the power of her personality that she won them round and was accorded an ovation.

Dora and William had ten children. But in 1811, bored and tired of playing second fiddle to her stage work, he left her. She died abroad, poor and friendless. William became king and married a German princess.

— 'PLEASE SIR, I WANT SOME MORE...' —

British composer Lionel Bart thought of writing a musical based on the Charles Dickens novel *Oliver Twist* after remembering the box for Oliver chocolate bars (his childhood favourite) – which depicted the orphan Oliver asking for more food. His 1960 show *Oliver!* went on to be his most successful, spawning worldwide productions to this day and an Oscar-winning 1968 film starring Ron Moody and Oliver Reed.

— THE MOST PROLIFIC FILM DIRECTOR EVER? —

With 55 films and counting to his credit, film director Allen Smithee (or Alan Smithee, as it is sometimes spelled) may well take the record for the most prolific and varied director ever. The range of his work stretches from episodes of *The Cosby Show* and *The Twilight Zone* to movies such as *The Barking Dog* and *Le Zombi de Cap-Rouge*. Not to mention *Dalton: Code Of Vengeance II*! And age won't limit him because he doesn't exist.

Smithee is a pseudonym insisted on by the Directors' Guild for when a real director insists that his own name is taken off the credits – usually because he feels his work has been tampered with or he hasn't been allowed to realise his vision. Then the Guild substitutes the name of Smithee. It is usually considered to be the hallmark of a really, really bad film

— SOME SPORTS STARS IN THE MOVIES —

• Bobby Moore, Pele, Osvaldo Ardiles, Mike Summerbee – footballers, appeared in *Escape To Victory* (1981)

• OJ Simpson – American football player, appeared in films including *The Towering Inferno* (1974) and *The Naked Gun* (1988)

• Kareem Abdul Jabbar – basketball player, appeared in movies including *Game Of Death* (1978) and *Airplane!* (1980)

• Hulk Hogan – wrestler, appeared in many films, including *Rocky III* (1982)

• Michael Jordan, Larry Bird, Charles Barkley, Patrick Ewing, Larry Johnson, Tyrone Bogues, Shawn Bradley – basketball players, appeared together in *Space Jam* (1996)

• Vinnie Jones – footballer, appeared in many films starting with *Lock, Stock And Two Smoking Barrels* (1998)

• Eric Cantona – footballer, appeared in *Elizabeth* (1998)

— THE POLITICIAN AND THE PLAYGIRL —

One of the 20th century's most infamous theatrical scandals involved David Mellor, Britain's heritage minister with responsibility for the arts, and the actress who besotted him. In 1992 Mellor, popularly dubbed the 'minister of fun', was exposed in a newspaper as an adulterer. He'd been having an affair with the little-known actress Antonia de Sancha.

She didn't stay unknown for long. What made the affair all the more memorable, and all the less dignified for Mellor, was that their lovemaking became notorious for the fact that the minister wore a Chelsea Football Club kit while in coitus. Another scandal broke soon after, and a little over two months after the de Sancha story, Mellor had resigned.

New revelations appeared in Richard Eyre's 2003 account of his time in charge of the National Theatre, which had coincided with Mellor's term of office. Mellor had, revealed Eyre, urged him to audition an actress friend of his. It was de Sancha, though Eyre had no idea then of the pair's special relationship. She failed the audition.

— THE FILMS OF RONALD REAGAN —

Everyone knows that Ronald Reagan was the actor who became US President. But how many can actually name a Reagan film? Just in case you get asked at a party, here's a few. (He made 60.)

Love Is On The Air (1937)
Swing Your Lady (1938)
Cowboy From Brooklyn (1938)
Brother Rat (1938)
Hell's Kitchen (1939)
Secret Service Of The Air (1939)
Knute Rockne All American (1940)
King's Row (1942)
For God And Country (1943)
Storm Warning (1951)
Hong Kong (1952)
Law And Order (1953)
The Jungle Trap (1954)
Hellcats Of The Navy (1957)
The Killers (1964)

— THE STAR TREK MOVIES AND THEIR FRENCH TITLES —

Film	Year	French Title
The Motion Picture	1979	*Star Trek, Le Film*
The Wrath Of Khan	1982	*La Colere De Khan*
The Search For Spock	1984	*A La Recherche De Spock*
The Voyage Home	1986	*Retour Sur Terre*
The Final Frontier	1989	*L'Ultime Frontiere*
The Undiscovered Country	1991	*Terre Inconnue*
Generations	1994	*Generations*
First Contact	1996	*Premier Contact*
Insurrection	1998	*Insurrection*
Nemesis	2002	*Nemesis*

— OSCAR'S FIRST BOW —

The first-ever Academy Awards were presented in 1929, with Emil Jannings the first winner, Best Actor for both *The Last Command* and *The Way Of All Flesh*. Best Picture went to *Wings*. Achievement In Directing (Comedy) went to Lewis Milestone for *Two Arabian Knights*, while Achievement In Directing (Drama) went to Frank Borzage for *7th Heaven*. Janet Gaynor won Best Actress for *7th Heaven*, *Street Angel* and *Sunrise*. And Special Awards went to Charles Chaplin 'for versatility and genius in acting, writing, directing and producing *The Circus*' and to Warner Bros 'for producing *The Jazz Singer*, the pioneer outstanding talking picture, which has revolutionised the industry'.

— THE LONGEST FILM EVER MADE —

Got two days to spare? The longest film ever made is believed to be *The Longest Most Meaningless Movie In The World*, a British underground movie produced by Anthony Scott in association with the Swiss Film Centre, London. Directed by Vincent Patouillard and premiered at the Cinematheque de Paris in October 1970, it lasts exactly 48 hours!

— THE VOICE OF HOLLYWOOD —

Self-dubbed as 'The Voice of Hollywood', one of the greatest singing voices of the silver screen musicals' heyday remained just that – a voice. Marni Nixon is the woman who made the stars sound good, literally. When Deborah Kerr's singing voice was judged not strong enough for the 1955 film of *The King And I*, and her voice double for the songs was killed in a car accident, Nixon was hired. She impressed industry-shakers so much that her career was set, though it would be mostly uncredited.

In 1957 Nixon doubled for Kerr's voice again in *An Affair to Remember*. Then came gorgeous singing performances – but seemingly coming from the mouths of Natalie Wood and Audrey Hepburn (who was less than ecstatic at not being allowed to sing her own numbers) – in *West Side Story* and *My Fair Lady*. Nixon finally appeared in her own right in *The Sound Of Music*, but playing the tiny part of a singing nun. In 1998, by then in her late sixties, Nixon was still in the dubbing business – supplying the singing voice for Grandmother Fa in the animated movie *Mulan*.

— BRANDO ON ACTORS —

'An actor's a guy who, if you ain't talkin' about him, ain't listening.' – Marlon Brando

— CINEMA'S FIRST BOW —

The first-ever public cinema was the Cinematographe Lumiere, situated in a former billiard hall in Paris's Grand Café at 14 boulevard des Capucines. It was run by cinema pioneers Auguste and Louis Lumiere. Despite a varied programme, however, only 35 people bothered to pay 1 franc to sample the new medium on opening day – 28 December 1895.

Since the rent of the room was 30 francs a day, it seemed that landlord Monsieur Borgo was wise in not taking the proffered alternative of 20 per cent of box-office takings instead. Not for long. Quickly the cinema caught on, and the box-office tills were ringing to the tune of 2,500 francs a day.

— THESPIS —

Actors are often called thespians. This refers to Thespis, one of the first great men of theatre. Somewhere between 600 and 525 BC, Thespis from Attica came up with the idea of an actor – otherwise known as the protagonist. His job was to interact with a chorus to tell a story. Not content with one groundbreaking invention, Thespis added another when he thought of the touring theatre company, carting actors around in a cart from which they declaimed. But then, touring theatre was never glamorous!

— THE *BLUE PETER* PETS —

Accusations of drug-taking and more may have dogged some of Blue Peter's (BP) presenters, but – apart from the elephant that relieved itself on the studio floor – the long-running BBC children's TV series (since 1958) has been marked by blameless and charming pets.

Petra – the first regular BP dog, after a predecessor made one appearance then died

Jason – cat, worked on BP for 27 years

Patch – puppy born to Petra in 1965

Freda – tortoise originally named Fred; later discovered to be female

Shep – dog; BBC-owned but host John Noakes was allowed to keep him

Jack and Jill – cats

Goldie – dog

Maggie and Jim – tortoises

Bonnie – Goldie's daughter

George – tortoise, over 80 years old

Willow – kitten; first BP pet to be neutered

Kari – cat

Oke – Kari's brother

Mabel – dog

Lucy – dog

Meg – dog, partial to cat food

— BAT-VILLAINS —

Before Tim Burton came along with his Hollywood-sized special effects, Batman meant 1960s TV, actor Adam West, his assistant Robin (Burt Ward) and his trusty utility belt. It also meant an array of hammy villains, including scenery-chewing performances from an array of talent.

Burgess Meredith as The Penguin
Julie Newmar (or Eartha Kitt) as Catwoman
Cesar Romero as the Joker
Frank Gorshin as the Riddler
Liberace as Chandell
Joan Crawford as the Devil
Joan Collins as Lady Fogg
Milton Berle as Louie the Lilac
Vincent Price as Egghead
Ethel Merman as Lola Lasagne
Pierre Salinger as Lucky Pierre
Cliff Robertson as Shame
Victor Buono as King Tut
George Sanders as Mr Freeze
Roddy McDowell as Bookworm
Tallulah Bankhead as the Black Widow

— MICHAEL DOUGLAS, PRODUCER EXTRAORDINAIRE —

Aside from his acting successes, Michael Douglas is among the canniest of movie producers. It is not that he hasn't had flops, but his record is astonishingly consistent.

Film	Year	Approximate Gross
One Flew Over The Cuckoo's Nest	1975	$112,000,000 (US)
The China Syndrome	1979	$51,718,367 (US)
Romancing The Stone	1984	$114,900,000 (W)
The Jewel Of The Nile	1985	$75,973,200 (US)
Flatliners	1990	$61,489,265 (US)
Face/Off	1997	$241,600,000 (W)

— POP STARS' SCREEN FLOPS —

How many times have we heard pop stars confess that 'all they ever really wanted was to act'? Well, many have tried – some with success, from Cher to Eminem. Others, well, take a look at this list. We warn you, it's not for the faint-hearted.

Prince – Film critic Leonard Maltin slated *Under The Cherry Moon* (1986) as 'a triumph of self-adoration and overall embarrassment'. The pop star directed and starred in the story about a con man who falls in love. It won five derisory Razzie awards – worst actor, director, original song, picture and supporting actor (and was nominated for three more).

Britney Spears – The pop nymphette decided to go big-screen with *Crossroads* (2002), the story of a gal who just wants to sing. Well, sing she did. But there wasn't much acting of worth, with *Rolling Stone* magazine's Peter Travers reporting, 'At the screening I attended, derisive laughter greeted one of Spears' stilted line readings.'

Mariah Carey – If Spears made a bad start, then Carey made a dreadful one. Her first lead was in *Glitter* (2001). The tale of, er, a gal who just wants to sing. 'She is comfortably out-acted by the cherrywood kitchen counter-top in her spiffy Manhattan apartment,' sneered *The Guardian*. 'Primarily a showcase for (Carey's) breasts,' sighed *The Washington Post*.

Madonna – After a film-stealing debut in *Desperately Seeking Susan* (1985), it has been a mostly slippery slope for the queen of pop. The high point was *Evita* (1996), the lower-than-low points the ludicrous erotic thriller *Body Of Evidence* (1993) and *Swept Away* (2002), directed by hubbie Guy Ritchie. Of the former, Roger Ebert in the *Chicago Sun-Times* opined, 'Madonna...nails down her title as the queen of movies that were bad ideas from the very beginning...I've seen comedies with fewer laughs.' As for *Swept Away*, it didn't even get shown in British cinemas after US critics slated it (winning the dubious distinction of 'no stars' in the *New York Daily News*)!

— WHAT DO SEAN CONNERY AND LARRY HAGMAN HAVE IN COMMON? —

Answer: They both got their showbiz breaks in the 1951 London production of Rodgers and Hammerstein's musical *South Pacific*. The director, deciding that his chorus looked too camp to be credible soldiers, sent for a bunch of muscular actors. Among them were Connery, a former Mr Universe contestant, and Hagman, who was the son of the show's leading lady, Mary Martin. Both went on to make their names as screen tough guys. Hagman was mean tycoon JR in *Dallas*, while Connery went on to create the role of James Bond.

— FIGHTING ANTI-SEMITISM: THE HILLCREST COUNTRY CLUB —

Despite the influence wielded by Hollywood's Jewish community in the early days of the studio system, anti-Semitism was still prevalent. Not only were Jewish actors and actresses expected to change their names to sound less Jewish, but also – status symbol of status symbols – most country clubs did not allow Jews as members. Even Louis B Mayer, the powerful boss of MGM and in the late 1930s one of America's highest earners, could not find a club that would let him in.

Until, that is, the Hillcrest Country Club was established as a Jews-only club – across Pico Boulevard from the 20th Century Fox Studios. And it soon had a membership list that, were it not for the prejudices, would have graced any club. Mayer joined, as did Sam Goldwyn, Danny Kaye, Jack Benny, George Burns and Groucho Marx. It was a kind of 'Who's Who (And Jewish) In Movieland'! Comedians, including Kaye, Marx and Milton Berle, even used to enjoy regular Friday lunches during which they'd test out new material on each other!

The point made, the Hillcrest eventually opened its doors to non-Jews. The Lebanese Catholic actor Danny Thomas was the first Gentile member.

— THE DOCTORS WHO —

At the time of writing the BBC has announced it's bringing back the cult TV series, started in 1963, about the famous regenerating timelord. Generations to date have played the character.

William Hartnell – the first Doctor, testy and impatient (replaced by Peter Cushing for the cinema films)

Patrick Troughton – the playful, recorder-playing second

Doctor Jon Pertwee – the third Doctor was more like a detective, with vintage car and gadgets

Tom Baker – mysterious and bohemian, the fourth Doctor had the soul of a traveller

Peter Davidson – the Doctor as ace cricketer

Colin Baker – the sixth Doctor was prone to mood swings, and verged on the camp

Sylvester McCoy – the seventh Doctor had a female assistant, Ace, with a powerful baseball bat

Paul McGann – the *Withnail And I* star became the Doctor for one blockbuster 90-minute special, and some audio versions

Richard E Grant – McGann's *Withnail* co-star plays the Doctor on a BBC animated online series. To come: **Christopher Eccleston**, who is set to play the Doctor in the new TV series, to hit British screens in 2005.

— *FRIENDS* FACTS #1 —

• The fountain in the opening credits can be found in Warner Bros Studios on Warner Boulevard, California. It's in the studio's Park Boulevard.

• An initial idea for the show's title was *Insomnia Café*.

— WOODY ALLEN ONE-LINERS #4 —

'The most important words in the English language are not "I love you" but "It's benign."'
– Harry, *Deconstructing Harry* (1997)

— MOVIE MOTORS —

Cars have long been central to the cinema. So here are some facts about cinematic motors.

In 1968, James Bond author Ian Fleming saw his other great creation brought to the big screen, *Chitty Chitty Bang Bang*. Although Fleming's fascination with cars runs through the Bond books, Chitty could float on water and fly – feats which the Bond producers repeated, with different cars, in *The Spy Who Loved Me* (1977) and *The Man With The Golden Gun* (1974) . In fact several cars were used in the filming of *Chitty*. The car used for the hovercraft scenes was lighter since some of it was constructed from aluminium instead of brass. It also had its engine taken out for the flying scenes, so that it would be light enough to hang from a helicopter. The car used in most of the shots, driving along roads, was built by Alan Mann in Hertfordshire in 1967 and was fitted with a Ford 3000 V6 engine and automatic transmission.

One of the great car chases occurs in *Bullitt* (1968). Steve McQueen became so enamoured of the one surviving Mustang used in filming (its twin was too damaged to use again) he tried, unsuccessfully, to buy it. During the chase, director Peter Yates asked the stunt drivers to drive at around 75 miles per hour. However, the drivers exceeded their orders, reaching speeds of over 110 miles per hour.

Another of the most famous car chases in cinema involves Gene Hackman careering across New York in *The French Connection* (1971). The sequence nearly turned gruesome when during shooting an unsuspecting mother pushing her baby across the road was nearly run over.

The most famous James Bond car is probably the Aston Martin DB5, which 007 drove in the 1964 *Goldfinger* (utilising the spectacular ejector seat), *Thunderball* (1965) and *On Her Majesty's Secret Service* (1969). Its special features included machine guns, oil dispenser, smoke screen, bulletproof shields, ejector seat, wheel hub tyre slasher blades, revolving licence plates and a tracking/homing device. The producers paid for the Aston Martin in *Goldfinger*, but it became so iconic and they never had to pay for a car again. Nowadays, it is a very lucrative product placement opportunity (Aston Martin paid a reported £100 million to have Bond drive their cars in 2002's *Die Another Day* and the following two 007 flicks).

The 1996 James Spader-starrer *Crash* is about people who get sexually aroused from being in car crashes.

1998's thriller *Ronin* featured plenty of vehicular bust-ups, and in filming the production trashed a costly 75 cars.

— TERMS USED IN VARIETY, VAUDEVILLE, REVUE AND PANTO —

angel – financial backer

bender – contortionist (somewhat derogatory)

call – instead of bows, variety performers would historically take a 'call', which consisted of standing to acknowledge the applause; they would only bow (which was seen as amateur) if royalty were present

date – a professional booking

dental acts – acts that involved gripping with the teeth

diddy – toilet (term used especially by female performers)

floats – an early term for floodlights, because light originally came from candles floating in water at the stage's edge

ghost – refers to getting paid. In two-show-a-day variety performers would be paid after the second show to stop them, ghost-like, vanishing early

hoofer – tap dancer

limes – spotlight operated from high in the theatre to illuminate the stars (hence, 'limelight'); the earliest spotlights were made by heating lime in a cylinder

segue – method of linking two acts with music

vamp – musicians' improvisations to accompany an act (a practice common in the less glamorous circuits – in the top dates the music was all rehearsed)

— THEATRE SEATING —

Typically, the seats immediately facing the stage, usually on a slightly lower level, are called the stalls. These might go back to a semi-raised level called the stalls circle. Then the first level up is usually the dress circle or grand tier (or, in America, the mezzanine). Above this you might get the balcony. Sometimes, an extra level between the dress circle and balcony could be called the upper circle. On the sides are the boxes and (with less good views) the slips. It varies somewhat from theatre to theatre. Here are a few examples.

Royal Opera House, Covent Garden, London:

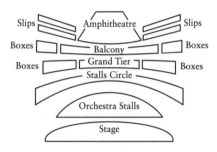

New Amsteram Theater, New York:

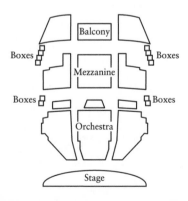

Royal Shakespeare Theatre, Stratford-upon-Avon:

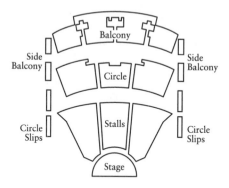

— SUPERSTITIOUS THESPS —

Thespy types are known for their superstitions. The trade is riddled with them, and unless a fledgling actor is aware of the major traditions, he or she may be accused of bringing the show down around everyone's ears. These are the most common.

- Don't whistle in the dressing-room.
- If more than one person washes their hands in the toilet basin at the same time, they must make the sign of the cross on the water, or a quarrel will follow.
- If an actress drops a comb, she must dance over it or she will lose her job.
- Some actors refuse to speak the last line of a play in rehearsals, worried that it will mean the show will flop.
- Never put shoes on a table.
- Never put peacock feathers or a bowl of goldfish on the stage.
- Never hang pictures in the dressing-room until after opening night.
- Never say 'Macbeth' (see The Scottish Play).

— ANDREW LLOYD WEBBER'S MUSICALS —

Title	Lyricist	Theatre/Opening
Joseph And The Amazing Technicolor Dreamcoat	Tim Rice	Colet Court School 1 March 1968
Jesus Christ Superstar	Tim Rice Mark Hellinger	New York 12 October 1971
By Jeeves	Alan Ayckbourn	Her Majesty's 22 April 1975
Evita	Tim Rice	Prince Edward 21 June 1978
Cats	TS Eliot	New London 11 May 1981
Song & Dance	Don Black	Palace 26 March 1982
Starlight Express	Richard Stilgoe	Apollo Victoria 19 March 1984
Phantom Of The Opera	Charles Hart Richard Stilgoe	Her Majesty's 9 October 1986
Aspects Of Love	Don Black Charles Hart	Prince Of Wales 17 April 1989
Sunset Boulevard	Don Black C Hampton	Adelphi 12 July 1993
Whistle Down The Wind	Jim Steinman	Nat. Theatre (US) 6 December 1996
The Beautiful Game	Ben Elton	Cambridge 26 September 2000
The Woman In White	David Zippel	Palace Late 2004

— OPERATION RED DAWN —

The military operation in Iraq that resulted in the arrest of deposed dictator Saddam Hussein in December 2003 was named after a cult movie. Operation Red Dawn took its name, according to newspaper reports, from the 1984 film *Red Dawn* starring Patrick Swayze, Charlie Sheen and Jennifer Grey. In the film, a group of high school students must become guerrilla fighters and defend their American town from invading foreign forces.

— ALCATRAZ MOVIES —

Few sights are as forbidding as the Rock. The Alcatraz prison stands, fortified, a short ferry-ride from the San Francisco jetties – once a cruel reminder for inmates of the luxuries they were missing. But with the freezing cold water and strong currents it might have been miles away. Movies have been obsessed with the idea of prisoners escaping from Alcatraz, and in some cases breaking into it.

Seven Miles From Alcatraz (1943) is a mid-war spin, as prisoners are driven to escape by the fear of enemy bomb attacks, and Alcatraz becomes the target of a Nazi plan.

Birdman Of Alcatraz (1962) has Burt Lancaster playing the famous 'Birdman' Robert Stroud, a man serving a life term who takes comfort from birds (the feathered kind). Though the movie moved public sympathy towards Stroud and letters were sent begging for his release, it glossed over his villainy. In fact, he killed two people in prison, wrote child pornography and complained to a parole hearing that he 'had a lot of people left to kill'.

Escape from Alcatraz (1979) has Clint Eastwood and Patrick McGoohan facing off in the story of Frank Morris's possible escape from the prison.

Terror At Alcatraz (1982) is a race to find Al Capone's buried treasure on the Rock, starring the Smothers Brothers – Dick and yo-yo expert Tom.

Terror On Alcatraz (1986) shows Alcatraz as the scene for a slasher flick with Morris (played by Aldo Ray) returning to the prison to collect a deposit box key and being disturbed by partying teenagers. One by one he makes sure they never annoy him again.

Murder In The First (1995) focuses on a prisoner illegally shut in solitary confinement for years. At the end of his sentence he is mad and quickly turns to murder. A young lawyer tries to save him by arguing that Alcatraz is to blame. A high-profile cast includes Christian Slater, Kevin Bacon and Gary Oldman.

The Rock (1996) features Sean Connery in action mode as the only man ever to break out of Alcatraz and now he has to break back in to foil the terrorists who have set up shop there to launch a nerve gas attack on San Francisco.

— GIELGUDISMS —

Late, great British actor Sir John Gielgud was almost as famous for his way with a faux pas as for his acting. Many became well known and much loved within theatre circles. Here's some of his best.

> Sitting with playwright Edward Knoblock in a London restaurant, Gielgud said of a passer-by, 'He's the most boring man in the world with the exception of Edward Knoblock (pause, realising whom he was with). I mean the other Edward Knoblock.'

> After watching Richard Burton in his own production of *Hamlet*, Gielgud popped backstage to say, 'We'll go to dinner when you're ready.' What came out was, 'We'll go to dinner when you're better.'

> Another Burton gaffe, Gielgud once said to Elizabeth Taylor, 'I don't know what's happened to Richard Burton. I think he married some terrible film star and had to live abroad.'

> He described Ingrid Bergman as a nice woman who could speak five languages, but 'can't act in any of them.'

> Gielgud once dolefully admitted that, 'I've dropped enough bricks to build another Great Wall of China.'

— OPERA – A SLIPPERY BUSINESS —

A performance of the rarely seen opera *La Vestale* by Gasparo Spontini at the 1980 Wexford Festival was the occasion for one of the most famous of stage disasters. The set designer had supplied a sharply sloped stage covered with white plastic to look like the tiles of ancient Rome. One night a stagehand forgot to apply the anti-skid spray.

The tenor entered at the top of the slope and immediately slid headlong all the way down before smashing into the footlights. He struggled back to his feet – still singing – and was slowly able to grab an altar in the middle of the stage, to which he held on for dear life. A female co-star, having seen this, walked on and managed to angle her own skid towards the altar, which the two of them clutched tightly. On came the soprano, who held her balance but realised that she would fall if she walked any further. So, still singing, she returned to the wings and took off her shoes and tights, which gave her enough grip to move in comparative safety. However, the chorus were next – and they had not been warned. As they entered, they each slid right down to the footlights, creating a fabulous heap of prone, singing bodies!

— HOW TO MAKE YOUR VERY OWN AMERICAN PIE —

Okay, so the actual pie unforgettably featured in 1999's *American Pie* was reportedly bought from Costco. But in case anyone you know wants to (gulp) replicate the scene, or perhaps wants to eat a similar dish in protest at the movie's waste of good food, here's a recipe for good old home-baked apple pie.

INGREDIENTS:
6–8 tart apples, peeled, cored and sliced
1 tablespoonful lemon juice
1/2 cup sugar
1/2 cup light brown sugar
1 teaspoonful cinnamon
2 tablespoonfuls butter
2 tablespoonfuls flour
1/8 teaspoonful salt
Pastry for double crust 9-inch pie

Take the peeled, sliced apples and sprinkle them with lemon juice. Mix flour, sugar, salt and spices and combine them with the apples. Line a 9-inch pie plate with half of the pastry. Then fill with the apple mixture and dot with butter. Put the crust on top of the pie, remembering to cut slits to allow steam to escape, then seal the edges. Bake at 400°F for 50 minutes.

What you now do with the pie is up to you – but whatever you do, make sure it's not scalding hot!

— WILDER ON THE BOX —

'I'm delighted with television because it used to be that films were the lowest form of art. Now we've got something to look down on.' – Billy Wilder

— HOW 3D WORKS —

First popular in the 1950s, 3D cinema made a brief comeback in the '80s with movies like 1983's *Jaws 3D*. Suddenly the shark was coming out of the screen! Or, in *Nightmare On Elm Street 6: The Final Nightmare*, Freddy Krueger's killer blades reached out towards our own hearts. When done well, 3D is spectacularly effective.

It works from the rule that our left and right eyes see things from different angles. The fusion of the images from each eye creates a sense of distance in our brain. 3D filming uses a camera with two lenses roughly set at the same distance apart as our eyes are (usually about 2.5"). The film then projects two images – one for the perspective of the left eye, one for the right – on the screen simultaneously.

Looked at with our naked eyes we see both images. However, 3D glasses solve this problem. Each lens has a filter that will block out one image. So each eye sees one image, and the brain fuses them to form a sense of one three-dimensional image!

These days the 3D illusion is enhanced with computer generated images, a technique which has sorted out the most common problem of 3D films – focus.

— THE WIT OF THOMAS BEECHAM —

Sir Thomas Beecham was one of the great conductors of the 20th century and famous for his wit. One of his finest, and funniest, moments occurred during a production of Bizet's *Carmen* that he was conducting at London's Royal Opera House in 1932. A horse accompanying the smugglers in Act Three suddenly turned its back on the audience, and copiously soiled the stage. A shocked silence fell over the house until Beecham's voice was heard clearly to say, 'A critic, by God.'

— US PRESIDENTS AND THE MOVIES —

• Jimmy Carter was an avid film fan. He ordered 465 personal screenings in four years. The first after his inauguration was *All The President's Men*, about Nixon and Watergate.

• Lyndon Johnson slept through most of the movies he watched.

• President Eisenhower didn't like the film star Robert Mitchum, claiming, 'he got tangled up with drugs,' and refused to watch any of his films. Reportedly one screening of a Western featured Mitchum and as soon as the actor appeared the president walked out.

• Both President and Eleanor Roosevelt loved films and the first lady wrote an article for *Photoplay* magazine entitled 'Why We Roosevelts Are Movie Fans'. She claimed that the family's favourites included *Snow White And The Seven Dwarfs* and anything with Shirley Temple. Roosevelt took *Casablanca* to screen for Winston Churchill during their secret meeting in January 1943, held in Casablanca itself.

• Richard Nixon loved *Patton* so much that he watched it many times, including the night before the secret bombing of Cambodia.

• Ronald Reagan was not only a film fan – having been a movie actor – he loved popcorn while he watched, usually getting through two bowls. During *Gandhi* he devoured three bowlfuls.

• Bill Clinton loves *High Noon*. But his White House screenings also ranged from comedies like *The Naked Gun* to more arty films including *Strictly Ballroom* and *Shine*.

— FLYING HIGH —

The man who holds the official record for having performed the most stage flights is the Japanese kabuki actor Ichikawa Ennosuke. Ennosuke, born in 1939, uses spectacular effects to make the ancient art of kabuki seem new and exciting. His shows are even referred to as 'super kabuki'! Ennosuka has flown across stage and audience – a stunt known as *chunori* – in over 5,000 performances since April 1968.

— THE MOST-WATCHED TV EVENT —

The most-watched international TV event was the funeral of Diana, Princess of Wales, on 6 September 1997, which drew reported figures of 2.5 billion viewers worldwide.

Previously the most-watched UK TV event had been an episode of the game-show *Sale Of The Century*. The Anglia TV programme hosted by Nicholas Parsons went out on the afternoon of 22 December 1978, when viewers were diverted because of a BBC strike. An amazing 21.2 million viewers watched it.

— THE FILMS OF JEAN-CLAUDE VAN DAM —

The poor man's posing action hero or under-rated screen icon? Take your pick, but anyway whether he merits it or not here's a list of Jean-Claude Van Dam's – or, as he likes to be known, 'the muscles from Brussels' or (reportedly) 'the Fred Astaire of karate' – movies to date.

Rue Barbare (1984)
Breakin' (1984)
Monaco Forever (1984)
No Retreat, No Surrender (1985)
Bloodsport (1988)
Black Eagle (1988)
Cyborg (1989)
Kickboxer (1989)
A.W.O.L./Lionheart/Wrong Bet (1990)
Death Warrant (1990)
Double Impact (1991)
Universal Soldier (1992)
Hard Target (1993)
Nowhere To Run (1993)
Street Fighter (1994)
Timecop (1994)
Sudden Death (1995)
Maximum Risk (1996)
The Quest (1996)
Double Team (1997)
Knock Off (1998)

Legionnaire (1998)
Coyote Moon (1999)
Universal Soldier: The Return (1999)
The Order (2001)
Replicant (2001)
Derailed (2002)
The Savage (2003)
Wake Of Death (2004)

— WEST END GHOSTS —

The Theatre Royal, Drury Lane, is haunted by a mysterious figure in 18th century clothes. Workers doing refurbishments found the skeleton of a man with a dagger in his ribs, dating from the 18th century. Could this be the remains of the unknown ghost?

Another Drury Lane ghost is never seen, only smelt. The 'lavender ghost' gives off a powerful scent of lavender – apparently it's the ghost of an incontinent actor who took a shine to several younger actors. He used to carry bags of lavender to counter the smell of urine.

Actor Donald Sinden claims to have once seen the ghost of Buckley, the 1860s manager of the Theatre Royal in the Haymarket. He was late for an entrance and ran down the stairs towards the stage, passing the show's star, Ralph Richardson, on the way. As he rushed past, Richardson said, 'Good evening.' It was only when he got to the stage and saw Richardson already was there that he realised that he must have encountered the theatre's ghost! At the same venue, a stagehand told another actor, Toby Stephens, of the time he had seen 'a black figure' in the wings. The stagehand went to tell the stranger to move, when he became caught in his gaze. He passed out, and felt unwell for a week.

— *FRIENDS* FACTS #2 —

• Joey's middle name is Francis, Rachel's is Karen, Chandler's is Muriel.

• Ross's pet monkey, Marcel, left when he got a part in the movie, *Outbreak* (which hinges on a monkey spreading a deadly virus).

— FILMING *THE BLUE PLANET* —

Much of the spectacular footage for the acclaimed 2001 BBC documentary series about the seas, *The Blue Planet*, was shot from a 60-foot sailing boat, *Silurian*. Skippered by whale researcher Kit Rogers and conservationist Jessie Lane, *Silurian* was converted into a floating shooting platform. In the five years the series took to make, they crossed the Atlantic five times and sailed around 30,000 miles.

Producer Alastair Fothergill sent submersibles down 4,500m under the oceans' surfaces with high-definition cameras. Had a cameraman attempted to swim at this depth he would have been instantly crushed to death by the pressure. For this reason cameramen were not allowed below 70m.

— STAN LEE'S SUPERHERO STABLE —

With the massive resurgence in super-hero movies, one of the biggest influences on today's cinema is arguably Stan Lee – the Marvel Comics guru who invented many of the best-loved comic characters. Here are some recent and, at time of writing, forthcoming Lee-inspired movies.

Film	Director	Stars
Blade (1998)	Stephen Norrington	Wesley Snipes Kris Kristofferson
Blade 2 (2002)	Guillermo del Toro	Wesley Snipes Kris Kristofferson
The X-Men (2000)	Bryan Singer	Ian McKellen Hugh Jackman
X-2 (2003)	Bryan Singer	Patrick Stewart Halle Berry
Spider-Man (2002)	Sam Raimi	Tobey Maguire Kirsten Dunst
Spider-Man 2 (2004)	Sam Raimi	Tobey Maguire Kirsten Dunst
The Hulk (2003)	Ang Lee	Eric Bana Jennifer Connelly
Daredevil (2003)	Mark Steven Johnson	Ben Affleck Jennifer Garner
Fantastic Four (2004)	tbc	tbc
Iron Man (2004)	tbc	tbc
Ghost Rider (2005)	Mark Steven Johnson	Nicolas Cage

— 'HOLLYWOOD' —

The iconic Hollywood sign, 50-foot-high letters perched near the tip of Beachwood Canyon's Mount Lee, the highest peak in Los Angeles. Though it nowadays stands as a monument to the huge American film industry, its roots are more mundane. Built in 1923 by property developers to advertise their new sites, it originally read 'Hollywoodland' and used to light up at night. A caretaker looked after the sign and lived in a cabin situated just behind one of the L's. It was only in the 1940s when the film business mushroomed that the last four letters were removed.

In 1976, vandals changed the sign to read 'HOLLYWEED', to applaud newly loosened marijuana laws. Then in 1978 it was altered to read 'HOLYWOOD' when Pope John Paul II visited. During the Iran-Contra scandal it briefly became 'OLLYWOOD', a reference to Oliver North, the official at the centre of the affair.

Best viewing points for the sign include Mullholland Drive, the Hollywood Freeway or, to get really close-up, drive north up Gower Street onto Beachwood Drive.

— THE THEME TO M*A*S*H —

Robert Altman's 1970 film M*A*S*H, from Richard Hooker's book, gave a satirical view of the lunacy of war – in this case the Korean War. M*A*S*H was a smash, both the movie and the TV series that followed it. The film is epitomised by the calming, edgy and hilariously catchy theme song, 'Suicide Is Painless', written by Mike Altman and Johnny Mandel.

Through early morning fog I see,
Visions of the things to be,
The pains that are withheld for me,
I realise and I can see...

CHORUS:
That suicide is painless.
It brings on many changes.
And I can take or leave it if I please.

I try to find a way to make,
All our little joys relate,
Without that ever-present hate,
But now I know that it's too late, and...

[CHORUS]

The game of life is hard to play,
I'm gonna lose it anyway.
The losing card I'll someday lay,
So this is all I have to say...

[CHORUS]

The only way to win is cheat,
And lay it down before I'm beat,
And to another give my seat,
For that's the only painless feat.

[CHORUS]

The sword of time will pierce our skins.
It doesn't hurt when it begins,

But as it works its way on in,
The pain grows stronger, watch it grin, but...

[CHORUS]

A brave man once requested me,
To answer questions that are key.
Is it to be or not to be?
And I replied, 'Oh why ask me?'

'Cause suicide is painless.
It brings on many changes.
And I can take or leave it if I please.

And you can do the same thing if you choose.

— MONTY PYTHON'S 'EX-PARROT' —

First broadcast on 7 December 1969, the dead parrot sketch in *Monty Python's Flying Circus* has become part of comedy folklore. Thousands of people can quote it – but do you know all the different terms John Cleese's Mr Praline uses to finally convince Michael Palin's shopkeeper that his bird is deceased?

'It's not pining; it's passed on. This parrot is no more. It has ceased to be. It's expired and gone to meet its maker. This is a late parrot. It's a stiff. Bereft of life, it rests in peace. If you hadn't nailed it to the perch, it would be pushing up the daisies. It's rung down the curtain and joined the choir invisible. This is an ex-parrot.'

— A BREATH OF FRESH AIR —

Theatre-going conditions in 1880s London were terrible. Gas fumes and overcrowding led to a distinctly uncomfortable experience. An 1884 study compared the air in the dress circles of some of the city's major theatres with the air in a sewer. The air in the sewer was healthier.

— SPRINGER SPEAK —

According to *The Times*, *Jerry Springer: The Opera* has the most swear words of any opera ever written: 8,283 to be precise!

— QUOTES FROM *THE OFFICE* —

'If you were to ask me to name three geniuses, I probably wouldn't say Einstein, Newton...I'd go Milligan, Cleese, Everett. Sessions.' (David Brent, series 1, episode 2)

'It's like an alarm clock's gone off, and I've just got to get away. I think it was John Lennon who said, "Life is what happens when you're making other plans." and that's how I feel. Although he also said, "I am the walrus, I am the eggman," so I don't know what to believe.' (Tim, series 1, episode 6)

'Well, there's good news and bad news. The good news is that...some of you will lose your jobs. Those of you who are kept on will have to relocate to Swindon, if you want to stay. I know, gutting. On a more positive note, the good news is, I've been promoted. So every cloud...you're still thinking about the bad news, aren't you?' (David Brent, series 1, episode 6)

'I can read women. And you've got to know their wants and their needs, and that can be anything from making sure she's got enough money to buy groceries each week to making sure she's gratified sexually after intercourse.' (Gareth, series 2, episode 2)

'"If you want the rainbow, you've gotta put up with the rain." Do you know which philosopher said that? Dolly Parton. And people say she's just a big pair of tits.' (David Brent, series 2, episode 6)

— FROST ON TELLY —

'Television is an invention that permits you to be entertained in your living-room by people you wouldn't have in your home.' – David Frost on CBS TV (1971)

— HOW SADLER'S WELLS GOT ITS NAME —

One of London's smartest theatres following its 1998 makeover, Rosebury Avenue's Sadler's Wells is established as one of the world's leading dance houses. It has been an integral part of the city's theatre-going life for so long that nobody really questions its curious name.

In fact, Sadler's Wells were just that. In 1683 entrepreneur Richard Sadler discovered a well in the garden of the Musick house he had built. Remembering that the area had been famous for the therapeutic properties of its wells in medieval times, Sadler advertised the well for those with 'dropsy, jaundice, scurvy, green sickness and other distempers to which females are liable', including the rather intriguing 'virgin's fever!' By 1685 Sadler's well was the height of fashion and he added entertainment. After a while the public lost interest in the waters and by the 18th century attractions such as jugglers, acrobats, wrestlers, singers, and even dancing dogs and a singing duck were the main draws. It found a great star in Joseph Grimaldi, who helped develop the English pantomime tradition in the early 19th century. And indeed pantomime as well as operetta and variety were the mainstay of the Wells for decades. Eventually the site declined, becoming a roller-skating rink and a fight venue. It reopened in 1879 as a music hall, then one of London's first cinemas. But in 1925 the great impresario Lilian Baylis arrived, and turned the theatre into one of the great lyric arts houses, where the Royal Ballet and English National Opera were forged, and it remains a major theatre. In a lasting homage to its beginnings, it retains the name of Sadler's Wells.

— OVER BEFORE IT ENDED —

An ill-fated production of *The Intimate Revue* at London's Duchess Theatre on 11 March 1930 closed without even fully completing one performance, making it the shortest theatre run ever! Scene changes took about 20 minutes each, so the management, seeing that most of the audience were leaving the theatre anyway, cut 7 scenes to bring the curtain down before midnight.

— *BUFFY* TOP TRUMPS —

In the official *Buffy The Vampire Slayer* Top Trumps card game, the card for Buffy Summers includes the following statistics.

Combat Daytime – 10
Combat Nighttime – 10
Fright Factor – 1
Killer Rating – 100 per cent
Intelligence – 75 per cent

So who can beat the fearsome Buffy? The Master is pretty scary, with a Fright Factor of 9 and 85 per cent intelligence. Willow is far cleverer than either with 99 per cent intelligence. Spike is reckoned to be just as frightening as The Master, while Giles has 100 per cent intelligence. You know who else can whip Buffy? Joyce Summers, her mother, with an 80 per cent intelligence factor. Just goes to show, mums always know best.

— SENSURROUND —

Among the various gimmicks designed to lure audiences into cinemas, one of the most memorable was Sensurround. Devised for the 1974 disaster film *Earthquake*, Sensurround is an audio special effects system which encodes signals on the film to create audio waves that cannot be heard by humans, but – in cinemas equipped with speakers (which distributors usually loaned to the cinemas) able to handle the low-end waves – it can be felt! Audiences experienced the sounds by feeling vibrations through their bodies and eardrums. In *Earthquake* it was intended to simulate the tremors of the quake and the rumbles were played at 110dB to 120dB and ranged from 16Hz to 120Hz – they fit the exact waveform of the 1972 Sylmar earthquake.

Only five films ever used Sensurround before the device was gently retired. Perhaps, after the powerful sound waves actually cracked the plaster in some cinemas, it was decided that it was too much trouble! The Sensurround movies were *Earthquake* (1974), *Midway* (1976), *Rollercoaster* (1977), *Battlestar Galactica* (1979) and *Zoot Suit* (1982). Each film presented a modified version of Sensurround, with *Zoot Suit* using Sensurround+Plus, a DBX noise reduction system without any rumble. It was – so far – Sensurround's last tremor.

— BIG SCREEN – IMAX —

IMAX cinemas use the largest screens commonly available. The word IMAX is an abbreviation of 'Image Maximum'. The BFI London IMAX Cinema has a screen 20 metres high and 26 metres wide. It's 12 times the size of the clockface of Big Ben.

— SOME *CASABLANCA* QUOTES —

Casablanca (1942), starring Humphrey Bogart, Ingrid Bergman and Claude Rains, was intended to be just another studio war film. No one could have foreseen that it would become one of the defining films of 1940s Hollywood, with a script so memorable that its lines would become second nature to millions (even if they are sometimes misquoted).

Ilsa: 'Play it, Sam. Play "As Time Goes By".'

Rick: 'Of all the gin joints in all the towns in all the world, she walks into mine.'

Ilsa: 'Kiss me. Kiss me as if it were the last time.'

Captain Renault: 'Realising the importance of the case, my men are rounding up twice the usual number of suspects.'

Captain Renault: 'I'm shocked, shocked to find out that gambling is going on here!' (Then, after he is handed his winnings) 'Oh, thank you very much.'

Rick: 'We'll always have Paris.'

Rick: 'Here's looking at you, kid.'

Rick: '...it doesn't take much to see that the problems of three little people don't amount to a hill of beans in this crazy world.'

Rick: 'Louis, I think this is the beginning of a beautiful friendship.'

— *THE FELLOWSHIP OF THE RING* —

Peter Jackson's film trilogy *The Lord Of The Rings* has been hailed by some as the greatest screen trilogy ever filmed. Certainly it's up there with *Star Wars* in terms of profitability. At the time of writing, *Lord Of The Rings: The Two Towers* holds 4th place in the all-time box-office ranking with takings of $921,100,000.

Not bad for a mostly unknown cast. So just who are the actors who became the fellowship of the ring?

Sean Astin (Sam Gamgee) – Son of John Astin (Gomez in *The Addams Family* TV series), Sean Astin was best known pre-*Rings* for his winning turn as Mikey in that lovable 1985 kids' adventure movie *The Goonies*.

Sean Bean (Boromir) – Not an international household name perhaps, but well known in his native England, Bean started his working life as a welder. He found success with the series of *Sharpe* TV films and as the villainous Alec Trevelyan in the 1995 James Bond movie *GoldenEye*.

Orlando Bloom (Legolas Greenleaf) – The English actor's only pre-*Rings* credit is the 1997 film *Wilde*, in the part of (ahem) 'Rentboy'. Reckoned by industry watchers to be one of the hottest prospects of the next decade.

Billy Boyd (Pippin) – A pretty obscure Scottish actor one day, a member of the Fellowship the next, Boyd's previous screen life had been confined to small films and an episode of TV detective series *Taggart*.

Ian McKellen (Gandalf) – Although McKellen had been a superstar to theatre fans for years, it was only more recently that cinemagoers grew to know his face. After years of cameos and arty ventures with limited audiences such as *Gods And Monsters* (which got him an Oscar nomination) and *Richard III*, he finally broke through to the A-list. The vast bulk of popcorn-munchers became aware of McKellen when he put on the beard of Gandalf and – at around the same time – the helmet of Magneto in the *X-Men* series.

Viggo Mortensen (Aragorn) – The New York-born, one-time professional truck driver Mortensen has built a career in solid supporting performances (remember the crippled Lalin in *Carlito's Way*?). Critics spotted him, audiences did so less, but the graft paid off when he beat Stuart Townshend to the plum role of Aragorn.

Dominic Monaghan (Merry) – Born and raised in Berlin, Monaghan's family moved to England when he was twelve. His only pre-*Rings* success came in the shape of a co-starring role in British TV detective series *Hetty Wainthropp Investigates*.

Elijah Wood (Frodo Baggins) – One of the relatively few child actors to 'make it' past puberty, Wood has impressed on screen in films like 1998's *Deep Impact* and *The Faculty*. But it's his work in the *Rings* movies that has made him one of the most recognisable actors on the planet.

John Rhys-Davies (Gimli) – One of Wales's busiest actors, Rhys-Davies is one of those thesps whose face is always vaguely familiar. That's because of memorable roles in big-budget movies – such as his opera-loving Sallah in the *Indiana Jones* films. With well over 100 films and TV programmes to his name, it's unlikely he cares much about not being a huge star.

— BLINK AND YOU'D MISS IT —

The shortest stage play ever is thought to be Samuel Beckett's *Breath*. It lasts for 35 seconds and includes only screams and heavy breathing.

— *LES MISERABLES* —

Les Miserables opened in London in 1985. Claude-Michele Schonberg and Alain Boublil wrote it, with English lyrics by Herbert Kreztmer. The original production was directed by Trevor Nunn and co-produced by Cameron Mackintosh and the Royal Shakepeare Company.

As of 2003, the show has since played over 36,000 professional performances worldwide to audiences totalling more than 48 million people. Productions have played in 38 countries and 213 cities. There have been 31 cast recordings and the show has been translated into English, Japanese, Hebrew, Hungarian, Icelandic, Norwegian, German, Polish, Swedish, Dutch, Danish, French, Czech, Castilian, Mauritian Creole, Flemish, Finnish, Argentinian, Portuguese, Estonian and Mexican Spanish.

Each performance uses 392 costumes and 101 cast and crew.

— ELLEN TERRY'S THEATRICAL FAMILY —

There have been some far-reaching theatrical dynasties (not least the Redgraves), but none quite so far-reaching as the family of the great British actress Ellen Terry, of whom the most famous member was John Gielgud. At *Ellen Terry's Jubilee Matinee* held at the Theatre Royal, Drury Lane, on 12 June 1906, no fewer than 22 members of her family appeared with her (including Gielgud's mother, Kate) in the dance from Shakespeare's *Much Ado About Nothing*. Officially this is the most family members ever to act on the same stage in one production!

— MULTICOLOURED GANGSTERS —

In 1992 writer and director Quentin Tarantino famously gave the hoodlum anti-heroes of his breakout movie *Reservoir Dogs* colours instead of names. It's a device that had also been used in the fabulous hijack (of a New York underground train!) film *The Taking Of Pelham One Two Three* in 1979. Here are the multicoloured gangsters and the actors who played them.

The Taking Of Pelham One Two Three

Role	Actor
Mr Blue (Bernard Ryder)	Robert Shaw
Mr Gray (Joe Welcome)	Hector Elizondo
Mr Green (Harold Longman)	Martin Balsam
Mr Brown (George Steever)	Earl Hindman

Reservoir Dogs

Role	Actor
Mr Orange (Freddy Newandyke)	Tim Roth
Mr White (Lawrence Dimmick)	Harvey Keitel
Mr Blonde (Vic Vega)	Michael Madsen
Mr Pink	Steve Buscemi
Mr Blue	Edward Bunker
Mr Brown	Quentin Tarantino

— BAGPUSS —

Bagpuss was a British TV animated series about the adventures of a cat with pink and white stripes that lives in a shop owned by Emily. In each episode Bagpuss wakes up and mends a different object with his friends, such as the mice of the Marvellous Mechanical Mouse Organ, Gabriel the toad (with a guitar), the 'very distinguished' woodpecker book-end Professor Yaffle and Madeleine the rag doll.

There were only 13 episodes ever made. Their titles were 'Ship In A Bottle', 'The Owls Of Athens', 'The Frog Princess', 'The Hamish', 'Flying', 'The Ballet Shoe', 'The Wise Man', 'The Giant', 'The Mouse Mill', 'The Elephant', 'Old Man's Beard', 'The Fiddle and Uncle Feedle'. The names of the mice were Charlie Mouse, Jenny Mouse, Eddie Mouse, Janey Mouse, Willy Mouse and Lizzie Mouse.

'When Bagpuss wakes up all his friends wake up too.'

— BEN JOHNSON'S BODY —

Ben Johnson was one of the best loved of Elizabethan playwrights and a personal friend of William Shakespeare. However, when he died in 1637, although he was granted a grave in Westminster Abbey, he was buried standing up – to save on costs.

— BRECHT AND THE BERLINER ENSEMBLE —

It was in 1948 that Bertolt Brecht returned to Berlin. The East German government promised to fund his own company and the result was the Berliner Ensemble at the Deutsches Theater. The playwright's production of his own *Mother Courage* gave the company a flying start in 1949 – with Brecht's wife Helene Weigel providing a legendary performance as a matriarch struggling to survive in wartime.

In 1954 the company moved to the Theater am Schiffbauerdamm and after Brecht died it was Weigel who took over. During these years the 296-strong ensemble built its reputation as one of the finest, definitive companies of the 20th century. These were the classic years of the Berliner Ensemble, which arguably ended with the death of Weigel in 1971, when Ruth Berghaus took over the reins.

— *PLAYBOY*'S FAVOURITE MOVIE NUDE SCENES —

In 2003 *Playboy*'s website unveiled their ten 'most memorable nude scenes of modern times. Here are their choices.

1) *Fast Times At Ridgemont High* (1982): In a dream sequence, Phoebe Cates pops her bikini-top on emerging from a pool, which rather impresses the watching Judge Reinhold!

2) *Swordfish* (2001): Halle Berry lowers her book, to startling effect when Hugh Jackman notices that she has no top on.

3) *Basic Instinct* (1992): Sharon Stone flashes a surprise in a police interrogation.

4) *Showgirls* (1995): Elizabeth Berkley and Rena Riffel show off their pole-dancing talents.

5) *Striptease* (1996): This features more pole-dancing, this time from Demi Moore.

6) *Short Cuts* (1993): Julianne Moore removes all clothes below the waist while in the middle of a blazing row with husband Matthew Modine.

7) *Revenge Of The Nerds* (1984): Surveillance cameras in the sorority girls' bathroom.

8) *Lifeforce* (1985): Space vampire Mathilda May seduces her victims with her feminine wiles.

9) *Pret-à-Porter* (1992): Robert Altman's satire on the fashion industry includes a scene-stealing nude collection on the catwalk!

10) *Working Girl* (1988): Melanie Griffith does the vacuuming in panties and high heels.

— WEST END THEATRE MAP —

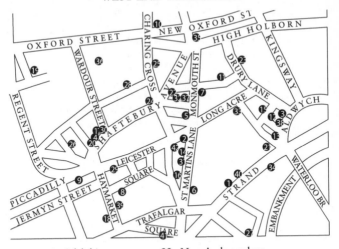

1 Adelphi	22 New Ambassadors
2 Alberry	23 New London
3 Aldwych	24 Palace
4 Apollo	25 Phoenix
5 Arts	26 Piccadilly
6 Coliseum	27 Playhouse
7 Cambridge	28 Prince Edward
8 Comedy	29 Prince of Wales
9 Criterion	30 Queens
10 Dominion	31 Royal Court Downstairs
11 Donmar	32 Royal Court Upstairs
12 Drury Lane	33 Royal Opera House
13 Duchess	34 Savoy
14 Duke of York's	35 Shaftesbury
15 Fortune	36 Soho
16 Garrick	37 St Martin's
17 Gielgud	38 Strand
18 Her Majesty's	39 Theatre Royal Haymarket
19 London Palladium	40 Vaudeville
20 Lyric	41 Whitehall
21 Lyceum	42 Wyndhams

— MICKEY MOUSE'S BIRTHDAY —

Mickey Mouse's official birthday falls on 18 November. He was 'born' when his black-and-white movie debut *Steamboat Willie* debuted at New York's Colony Theater on that date in 1928. In 2003 Walt Disney World celebrated their favourite mouse turning 75 (and not looking a day older than he did in 1928!) with 75 6-foot tall, 700-pound statues of Mickey in various poses inspired or designed by personalities including Andre Agassi, Ellen DeGeneres and Janet Jackson.

— THE OSBOURNES —

When Music Television (MTV) started following the eccentric family of singer Ozzy Osbourne in 2002 the eccentric brood caught the public imagination. Viewership for some episodes rocketed to a reported seven million-plus in the US alone. Here are the principal 'characters' in *The Osbournes*.

Ozzy – 'The Prince Of Darkness' or, as MTV calls him, 'America's favourite father'.

Sharon – Ozzy's wife

Kelly – Ozzy's daughter

Jack – Ozzy's son

Melinda Varga – The Osbournes' nanny

The Osbournes' pets – Lola (dog), Minnie (dog), Maggie (dog), Baby (dog), Lulu (dog), Martini (dog), Pipi (dog), Puss (cat)

NB: Another daughter of Sharon and Ozzy, Aimee, refused to participate in the series.

— YIDDISH THEATRE, A POTTED HISTORY —

Yiddish theatre was the Jewish theatre genre that used Yiddish, the common language of European Jews before the establishment of Israel in 1948. Originally it was a religious celebration. Ashkenazi Jews from northern and eastern Europe established the tradition of a play on the festival of Purim in the 18th and 19th centuries. Then, during the Jewish enlightenment era, playwrights began writing for the wider public – who spoke Yiddish.

The fathers of Yiddish theatre include Solomon Ettinger (1800–56) who in 1826 wrote *Serkele*, one of the first-known Yiddish plays. In 1876 Romania, Abraham Goldfaden became writer-in-residence for the earliest professional Yiddish theatre, the Broder Singers. Goldfaden expanded his troupe and toured. But, banned from Russia in 1883 and having played the rest of Europe, they moved to New York – where they opened their own theatre.

Yiddish theatre had two official 'golden epochs'. The first was started by Jacob Gordin's play *Siberia* (1892) – which incorporated social realism and kick-started the politically charged Yiddish plays of that time. Yiddish theatre's 'angry young men' included David Pinski (1872–1959), Leon Kobrin (1872–1946) and Solomon Libin (1872–1955). This period also saw the emergence of arguably Yiddish theatre's first acting superstar, Jacob Adler (father of the American method-acting guru Stella Adler). The centre for Yiddish theatre at this time was New York, where such companies were very common.

The 'second golden epoch' came a decade and a half later, and reached far further than New York, as an expressionistic art theatre movement. In 1908 Odessa the playwright Hirschbein started a Jewish theatre that became very influential, with productions including the Vilna Troupe's *The Dybbuk* (by Shloime Ansky) in 1919 and the polemic Moscow State Jewish Theatre. This period saw the emergence of New York's Folksbiene Company, and the left-wing Artef Theatre.

Yiddish Theatre has more of a cult/nostalgia following in the 21st century, with companies such as the Polish Yiddish State Theatre and the Romanian Yiddish State Theatre still flying the flag.

— BANNING THEATRE —

In 1737, England passed the Licensing Act, which gave the Lord Chamberlain the power to license plays – which is where the phrase 'legitimate theatre' comes from. The power wasn't revoked until 1968, during which time many plays today acknowledged as masterpieces were branded unfit for public consumption and banned from anywhere other than private clubs. If theatres defied the ban, they could be shut down. Among those blacklisted in the 20th century:

- WS Gilbert and Arthur Sullivan's *The Mikado* – temporarily banned in 1907 to avoid insulting the visiting Crown Prince of Japan
- Strindberg's *Miss Julie* – on moral grounds
- Pirandello's *Six Characters In Search Of An Author* – on moral grounds
- Laurence Houseman's *Victoria Regina* – banned 1934, for portrayal of Royal Family members
- Samuel Beckett's *Endgame* – banned 1958, due to references to the non-existence of God
- Eugene O'Neill's *Desire Under The Elms*
- Arthur Miller's *A View From The Bridge*
- John Osborne's *A Patriot For Me* – allowed only private club performances in 1964
- Fernando Arrabal's *Car Cemetery* – banned 1968, for a 'blasphemous' crucifixion scene, this was the last play to be denied a licence by the Lord Chamberlain

— KING OF THE STUNTMEN —

Known as the most prolific stuntman in the film business (he holds the Guinness World Record for this category), Vic Armstrong's career spans nearly 40 years. From an uncredited beginning in *Arabesque* (a 1966 spy film starring Gregory Peck and Sophia Loren), Armstrong went on to risk his neck in over 200 films. He doubled for Harrison Ford in the *Star Wars* and *Indiana Jones* series and elsewhere, as well as for Christopher Lee, Donald Sutherland, Jon Voight, Christopher Reeve in the *Superman* movies and every 007 in the James Bond series. He has co-ordinated stunts for many films, including *Indiana Jones And The Last Crusade* (1989), *Tomorrow Never Dies* (1997),

Charlie's Angels (2000), *Die Another Day* (2002) and *Gangs Of New York* (2002).

Part of a family of stuntpeople, Armstrong's wife Wendy Leech is a stuntwoman whom he met when they doubled for Christopher Reeve and Margot Kidder in 1978's *Superman*. His two sons and two daughters work in stunts and special effects. Although Armstrong senior has suffered several broken limbs, his work has left him mostly unscathed.

— RAT-PACKERS —

It was Katharine Hepburn who, casting a cynical eye on Frank Sinatra and his pals lounging around after a five-day drinking binge, told them that they looked like a 'rat pack'. The name stuck, and rat-packers Sinatra, Dean Martin, Sammy Davis Jr, Joey Bishop and Peter Lawford became one of the most popular stage acts of the 20th century (they had screen hits too, with films like 1960's *Ocean's Eleven*). For seven years they regularly held court at the Sands hotel in Las Vegas, crooning and making fun of each other and delighting their audiences. Sinatra, leader of the pack, was known as the 'Chairman of the Board'.

> 'The satisfaction I get out of working with these two bums is that we have more laughs than the audience.'
> – Dean Martin

> 'Between us we knew everyone in show business.'
> – Sammy Davis Jr

> 'Being a star has made it possible for me to get insulted in places where the average Negro could never hope to get insulted.'
> – Sammy Davis Jr

> 'I'm trying to figure it out, chairman of what board? People come up to me and seriously say, "Well, what are you chairman of?" And I can't answer them.'
> – Frank Sinatra

— THE *GREMLINS* RULES —

In 1984 a cute film about a cuddly little creature turned halfway through into a vicious horror flick, as the creature multiplied and his fellow 'Mogwais' turned into murderous *Gremlins*. Why? Because, as every fan of this movie knows, the humans didn't stick to the three basic rules that you have to follow when dealing with these cuties.

1) Don't expose them to bright lights, especially sunlight
2) Never get them wet
3) Never, ever feed them after midnight!

— HEARTS OF GOLD —

The hooker with a heart of gold is one of cinema's staple stereotypes. They're almost always female, with memorable male prostitutes comparatively rare (Jon Voight in *Midnight Cowboy* springs most readily to mind). Here are ten of the most famous kind-hearted hookers.

Mary Magdalene
The original pro with feelings, every Jesus flick worth its bread and fish features Mary Magdalene. A selection includes Carmen Sevilla in *King Of Kings* (1961), Yvonne Elliman in *Jesus Christ Superstar* (1973), Anne Bancroft in *Jesus Of Nazareth* (1977), Barbara Hershey in *The Last Temptation Of Christ* (1988) and Monica Bellucci in *The Passion Of The Christ* (2004).

Irma La Douce (Shirley MacLaine)
In *Irma La Douce* (1963) the Oscar-nominated MacLaine is the prostitute who wins the heart of Jack Lemmon's ex-policeman. Unwillingly he becomes her pimp, and her sole client. Adapted from the 1950s stage musical by Alexandre Breffort, Marguerite Monnet, Julian More, Monty Norman and David Heneker.

Amy Post (Sally Field)
Field's lonely call girl joins Tommy Lee Jones to hitchhike to California in *Back Roads* (1981).

Simone (Cathy Tyson)
Bob Hoskins' tough guy finds a job escorting well-to-do prostitute Tyson in Neil Jordan's classic Brit-flick *Mona Lisa* (1986).

Vivian Ward (Julia Roberts)
In *Pretty Woman* (1990), Roberts is swept off the street by Richard Gere's kerb-crawling millionaire.

Alabama Whitman (Patricia Arquette)
Arquette's hooker hooks up with Christian Slater in the 1993 Tony Scott/Quentin Tarantino collaboration *True Romance*.

Sera (Elisabeth Shue)
Shue's Las Vegas working girl sticks around while Nicolas Cage drinks himself to death in 1995's *Leaving Las Vegas*. She got an Oscar nomination, so it was worth it!

Linda Ash (Mira Sorvino)
The same year, Sorvino actually picked up an Oscar as the real mother of Woody Allen's adopted son in 1995's *Mighty Aphrodite*.

Lynne Bracken (Kim Basinger)
Basinger also collected a golden statuette as the femme fatale who seduces both Russell Crowe and Guy Pearce in 1997's *LA Confidential*.

Fantine (Uma Thurman)
Thurman played the down-on-her-luck Fantine in the starry 1998 movie of Victor Hugo's *Les Miserables*. However, the part had already been played on film by – among others – Florence Eldridge in 1935 and Angela Pleasance in 1978. In the long-running stage musical, incidentally, the role was created by Patti LuPone.

— THE MOST CLICHED MOVIE LINE —

It is thought that the most clichéd line in screen history is 'Let's get out of here.' A survey assessed 150 American movies made between 1938 and 1974 and found that no less than 84 per cent of Hollywood productions use it, 17 per cent more than once.

— KILLER PLANTS —

In real life the desire to improve your home environment with a few nice plants is usually harmless and rather pleasant. In the strange world of the movies, however, it can be a fatal mistake!

- The 1956 horror classic *Invasion Of The Body Snatchers* (remade with Donald Sutherland and Jeff Goldblum in 1978) sees plants from outer space take over the bodies of humankind. Enough to make you not want to water the flowers for a month! Key Line (from 1956 version): Dr Miles J Binnell, 'They're here already! You're next! You're next! You're next!'

- In a crater 100 m below sea level, a naval expedition find flesh-eating plants in *The Land Unknown* (1957). Key Line: Dr Carl Hunter, 'You're alone – alone. Do you hear me? Always alone!'

- *Angry Red Planet* (1960) depicts a Mars full of man-eating plants (as well as assorted monsters). Key Line: Martian Voice, 'Warn mankind not to return unbidden.'

- Jonathan Haze battled with the giant, carnivorous plant that promised to solve his woman problem in return for food – in *Little Shop Of Horrors* (1960). Remade in 1986 as a musical starring Rick Moranis.
Key Line: Audrey II, 'I'm just a mean green mother from outer space and I'm bad!...Feed me, Seymour!'

- *Day Of The Triffids* in 1962, starring Howard Keel, featured a meteor shower that sparked a plant rebellion. Key Line: Tom Goodwin, 'Keep behind me. There's no sense in getting killed by a plant.'

- *Attack Of The Mushroom People* (1963), otherwise known as *Matango* or *Fungus Of Terror*, is a Japanese sci-fi movie about survivors of a shipwreck turning into mushrooms.

- Equipped with one of the strangest titles ever to grace a billboard, *The Navy Vs. The Night Monsters* (1966) has some rare tree specimens turning into acid-spouting monsters who take on a south seas naval base.

• *Maneater Of Hydra*, otherwise known as *Island Of The Doomed*, is a 1967 yarn about trees that suck the blood of their victims.

• Edward D Wood Jr, better known as Ed Wood, is generally credited as the worst filmmaker of all time, and in 1970 *The Double Garden* (also known as *The Venus Flytrap* and *The Revenge Of Dr X*) is a classic of its kind. An insane NASA scientist uses the power of a storm to turn a plant into a people-muncher.
Key Line: Dr Bragan, 'How in the hell can anybody be so utterly stupid as to build a rocket base on the coast of Florida?'

• Andy Warhol follower Joe Dallesandro stars as a half-man, half-tree who entices the unsuspecting into his garden, in the surreal *Seeds Of Evil* (1974). Key Line: Poster-line, 'Garden of LOVE, garden of DEATH. He plants the seeds of evil.'

• And, spoofs though they may be, *Killer Tomatoes* (1978), *Return Of The Killer Tomatoes* (1988), *Killer Tomatoes Strike Back* (1990) and *Killer Tomatoes Eat France!* (1991) are all about really nasty, er, killer tomatoes.
Key Line: Swan, 'We have to convince the little housewife out there that the tomato that ate the family pet is not dangerous!'

• In the horror compendium *Creepshow* (1982) a farmer (played by horror maestro and the film's writer Stephen King) finds a meteor that turns everything – including him – into plants. Key Line: Jordy Verrill, 'Meteor s**t!'

• Seeds of an alien plant possess the poor folk of Comet Valley in *Seed People* (1992).

— WHEN THE BUTLER REALLY DID IT —

There are times – not many, mind – when the old cliché is true, and the butler really did do it. Before we reveal some mysteries where the trusty manservant proved less than trustworthy, be warned – we're giving away the endings here!

Film	Butler Played By
Murder By Death (1976) (the butler sort of did it)	Alec Guinness
Murder On The Orient Express (1974) (the butler, amongst others)	John Gielgud
Clue (1985)	Tim Curry
The Shining (1980) (the butler is the original murderer)	Philip Stone

— SOME SHOWBIZ FOLK IN POLITICS —

Vaclav Havel – Czech stagehand-turned-playwright who wrote and spoke against the Communist takeover of Czechoslovakia in 1948. Imprisoned between 1978 and 1983, and again in 1989, but that same year the 'Velvet Revolution' turned his fortunes around. He became president of Czechoslovakia and – when the country split into two – of the Czech Republic in 1993.

Ronald Reagan – No actors have turned to politics more successfully than Ronald Wilson Reagan, who quit a 20-year film career to become Governor of California in 1966. He won the Republican Presidential nomination in 1980 and won with 489 electoral votes next to Jimmy Carter's 49. He served as the 40th president of the United States between 1981 and 1989.

Clint Eastwood – The tough-guy film actor was elected mayor of Carmel-by-the-Sea, California, in 1986.

Sonny Bono – The former on-stage and off-stage singing partner of Cher, Bono became mayor of Palm Springs in 1988, and was elected to the US Congress as a representative from the state of California in 1994.

Cicciolina – A Hungarian-born pornographic film actress (real name Ilona Staller) who was elected to the Italian Parliament in 1987. She continued acting in hardcore roles for two years after her election. In the build-up to the 1990 Gulf War, Cicciolina offered to sleep with Saddam Hussein if he would embrace peace, saying, 'I am available to make love with Saddam Hussein to achieve peace in the Middle East.' She repeated the offer in October 2002. Given to political statements that sometimes involve mentioning parts of her anatomy, such as, 'My breasts have never done anyone any harm, while Bin Laden's war has caused thousands of victims.'

Glenda Jackson – One of the most successful of English actresses, both on stage and screen, the star of *Women In Love* (1969) retired from acting in 1992 to become a Labour MP. In 1999 she briefly stood for election as mayor of London.

Arnold Schwarzenegger – The *Terminator* swapped the cameras for the podium in 2003 to successfully run as governor of California, announcing his candidacy in true showbiz style, on *The Tonight Show With Jay Leno*. In a televised debate with a female rival for the governorship, he brushed aside her comments by suggesting that he had the 'perfect part' for her, in *Terminator 4*. Despite his new job, Schwarzenegger has not yet ruled out more movie acting.

Gary Coleman – Actor who became internationally famous for his role as Arnold Jackson in the 1978 TV series *Diff'rent Strokes*, ran unsuccessfully against Schwarzenegger for the California governorship in 2003.

— JOHN WILLIAMS: COMPOSING FOR ALIENS —

John Williams is among the most prolific of film composers, having written music for over 200 titles. Among the blockbusters he has worked on are the *Harry Potter* and *Star Wars* movies. One of his most rewarding (in every way) collaborations has been with Steven Spielberg, who has used Williams in all but one of his films.

In 1977's *Close Encounters Of The Third Kind*, Spielberg even made Williams's music the focus of the plot. A simple, even childish musical theme became the aliens' hypnotic siren-call:

— WHISTLING IN THE THEATRE —

Whistling in the theatre is frowned upon. Why? For years it was sailors who rigged the ropes for theatres because of their expertise with knots, but, they would always whistle before throwing a rope down from the flies to warn those below to watch out. Whistling was therefore a signal to duck and run!

— SOME PROMINENT SCREEN SPANKINGS —

Forsaking All Others (1934) – Clark Gable spanks Joan Crawford, but it is 'off-screen,' left to sound effects and the imagination.

Kiss Me Kate (1953) – Howard Keel gives Kathryn Grayson an on-stage spanking as part of their ongoing feud (and after she's hit him several times). Subsequent TV versions starred Alfred Drake and Patricia Morrison (1958), Robert Goulet and Carol Lawrence (1968), and Brent Barrett and Rachel York (2003).

McLintock! (1963) – John Wayne administers a full-blown spanking, though he'd previously slapped a lady's posterior in *The Quiet Man* (1952).

If... (1968) – Malcolm McDowell and friends are given corporal punishment in the boarding school where they eventually rebel.

Monty Python And The Holy Grail (1975) – Michael Palin's Sir Galahad braves the 'terrors' of Castle Anthrax, which is entirely populated by sexually frustrated women who ask for a 'good spanking'. Launcelot reluctantly saves him.

Secretary (2002) – Maggie Gyllenhaal assumes the position for boss James Spader as they embark on a sado-masochistic relationship.

The king of movie spanking is Gene Autry. As an old man he had the spanking removed from his films because – reportedly – he didn't want to be remembered as unkind to women. However, Autry spanks Barbara Pepper in *Sagebrush Troubador* (1934), Adele Mara in *Twilight On The Rio Grande* (1947), Gail Davis in an episode of *The Gene Autry Show* (1960) and there were more.

— THE EVOLUTION OF BULGARIAN THEATRE —

Bulgaria discovered theatre comparatively late, partly because of Turkish rule between 1396 and 1878, which forbade visits by foreign theatre companies and stamped out most Bulgarian culture. So it wasn't until the 1840s that a schoolteacher named Iordan Djinot began staging dramatic dialogues, all with moral or patriotic themes. The idea quickly spread throughout Bulgaria, and by the 1850s amateur drama groups were staging translations of foreign plays by the likes of Schiller, Goldoni and Moliere. It was another schoolteacher, SI Dobroplodnij, who wrote the first original Bulgarian play, *Mikhail*, premiered by his students in a Shumen café in August 1856. But even this was based on a Serbian story. However, Dobroplodnij inspired several pupils, including Dobri Vojnikov and Vasil Drumen, to write their own plays, and though both were exiled for their trouble, they wrote powerful works for Bulgarian émigrés in Romania. This period of Bulgarian theatre – concentrating on tales of Bulgarian patriots fighting the Turkish regime – is known as hayduk drama.

When the Turks left in 1878 formal theatres were built, with the National Theatre of Sofia opening in January 1907. The playwright-hero of the turn of the century, a man whose tales of the liberation from Turkey inspired the nation, was Ivan Vazov (1850–1921). His best-remembered work *Khushove* (1894) is still frequently performed in Bulgaria

When ties with Russia were re-established after World War I, Bulgaria was very influenced by Soviet theatre. Bulgarian actors would travel to Russia for training, and in 1925 the Russian actor NO Massalitinov took over the Bulgarian National Theatre. Good homegrown playwrights such as Yordan Yovkov and comedy-writer Stefan L. Kostov were rife, and after World War II Bulgarian drama moved forward again. The old hayduk style found new meat in depicting communists fighting the Nazis and after Stalin's death there were new freedoms in what could be portrayed on stage. These days Bulgarian theatre is moving forward, with some new writers even making their marks abroad in more established theatre communities (Hristo Boytchev's play *The Colonel Bird* won the British Council's 1996 International New Playwriting Award and was performed at London's Gate Theatre in 1999).

— THE EVOLUTION OF STAND-UP COMEDY —

When asked to 'describe the evolution of stand-up comedy', funnyman playwright Neil Simon quipped, 'The absence of chairs.'

— A WEEK'S WORTH OF *SEX AND THE CITY* ADVICE —

In case you're one of those people who live their lives by the sage words of Carrie and friends in HBO's TV series *Sex And The City*, we've prepared a week's worth of handy quotes from the show...

Monday – Carrie: 'The universe may not always play fair, but at least it's got a hell of a sense of humour.'

Tuesday – Carrie: 'Someone once said that two halves make a whole. And when two halves move in together, it makes a whole lot of stuff.'

Wednesday – Carrie: 'Miranda was a huge fan of the Yankees. I was a huge fan of being anywhere you could smoke and drink at two in the afternoon without judgment.'

Thursday – Carrie: 'The gay straight man was a new strain of homosexual male spawned in Manhattan as the result of overexposure to fashion, exotic cuisine, musical theatre and antique furniture.'

Friday – Samantha: 'Money is power, sex is power, therefore, getting money for sex is simply an exchange of power.'

Saturday – Carrie: 'I like my money right where I can see it; hanging in my closet.'

Sunday – Carrie: 'Maybe the past is like an anchor holding us back. Maybe, you have to let go of who you were to become who you will be.'

— MERCHANDISING *THE SOPRANOS* —

Home Box Office (HBO)'s crime family TV drama has been such a hit that spin-off merchandising products are rife. Some of the more fun purchases include:

- The Artie Bucco line of dressings and sauces, including Creamy Caesar, Marinara, Barbecue and Fra Diavolo Marinara
- Artie Bucco's Grill Tower
- *The Sopranos* Bada Bing Tie
- *The Sopranos* Barone Sanitation Cap
- *The Sopranos* Satriale's Pork Store T-Shirt
- *The Sopranos* Bada Bing Babe Silhouette T-Shirt

— THE EARLY DAYS OF AL JOLSON —

Born Asa Yoelson in 1885 in the distinctly non-showbizzy surrounds of Snrednicke in Lithuania, the man who became one of the most famous entertainers on the planet knew humble beginnings. His father Moses Yoelson emigrated to Washington, DC, at the end of the 19th century and, when he had scraped together enough money, sent for Yoel, his three siblings and his mother. It was when his mother died that Asa made his first steps into singing, crooning on street corners for a few pennies to help support the family. Moses, however, never wanted the life of an entertainer for Asa, encouraging him to follow him and become a cantor.

When his father married again the adolescent Asa – who had changed his name to Al – left for New York to be a singer. He landed odd jobs singing in McGirk's restaurant, with military bands and, a little later, as a singing waiter. He changed his name again, to Harry Yoelson, and teamed up with his friend Fred E Moore. Just when things seemed to be a bit steadier, his voice broke. Ever resourceful, Harry Yoelson became Al again and found a new partner in his brother Harry (who himself had changed his name from Hirsch!). Al whistled while Harry sang, until the vocal crisis was over and they joined Joe Palmer as a triple act. The only problem: the names Joelson, Palmer and Joelson were too long for the posters. Which is when Joelson became Jolson. By 1907 Harry and Joe had left, leaving Al Jolson as a solo performer. Moving to San Francisco, he coined his catchphrase – 'You ain't heard nothin' yet!' – and was spotted by Lew Dickstader, the minstrel show impresario. The rest, as they say, is history...

— ALFRED HITCHCOCK'S CAMEOS —

The master of suspense frequently made witty cameo appearances in his films, so that part of the fun for viewers would be seeing if they could spot the distinctively rotund director. Here, for Hitchcock completists, is a list of all Hitch's big-screen cameos.

Film	Cameo
The Lodger (1926)	Twice, once at a desk in a newsroom, and then in a crowd watching an arrest.
Easy Virtue (1927)	He walks past a tennis court, walking stick in hand.
Blackmail (1929)	He looks annoyed by a little boy as he tries to read his book on the underground train.
Murder (1930)	He is seen walking past the murder-house.
The 39 Steps (1935)	As Robert Donat and Lucie Mannheim escape from the theatre, Hitchcock can be seen throwing away some rubbish.
Young And Innocent (1938)	Outside the courthouse, holding a camera.
The Lady Vanishes (1938)	He's smoking a cigarette in Victoria Station.
Rebecca (1940)	As the mischievous George Sanders finishes a phone call the director can be seen taking a stroll nearby.
Foreign Correspondent (1940)	After Joel McCrea leaves the hotel, Hitch is engrossed in a newspaper.
Mr. And Mrs. Smith (1941)	He passes Robert Montgomery in the street.
Suspicion (1941)	Popping a letter in the post.
Saboteur (1942)	When the saboteur's car stops in front of Cut Rate Drugs in New York, who should be standing there but...?
Shadow Of A Doubt (1943)	Playing cards on a train to Santa Rosa.
Lifeboat (1944)	Although the whole film is set on a lifeboat, Hitch manages to make an appearance, in a newspaper advert for the Reuco Obesity Slayer. (He's in both the 'before' and 'after' pictures!).
Spellbound (1945)	Carrying a violin case as he leaves an elevator at the Empire Hotel.
Notorious (1946)	Drinking champagne in Claude Rains's mansion.

Film	Cameo
The Paradine Case (1947)	Getting off a train at Cumberland Station.
Rope (1948)	His silhouette is seen on a neon sign.
Under Capricorn (1949)	Twice – once wearing a coat and hat during a parade in the town square, the next time on the steps outside Government House with two other men.
Stage Fright (1950)	He gazes at Jane Wyman when she is disguised as Marlene Dietrich's maid.
Strangers On A Train (1951)	Getting on to a train, holding a double bass.
I Confess (1953)	Walking past the top of a staircase immediately after the opening credits.
Dial M For Murder (1954)	In a photograph in Grace Kelly's apartment (as part of a class reunion pic).
Rear Window (1954)	He winds up the clock in the composer's apartment.
To Catch A Thief (1955)	Sitting to Cary Grant's left on a bus.
The Trouble With Harry (1955)	Walking past a parked limousine.
The Man Who Knew Too Much (1956)	Facing away from the camera, watching acrobats in the Moroccan marketplace.
The Wrong Man (1956)	He narrates the prologue.
Vertigo (1958)	Walking along a street.
North By Northwest (1959)	At the end of the opening credits, Hitchcock just misses his bus.
Psycho (1960)	As Janet Leigh returns to her office, Hitchcock can be seen through the window, wearing a cowboy hat.
The Birds (1963)	Walking out of a pet shop with two white terriers (actually Hitchcock's own dogs).
Marnie (1964)	Walking along a hotel corridor.
Torn Curtain (1966)	Sitting in a hotel lobby holding a baby.
Topaz (1969)	Being pushed in a wheelchair in an airport – until he gets up, shakes a man's hand and walks away!
Frenzy (1972)	In a crowd, the only one not applauding the man speaking.
Family Plot (1976)	Seen in silhouette through a door of the Registrar of Births and Deaths office. (Hitchcock himself died four years later.)

— NEW YORK STORIES —

Leonard Bernstein's hit musical *West Side Story* (which opened in New York in 1957), a modernisation of *Romeo And Juliet* that tells of gang warfare in New York between Puerto Rican immigrants and native thugs, originally had a different plot. Bernstein and book-writer Arthur Laurents planned to write it as *East Side Story*, with warring Jews and Catholics. However, they actually sat down to write it six years after they first had the idea, by which time they decided that Jews and Catholics were yesterday's feud, and so were born the Jets and the Sharks!

— 'A FEW OF MY FAVOURITE THINGS' —

In Rodgers and Hammerstein's musical *The Sound Of Music*, Maria and the children sing about their favourite things.

- Raindrops on roses
- Whiskers on kittens
- Bright copper kettles
- Warm woollen mittens
- Brown paper packages tied up with strings
- Cream coloured ponies
- Crisp apple strudels
- Doorbells
- Sleigh bells
- Schnitzel with noodles
- Wild geese that fly with the moon on their wings

— RADIO CITY MUSIC HALL —

Open for business on 27 December 1932, a collaboration between John D Rockefeller Jr, the impresario SL 'Roxy' Rothafel and media company RAC, resulted in the largest indoor theatre in the world, Radio City Music Hall. Located at 1260 Avenue of the Americas, it occupies the length of an entire block of New York City. Its auditorium measures 160 feet from back to stage and is 84 feet high. The Great Stage has a proscenium arch 60 feet high and 100 feet wide. Its gold-coloured curtain is the most vast stage curtain in the world. The Hall contains over 25,000 lights. It also functions as the world's largest cinema, with 5,910 seats.

— TRUE SCREEN 'PREDICTIONS' —

Movies have been around for over 100 years, and TV for not much less. But inevitably, devices which seemed the height of sci-fi fantasy when they first appeared on the big or small screen are now common, or could soon be. Here are some 'futuristic' TV predictions that came true.

Telephones where you can see as well as hear the caller – *Star Trek*'s Starship Enterprise used to call up a friend or enemy on screen in the 1966 TV series as the apex of 2260's technology. It is now an increasingly common feature of our mobile phones.

Sticking with *Star Trek*, the **transporter** may have been dreamed up as a way of speeding up continuity (to save the series from showing the Enterprise landing and taking off all the time), but it became one of the series's most popular features. Teleportation of humans may still be impossible, but the first steps have been taken towards teleporting objects. In February 2002 *New Scientist* magazine reported the invention of 'entanglement' teleporting. This uses the theory of 'quantum entanglement', in which two particles can be made to behave as one no matter how far apart they are. By measuring the state of one particle you can determine the state of the other. Laser beams have already been successfully teleported, and the thought of using larger objects in the future is tantalisingly close.

In the 1987 alien-vs.-men hit *Predator* the super-sophisticated extraterrestrial tipped the scales by using a **cloaking device** to make him invisible to his opponents' eyes. (Yes, this device was also a feature of *Star Trek* but didn't mention that for variety's sake!) The same trick was used in the 2002 James Bond film *Die Another Day*. Only by that time it was quite possible. The US military and others are investigating the uses of nanotechnology for camouflage purposes – specifically the way that tiny cameras in a vehicle or even on a coat could project an image onto the vehicle/clothing's other side, rendering anything inside 'invisible' to anyone watching.

— THE REAL VON TRAPP FAMILY – AND WHAT
HAPPENED NEXT —

The 1959 musical by Richard Rodgers and Oscar
Hammerstein II is based on the true story of the von
Trapp family – telling about Maria, the novice nun who
came to look after Captain von Trapp's children in
Austria, married their father, and the family's flight from
the Nazis. There are differences, for instance the fact that
Maria came to look after only one daughter (who had
contracted rheumatic fever), but the broad facts are true.
Maria and the captain were married on 26 November
1927.

The musical has the family, led by the just-married
captain and Maria, making their escape under cover of a
singing competition, fleeing to hike across the Alps. In
fact, the couple were expecting his tenth child, Johannes,
when in 1938 they organised what to all intents and
purposes was one of their regular mountain hikes. They
boarded a train and travelled through the Alps to Italy, on
through Switzerland and then from France to London.
From there they took a boat to America.

Suddenly, the once-rich von Trapps were poor refugees.
They urgently needed work, and the only thing they all
knew how to do together was to sing. So the Trapp
Family Singers started taking on singing jobs at weddings
and birthdays – and they were so successful that they
eventually played palaces and concert-halls across
America and Europe. By 1939 they had saved $1,000 and
bought a 600-acre farm property in Stowe, Vermont. The
mountain town reminded them of their native countryside
near Salzburg. Although they continued touring the world
for another 15 years, Stowe became their beloved home.
Maria named the house *Cor Unum* (One Heart).

In 1947 Captain Georg Ritter von Trapp passed away.
Maria dedicated herself to spreading the joy of music as
widely as possible, opening in Stowe the Trapp Family
Music Camp. Its popularity meant they needed larger
accommodation and so was built the Trapp Family

Lodge. Inevitably, though, the children left to pursue their own lives and marriages and the Music Camp was closed in 1957. Maria, Father Wasner and three of the children (Maria, Rosemarie and Johannes) left to do missionary work in the South Pacific, building schools, a church and reporting back to the church. When they returned, they devoted themselves to running the Trapp Family Lodge, which still operates today, run by the youngest of the von Trapp children, Johannes. Maria died in 1987, and is buried alongside the captain next to the Lodge.

The children:

Rupert (born 1911) became a medical doctor and died aged 80. He had six children.

Agathe (born 1913) moved to Baltimore and works in a kindergarten.

Maria (born 1914) stayed as a missionary in New Guinea for 27 years, then moved to Stowe.

Werner (born 1915) has six children, and lives as a farmer in Waitsfield, Vermont.

Hedwig (born 1917) worked at the Lodge until she died in 1972.

Johanna (born 1919) returned to Austria with her husband, had six children, and died in Vienna in 1994.

Martina (born 1921) died giving birth in 1951.

Rosemarie (born 1929) lives in Stowe.

Eleonore (born 1931) got married in 1954 and had seven children.

Johannes Georg (born 1939) is president of the Trapp Family Lodge, and has two children.

— DVD 'EASTER EGGS' —

Some DVD releases contain hidden features, known as 'Easter Eggs', which can be uncovered if you know where to look. It adds to the general fun of the format. Especially if you're in the know! Here are some Easter Egg giveaways (they do not all work on all regional releases, however).

The West Wing: Season 1 contains a joke documentary on White House security chief. To access: On the fourth disc of the set, go to the main menu and press the 'left' arrow, followed by the 'right' arrow. A star should be highlighted on the screen. Press enter.

Priscilla, Queen Of The Desert contains text and images about early drag queens. To access: At the main menu, press 'up' arrow. A star should be highlighted. Press enter.

Pirates Of The Caribbean: The Curse Of The Black Pearl contains several, but the best by far is a hidden interview with Rolling Stones guitarist Keith Richards, talking about how Johnny Depp based his characterisation on him. To access: On disc 2's main menu, select the 'Moonlight Serenade' scene progression. Highlight the 'Main Menu' option and press the 'down' arrow twice. One of the skeleton's teeth will be highlighted. Press enter.

Moulin Rouge contains several, but the best is a hidden joke reel. To access: On disc 2's main menu, select 'More'. At the next screen, highlight 'Back' and press the 'down' arrow. A fairy will be highlighted. Press enter.

The Lord Of The Rings: The Two Towers (extended edition) has Gollum's speech at the MTV Movie Awards. To access: On disc 1, choose 'Select A Scene' from the main menu. Go to the last page. Highlight 'Of Herbs And Stewed Rabbit' and press the 'down' arrow. The ring appears. Press enter.

The Office, series 1 has Peter Purves 'Who Cares Wins' training video and David Brent singing 'Free Love Freeway'. To access i), insert disc 2, and select the deleted scene '*Slough* by John Betjeman'. When the text introduction dims press 'enter'. To access ii), insert disc 1, and when the phone rings on the main menu, press enter.

Blade II contains the movie's director, Guillermo Del Toro, playing with a sex toy. To access: On disc 2, go to the Production Workshop. Select 'Visual Effects' and highlight 'Progress Reports'. Press the 'right' arrow, then 'up'. A vampire graphic will appear. Press enter.

The Godfather Trilogy (Box Set) has various, the best of which is an amusing montage of foreign language clips and a scene from HBO's *The Sopranos* where the main characters watch and discuss a pirate copy of *The Godfather* DVD. To access the first: On the 'Extra Features' disc, select 'Set Up', then press the 'right' arrow. A globe will appear. Press enter. For the second: On the 'Extra Features' disc, select 'Galleries', then 'DVD Credits'. Use the 'Next' option to go to the end of the credits and eventually the scene will start.

Star Wars Episode 2: Attack Of The Clones also has various, including a 3-minute out-takes selection. To access: On disc 1, select 'Language Selection'. Then select the THX logo and press the following numbers – 1,1,3,8. You may need to press enter between each. If that doesn't work, press 11,3,8.

— *PIRATES OF THE CARIBBEAN* – GETTING BACK TO THEIR ROOTS —

The 2003 action movie *Pirates Of The Caribbean: The Curse Of The Black Pearl* featured plenty of swashbuckling from Johnny Depp, Orlando Bloom, Geoffrey Rush et al. However, there were numerous references to its theme-park ride origins (the film is named after the ride at Florida's Walt Disney World), scenes that actually feature in the ride – except that instead of a real-life Depp and co, visitors get animatronic models! The references include:

- The singing of the song 'A Pirate's Life For Me'
- The sign from which hang dead pirates, seen by Johnny Depp at his first, seaborne, entrance
- The prisoners in jail trying to attract the attention of a dog who holds the keys in its mouth
- The town burning which features a redheaded prostitute and a pirate drinking rum pouring out of a bullet-ridden barrel
- A man sleeping with pigs
- The line 'Dead men tell no tales'
- A skeleton on the Isla de Muerta
- A man being dropped into a well
- A skeletal pirate drinking, with the wine visibly pouring through his ribcage

— FOUR STYLES OF THEATRE CURTAIN —

The use of curtains to hide a theatre's stage was started in Roman times, but dropped out of fashion until enclosed theatres came into being in 16th and 17th century Europe. The main front curtains (ie. aside from any advertising or safety curtain) can use one of a variety of operating systems. Here are the four most common:

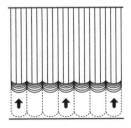

French Valance, or Festoon

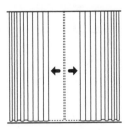

Draw, or Traverse

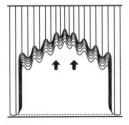

Countour Curtain

Tab, or Tableau

— THE REAL *BABE* —

The 1995 pig-with-a-heart film *Babe* planted its star firmly in cinemagoers' hearts. Although the sheep-pig was a strongly defined screen character, though, Babe himself was in fact played partly by an animatronic double and the rest of the time by – because baby pigs grow so fast – no fewer than 48 actual Yorkshire pigs!

— *FRIENDS* FACTS #3 —

• Chandler's roommate before Joey was Kip. After Joey, there was Eddie, who was mad and so (after some difficulties) was got rid of. After that, the apartment was always occupied by one of the Friends, though Chandler moved out to live with Monica in the apartment opposite.

• Phoebe has performed more than 25 songs on the show since it began.

— 'OH, YES IT IS!' —

The history of the English Christmas tradition of pantomimes is, appropriately for such a boisterous theatrical experience, a classic story of scene stealing. The word pantomime comes from the Roman pantomimes – which was the name given to a performer who used gestures and movements, accompanied by music and song, to tell a story of high passion. Then in the 18th century, an attempt to revive this ancient style was based on the misunderstanding that they were serious dance pieces.

So as not to over-stretch the dancers, stylised, acted tales were introduced to open the evenings and lead to the main event – these were based on popular stories of the day such as *Cinderella*, *Red Riding Hood* and *Aladdin*. Actresses were traditionally cast as the heroes and comedians would play the elderly ladies, who became known as the dames. These fun diversions, known as pantomimes, became so popular that they became longer and longer, finally becoming the sole, full-length evening's entertainment.

The leading English theatres competed to provide the most spectacular pantomimes, which traditionally run from Boxing Day to March. Some actors became so popular in pantos that they acted in nothing else. The form has evolved over the centuries, but as well as the dame and feminine hero, its stylised origins are still evident in the ritual chants of 'Oh yes it is! Oh no it isn't!' and, of course, 'Behind you!'

— VIDEO SYSTEMS —

There are three main television broadcast standard systems generally used around the world – National Television System Committee (NTSC), Phase Alternating Line (PAL) and Sequential Couleur Avec Memoire (SECAM). So when we buy video tapes and machines, they have to be compatible with the TV system in the buyer's home country. For this reason, a video bought in the US will not play on regular video players in the UK; because the US uses NTSC, while the UK employs PAL. Here is a bit about each system, including (some of) the countries in which each is standard.

NTSC: This was the first colour broadcast TV system and was introduced in the US in 1953. Runs on 525 lines per frame. Used by countries including:

American Samoa, Aruba, Bahamas, Barbados, Bolivia, British Virgin Islands, Canada, Chile, Columbia, Costa Rica, Cuba, Diego Garcia, Dominica, Dominican Republic, Ecuador, El Salvador, Galapagos Island, Grenada, Guatemala, Guyana (Republic), Haiti, Hawaii, Honduras, Jamaica, Japan, Johnston Islands, South Korea, Mariana Islands, Marshall Islands, Mexico, Micronesia, Midway Islands, Montserrat, Myanmar, Nicaragua, Okinawa, Palau, Panama, Peru, Philippines, Puerto Rico, Samoa, St Lucia, Surinam, Taiwan, Trinidad & Tobago, United States Of America, Venezuela, Vietnam, Virgin Islands

PAL: Used from the early 1960s, common in Europe (though not France). It uses a wider channel bandwidth than NTSC, so giving better picture quality, and runs on 625 lines per frame. Used by countries including:

Abu Dhabi, Afghanistan, Albania, Algeria, Argentina, Australia, Austria, Bahrain, Bangladesh, Belgium, Botswana, Brazil, Brunei, Cameroon, Canary Islands, China, Croatia, Cyprus, Denmark, Dubai, Egypt, Eritrea, Ethiopia, Falkland Islands, Faroe Islands, Fiji, Finland, Gambia, Germany, Ghana, Gibraltar, Guinea, Holland,

Hong Kong, Iceland, India, Indonesia, Ireland, Israel, Italy, Jordan, Kenya, Kuwait, Laos, Lebanon, Lesotho, Liberia, Liechtenstein, Macau, Macedonia, Madeira, Malawi, Malaysia, Maldives, Malta, Montenegro, Mozambique, Namibia, Nepal, Netherlands, New Zealand, Nigeria, Norway, Oman, Pakistan, Papua New Guinea, Paraguay, Peru, Philippines, Puerto Rico, Qatar, Sardinia, Saudi Arabia, Serbia, Seychelles, Sierra Leone, Singapore, Slovakia Republic, Slovenia, Solomon Islands, Somalia, South Africa, Spain, Sri Lanka, Sudan, Swaziland, Sweden, Switzerland, Syria, Tanzania, Thailand, Tonga, Turkey, Uganda, United Arab Emirates, United Kingdom, Uruguay, Vatican, Yemen, Yugoslavia, Zambia, Zanzibar, Zimbabwe

SECAM: Introduced in the early 1960s, SECAM is used in France. Although it uses the same bandwidth as PAL, SECAM transmits the colour information sequentially and runs on 625 lines per frame. Used by countries including:

Azerbaijan, Belarus, Benin, Bulgaria, Burundi, Cambodia, Central African Republic, Chad, Congo, Estonia, France, Gabon, Georgia, Greece, Guadeloupe, Guyana French, Hungary, Iran, Iraq, Ivory Coast, North Korea, Kyrgyzstan, Latvia, Libya, Lithuania, Luxembourg, Madagascar, Mali, Martinique, Mauritania, Mauritius, Monaco, Mongolia, Morocco, New Caledonia, Niger, Poland, Polynesia, Romania, Russia, Rwanda, Saudi Arabia, Senegal, St Pierre, Syria, Tahiti, Tajikistan, Togo, Tunisia, Turkmenistan, Ukraine, Uzbekistan, Wallis Island, Zaire

— THE LONGEST SCREEN KISS —

In 1941's film *You're In The Army Now* Regis Toomey and Jane Wyman found that military life was not quite as restrictive as may have been thought when they locked lips for three minutes and five seconds, officially the longest screen kiss ever!

— BIT-PART SUPERSTARS —

Here are some actors who had walk-on roles in movies, before breaking through to superstardom.

Richard Dreyfuss had two lines in *The Graduate* (1967).

Sophia Loren was a crowd-scenes extra in *Quo Vadis* (1951).

Kiera Knightley played one of Natalie Portman's hand-maidens in *Star Wars, Episode One: The Phantom Menace* (1999).

Samuel L Jackson was a would-be robber of a fast-food restaurant, but he was swiftly beaten by Eddie Murphy and Arsenio Hall in *Coming To America* (1988).

Cuba Gooding Jr got a haircut in the barber's shop in *Coming To America*.

Tim Robbins replaces Maverick's best friend Goose in *Top Gun* (1986) – a tiny role but he gets to ride in Tom Cruise's jet!

Danny Aiello plays the much-talked-about (but only seen for a fleeting few moments before being shot) Tony Rosato in *The Godfather, Part II* (1974).

Pierce Brosnan played 'First Irishman' in English gangster thriller *The Long Good Friday* (1980). It's a sinister, if super-small role.

— THE MARKETING PLOYS OF DAVID MERRICK —

David Merrick (1912–2000) was the pre-eminent Broadway theatre producer of his era. Bullish, temperamental and brilliant ('the abominable showman', as his biographer Howard Kissel has it, the 'adult terrible' as some newspapers put it), he became famous as much for his imaginative marketing campaigns as for his shows – ingenious schemes, blustering sallies often designed to defeat disapproving critics.

Editors routinely felt the lash of Merrick's tongue. Not one to be cowed by reviewers, after Frank Aston of the *World-Telegram*

And Sun newspaper gave Merrick's 1960 show *Do Re Mi* its only bad review (calling it 'an extravagant disaster'), the impresario phoned Aston's editor. 'Your notice,' he stormed according to Kissel, 'is the greatest journalistic blunder since the *Chicago Tribune* announced the death of Thomas E Dewey.' The editor removed the offending phrase in later editions.

But all Merrick's audacity was on display in his promotional work for the 1961 Jule Styne show, *Subways Are For Sleeping*. Merrick generated publicity with ceaseless imagination. He took out ads urging all winners of Miss Subway competitions to report to his office to audition. (None were accepted but it yielded column inches.) Additionally, he had posters put up in New York subway stations that read, 'Subways are for sleeping.' There was nothing to say that it was an ad for a show, and after police complained to the Transit Authority that the posters were encouraging people to sleep in the subways (which was illegal) the posters were banned. Merrick then started fuming about 'censorship' and publicly called the Transit Authority 'squares'. He also paid for his lawyer to fight the case of Bruno Bella, who had recently been arrested for sleeping on the subway.

He wasn't finished, even when Bella asked to be allowed to remain in prison since it offered better sleeping conditions than the streets. In the quiet theatre month of February, Merrick offered cash prizes in a competition for photos of people sleeping in subways.

Then came his most notorious stunt. Out-of-town tryouts had convinced Merrick that *Subways* would not find favour with the critics. So he had his assistant look in the telephone directory for people with the same names as the major reviewers. He then paid for them all to see the show and collected favourable quotes from them afterwards. When the 'real' critics wrote their bad notices, Merrick ran ads in the *New York Times* and the *Herald Tribune* with his own group's quotes on (he included small photos so as not to be accused of fraud). Despite having arranged for artwork delivery so close to the deadline that the copy would not be properly checked, The *New York Times* version was stopped just in time. However, the *Herald Tribune* ran the ad. When he was taken to task, Merrick went on the attack, saying that his group were real people, and he offered to lend them to other producers!

— WORLDWIDE *WEAKEST LINKS* —

BBC game show *The Weakest Link*, featuring Anne Robinson as a surly presenter who specialises in sour put-downs, has become world-famous for its catchphrase. As contestants lose a round, Robinson dismisses them with a curt, 'You are the weakest link, goodbye!' By 2004, the format had been sold to over 75 countries around the world and the catchphrase has been uttered in many languages. To give you a taste, here it is in ten dialects.

French: *Vous etes Le Maillon Faible, au revoir!*
German: *Du bist der Schwachste, du fliegst, unf tschuss!*
Dutch: *Jij bent De Zwakste Schakel, tot ziens!*
Italian: *Sei la anello debole, serrabarda!*
Russian: *Vy samoye Slaboe Zveno, Proschayte!*
Mandarin (China), in English phonetics: Qiang zhe dui kang, zhi you Zhi Zhe Wei Wang, ni bei tao tai le, Zai Jian!
Mandarin (Taiwan), in English phonetics: Ni shi zhe ge hui he bei tau tai zhe, zai jian!
Turkish: *Zincirde en zayif halkasin, gur-gur!*
Hungarian: *Te vagy A Leggy'ngebb Lancszem, Viszlat!*
Hebrew, in English phonetics: Ata hahulia hahalasha, shalom!

— WILLIAM CHARLES MACREADY: A DANGEROUS ACTOR —

British actor Macready (1793–1873) was one of the two theatre titans of his day, alongside the great Edmund Kean. And he was prepared to go to violent ends for his art. One night, in a Manchester performance of *Macbeth*, he came off-stage for the murder of King Duncan (after which he has to stagger back on gazing in horror at the blood on his hands) to find that his servant had forgotten to be ready with fake blood. Seeing a friend of the stage-manager who had been allowed to watch the show from the wings, Macready punched him hard in the nose, then bathed his hands in the resulting blood and hurried back to the stage. After he came off again he apologised to the startled fan, and gave him a £5 note as compensation.

— MORALITY AND THE MOVIES: THE HAYS CODE —

In the 1920s Hollywood was rocked by three scandals: the Fatty Arbuckle murder trial, the killing of William Desmond Taylor and the death from drugs of actor Wallace Reid. There was widespread worry that Hollywood was becoming a place of lawlessness, corruption and loose morality.

So in 1922 the Motion Picture Association of America was set up as a self-governing body for the film community. Headed by Will Hays, it vowed to make Hollywood a moral place. As movie audiences in America reached record levels after the Depression, Hays passed the Production Code – more popularly known as the Hays Code. Taking effect from 31 March 1930, the code bound major Hollywood studios for two decades.

It forbade nudity, the depiction of illegal drug use, childbirth, venereal disease, suggestive dances and profanity (when Clark Gable said, 'Frankly my dear, I don't give a damn,' in *Gone With The Wind* (1939), there was an outcry despite the fact that he stressed the word 'give'), as well as forbidding the ridicule of religion. Criminals on screen clearly must be shown to be wicked, as must adultery and squalid sex. Marriage must be presented as sacred. Bedrooms had to be treated with 'good taste and delicacy' – in practice, if a man or woman sat on a bed, they had to keep one foot on the floor. A husband and wife usually had to have separate beds (even if they were married in real life, like Lucille Ball and Desi Arnaz)!

The first test case came in 1934, when *Tarzan And His Mate* had short nude scenes chopped out on the Production Code's authority. But when the studio system changed in the 1950s production companies began to disobey the code – key films to defy it being *The Bicycle Thief* (1948), *The Moon Is Blue* (1953) and *The Man With The Golden Arm* (1955). It collapsed during the 1960s, the decade which saw an explosion of explicitness in the cinema and which led to the establishment of the modern classification system.

— SOME UNLIKELY BUT TRUE MOVIE TITLES —

- *Zombies On Broadway* (1945)
- *Bela Lugosi Meets A Brooklyn Gorilla* (1952)
- *Eegah* (1962)
- *Zotz!* (1962)
- *Rat Pfink A Boo Boo* (1965) – should have been called *Rat Pfink And Boo Boo*, but the title designer made a mistake, and there weren't the funds to correct it!
- *Faster Pussycat! Kill, Kill!* (1966)
- *The Incredibly Strange Creatures Who Stopped Living And Became Mixed-Up Zombies* (1967)
- *Oh Dad, Poor Dad, Mama's Hung You In The Closet And I'm Feeling So Sad* (1967)
- *Cottonpickin' Chickenpickers* (1967)
- *Satan's Cheerleaders* (1977)
- *Surf Nazis Must Die* (1987)
- *Night Of The Day Of The Dawn Of The Son Of The Bride Of The Return Of The Terror* (1991)

— THE BIRTH OF DOGSTAR —

Many actors have tried to make it in the pop world. Some, like Bruce Willis and Johnny Depp, even assembled their own bands. One of the best-known such bands is Dogstar, which boasts Keanu Reeves as bass player.

Dogstar got together in 1991 after the *Matrix* star and drummer Robert Mailhouse met in a Hollywood supermarket and found they both loved music and hockey. (Reeves started the conversation by quizzing Mailhouse about the Detroit Redwings jersey he was wearing.) They added guitarist/singer Bret Dormrose and formed Dogstar. The name comes from Henry Miller's book *Sexus*, where Dogstar is identified as the brightest star in the sky.

In 1995 the band opened for Jon Bon Jovi in Australia, played alongside David Bowie and were signed by Zoo Entertainment/BMG. Their albums include *Quattro Formaggi*, *Our Little Visionary* and *Happy Ending*. However, in 2003 Reeves and Mailhouse joined a new band, Becky (also comprising Rebecca Lord and Paulie Kosta).

— HOW TO MAKE FAKE BLOOD —

There are various ways of making stage/screen blood, and different lighting and actors' complexions can require different shades. The best way is to experiment and find what works best. (For the shower scene in 1960's *Psycho* Alfred Hitchcock found that red didn't look red on black and white film, so he used Bosco chocolate syrup instead.) Here are a few recipes that may be worth trying – be careful, they may stain and may not be edible, keep away from eyes and mouth.

1) Ingredients: 25g potassium thiocyanate, 5g ferric chloride, table salt. Add a few ml of water to two jugs. Add the potassium thiocyanate to one jug, the ferric chloride to the other. Then put a pinch of salt in each. Each fluid is clear, but when they touch they will turn red. So you coat the body part to be 'cut' with the contents of one jug, and the weapon doing the 'cutting' with the other, and when they touch, you'll get red 'blood'!

2) Ingredients: Chocolate Angel Delight (powdered desert mix – any similar mixture will probably work), Chinese bright red food colouring. Add water and the food colouring to the Angel Delight, experimenting with different amounts of water for different thickness. If you add a little green dishwashing detergent it will help when washing the blood out of clothes – but don't add too much, or you'll find bubbles and lather everywhere!

— HANDY PHRASES IN KLINGON —

Hello	*nuqneH*
Yes	*HIja'*
No	*ghobe'*
What time is it?	*'arlogh Qoylu'pu'*
What do you want?	*nuqneH*
Where is the bathroom?	*nuqDaq 'oH puchpa''e'*
Happy birthday	*goSIIj DatIvjaj*
Do you speak Klingon?	*tlhIngan Hol Dajatlh'e'*
Where do you keep the chocolate?	*Nuq Daq yuch Dapol*
May your dishes be always served alive	*reH nay'meylIjyIn Dujablu'jaj*
Your mother has a smooth forehead	*Hab SoSlI' Quch!*

— SONGS HEARD IN *HIGH FIDELITY* —

High Fidelity (2000), directed by Stephen Frears and adapted from Nick Hornby's book, stars John Cusack as Rob, a record store owner obsessed by music. Not surprisingly, the movie gets through dozens of songs – over 60, in fact. Here's a complete list of all the tracks featured in the movie.

'You're Gonna Miss Me' The Thirteenth Floor Elevators
'Who Loves The Sun' The Velvet Underground
'The Inside Game' Royal Trux
'I Want Candy' Bow Wow Wow
'Robbin's Nest' Illinois Jacquet
'The Night Chicago Died' Mitch Murray and Peter Callander
'Crocodile Rock' Elton John
'Rock Steady' Aretha Franklin
'Chapel Of Rest' Dick Walter
'Crimson And Clover' Joan Jett & The Blackhearts
'Suspect Device' Stiff Little Fingers
'Most Of The Time' Bob Dylan
'Seymour Stein' Belle & Sebastian
'Dry The Rain' The Beta Band
'La Boob Oscillator' Stereolab
'Jacob's Ladder' Neil Peart, Gary Weinrib and Alex Zivojinovich
'We Are The Champions' Queen
'The Anti-Circle' The Roots
'Walking On Sunshine' Katrina And The Waves
'I'm Glad You're Mine' Al Green
'Everybody's Gonna Be Happy' The Kinks
'Baby Got Going' Liz Phair
'Your Friend And Mine' Love
'Homespin Rerun' High Llamas
'Little Did I Know' Brother JT3
'Shipbuilding' Elvis Costello and The Attractions
'Hit The Street' Rupert Gregson-Williams
'I'm Wrong About Everything' John Wesley Harding
'Tonight I'll Be Staying Here With You' Bob Dylan
'I Get The Sweetest Feeling' Jackie Wilson
'I Can't Stand The Rain' Ann Peebles
'Getting It Together' Grand Funk Railroad
'Let's Get It On' Marvin Gaye and Ed Townsend
'The River' Bruce Springsteen
'Soul Surfer' James Cooperthwaite and Oliver Vessey

'I Believe (When I Fall In Love It Will Be Forever)' Stevie Wonder
'Baby, I Love Your Way' Peter Frampton
'Oh! Sweet Nuthin' The Velvet Underground
'My Little Red Book' Love
'Jesus Doesn't Want Me For A Sunbeam' The Vaselines
'This India' Harbhajhn Singh and Navinder Pal Singh
'Shooting Star' Bob Dylan
'Cold Blooded Old Times' Smog
'Tread Water' De La Soul
'On Hold' Edith Frost
'The Moonbeam Song' Harry Nilsson
'Hyena 1' Goldie
'Juice (Know The Ledge)' – Eric B and Rakin
'I'm Gonna Love You Just A Little More, Babe' Barry White
'Doing It Anyway' Apartment 26
'Always See Your Face' Love
'What's On Your Mind' Eric B and Rakim
'Soaring And Boring' Plush
'Where Did You Get Those Pants' Fishbone
'Leave Home' The Chemical Brothers
'Good And Strong' Sy Smith
'Loopfest' Toby Bricneno and Jay Cryka
'Mendocino' Doug Sahm

— JOHN OSBORNE'S NOTORIOUS POSTCARDS —

English playwright (of *Look Back In Anger* among others) and the original 'angry young man' of 1960s theatre John Osborne was not only one to hold grudges, he seldom kept them to himself. During his lifetime he sent a slew of angry postcards to those who he felt had slighted him or his work.

The Times theatre critic Benedict Nightingale remembers getting an unsigned postcard warning, 'Safer for your health to stay clear of downtown Chichester,' signed 'Chichester British Playwrights Mafia Headquarters'.

The Daily Mail's diminutive Jack Tinker had a postcard addressing him as Miss Tinker and informing him that he too was in line for a fatality, while Osborne labelled the *Evening Standard*'s Nicholas De Jongh 'a second-string pouf'. John Peter of *The Sunday Times* had a card calling him a dim Hungarian.

— SOME TOP TAG-LINES —

'Six Men. Full Moon. No Chance.' *Dog Soldiers* (2002)

'Just when you thought it was safe to go back into the water.' *Jaws 2* (1978)

'Just when you thought it was safe to go back in the water – you can't get to it.' *Blood Beach* (1981)

'In space no-one can hear you scream.' *Alien* (1979)

'He wasn't the messiah. He was a very naughty boy.' *The Life Of Brian* (1979)

'A comedy about truth, justice and other special effects.' *Wag The Dog* (1997)

'Does for rock and roll what *The Sound Of Music* did for hills.' *This Is Spinal Tap* (1984)

'Be afraid. Be very afraid.' *The Fly* (1986)

'Please do not disturb Evelyn. She already is.' *Mountaintop Motel Massacre* (1986)

'A tale of murder, lust, greed, revenge, and seafood.' *A Fish Called Wanda* (1988)

— THE WAR OF THE WORLDS —

Okay, so this is a radio story. I'm cheating. But since it features the great screen and stage star Orson Welles I'm hoping to get away with it...

In 1938, Welles took his Mercury Theatre Company onto the radio with a series of live broadcasts of plays, starting with *Julius Caesar* on 11 September and followed by *Jane Eyre*, *Sherlock Holmes*, *Oliver Twist*, *Around The World In Eighty Days* and others. One of these, the 30 October performance of HG Wells's *The War Of The Worlds*, was to become one of the most extraordinary and famous broadcasts ever.

The show started normally enough, with the company introduction and obviously stagey opening narration. However, the tale had been updated to 1930s America, and soon moved to the device of fake newsflashes, detailing an invasion of Martians. What happened every week happened at this point (around 8:12pm) – a rival station's popular ventriloquist, Edgar Bergen, took a rest while a singer took over. Bored, many of his listeners (12 per cent on this night) turned the dial to find something more interesting until Bergen returned. They found what they took to be real newsflashes about aliens attacking the Earth! The Secretary of the Interior himself seemed to say, '...we must continue the performance of our duties...so that we may confront this destructive adversary with a nation united, courageous, and consecrated to the preservation of human supremacy on this Earth.'

Six million people heard this and were afraid. Three times during the programme, with the switchboard now overwhelmed with enquiries as to whether Martians really were invading, announcements were made to say that this was just a play. Panic spread around the country, clusters of people convinced that they were in mortal danger – in one block of flats, all the residents took flight with wet towels around their mouths and noses as makeshift gas masks, terrified church congregations gathered to pray, weddings were interrupted, people left their homes.

Welles himself finished the broadcast by repeating that the play was 'the Mercury Theatre's own version of dressing up in a sheet and jumping out of a bush and saying "Boo!"' and reminded everyone to remember the 'lesson', 'that grinning, glowing, globular invader of your living room is an inhabitant of the pumpkin patch...that was no Martian...it's Halloween'. He soon knew real fear himself, as the station was besieged by reporters and angry listeners, and even received bomb threats. He eventually made a public apology.

— SOME SONGS WHICH MENTION FILM STARS —

Song	By...	Mentions...
'American Pie'	Don McLean	James Dean
'Celluloid Heroes'	The Kinks	Valentino
		Bette Davis
		George Sanders
		Mickey Rooney
		Marilyn Monroe
'Junior's Farm'	Paul McCartney	Ollie Hardy
'Bette Davis Eyes'	Kim Carnes	Bette Davis
'You're The Top'	Cole Porter	Fred Astaire
		Greta Garbo
'We Didn't Start The Fire'	Billy Joel	Marilyn Monroe
'Vogue'	Madonna	Fred Astaire
		Bette Davis
		Marlon Brando
'Electrolite'	REM	James Dean
		Steve McQueen
		Martin Sheen
'Robert De Niro's Waiting'	Bananarama	Robert De Niro
'Marilyn Monroe'	Willy Russell	Marilyn Monroe
'Puttin' On The Ritz'	Irving Berlin	Gary Cooper
'Candle In The Wind'	Elton John	Norma Jean Baker/
		Marilyn Monroe
'Roy Rogers'	Elton John	Roy Rogers
'The Song About Me And Shirley MacLaine'	Danny Wilson	Shirley MacLaine
'Michael Caine'	Madness	Michael Caine
'Donna (the Prima Donna)'	Dion	Zsa Zsa Gabor
'Always True To You In My Fashion'	Cole Porter	Clark Gable
'Send The Marines'	Tom Lehrer	John Wayne
		Randolph Scott

— BOGIE AND DIANA —

Humphrey Bogart was distantly related to Diana, Princess of Wales. They were, in fact, seventh cousins. She was also related to Rudolf Valentino.

— THE *KARATE KID* CRANE KICK —

The 1984 movie *The Karate Kid* depicts the bullied Daniel (Ralph Macchio) being taught Karate by his mysterious neighbour Mr Miyagi who, we learn, is a Karate expert from Okinawa.

The style of Karate taught by Miyagi is most likely *Te*, which was brought to Okinawa from China around 400 years ago. The character Miyagi was named after the real-life Chogun (or *Sensei*) Miyagi, who created his own style of karate-jutsu called *Goju Ryu*. However, the much imitated 'crane kick' as well as the sequel's 'drum technique' seem to be fictional. The first is a jumping front-kick (in fact Macchio has admitted it was meant to be performed with the right leg jumping, kicking and then also used for landing – as the character's left leg was injured, but the actor could not do this), the second a series of roundhouse punches.

The Crane Kick

— THE BIGGEST TOPS —

Perhaps the most famous circus owner of all time is Phineas Taylor Barnum (1810–1891). Born in Connecticut, he became a showman when he moved to New York City in 1835 and displayed a black woman in his service as the nurse of George Washington, aged over 160. When the woman died she was found to be no more than 70. In 1842 he mounted an immensely successful exhibition of Charles Stratton, or 'General Tom Thumb'. But it was after he retired in 1857 that he ran into debts and creditors forced him back into business. His response? 'The Greatest Show On Earth', a circus-cum-freak show which in 1871 merged with James Bailey's outfit to become the Barnum & Bailey Circus. After Barnum's death in 1891 another circus company, Ringling Brothers, bought Barnum & Bailey. It survives today, retaining the title 'The Greatest Show on Earth'.

Over in England, 'Lord' George Sanger was the most celebrated and successful 19th century circus impresario. Always impeccably dressed, Sanger insisted on wearing a top hat and diamond tie-pin. He opened his first circus in 1853 with his brother. They soon introduced lions, which brought in huge audiences. Sanger married the 'Lion Queen' from Wombwell's Menagerie, who of course joined her husband's company to perform serpent dances in the lions' cage. Sanger was soon a household name and rich enough to buy Asteley's Ampitheatre as a permanent home for his shows. Not that he gave up touring – he would brag that every town in England with a population of over 100 had been visited by Sanger's circuses.

In the 20th century, circuses continued to flourish, even though in many places the accent moved away from live animals to acrobatics. Started in 1971, the Moscow State Circus operates from its 3,400-seater base in Moscow and tours extensively.

But the biggest success story of recent times is the Canadian Cirque De Soleil. Founded in June 1984 by Guy Laliberte, who ran away from home to be a street musician and fire-eater in his teens, he dreamed of a new kind of circus – combining circus arts and street entertainment, with no animals. First performing in an 800-seater big top in Quebec, the company swiftly gained a reputation for jaw-dropping spectacle and theatrical flair. In 1987 Laliberte gambled the company's entire finances on performing for free but with top billing in Los Angeles – they didn't even have petrol money to get home afterwards, but it worked and Cirque got noticed in America. It was fully expanded to an international operation, so that by 2004 Cirque De Soleil employed over 2,500 people from over 40 countries and was simultaneously running nine shows, including *Quidam*, *Saltimbanco*, *La Nouba* and *Dralion*. The company had been seen by over 40 million spectators, and had 4 permanent theatres in Orlando, Las Vegas (2) and New York. 2002 brought revenues totalling around $325 million.

— SCREEN CHARACTERS' FAVOURITE DRINKS —

Some characters are quite specific about their tipples of choice. Here, in case they ever pop round, is a brief guide.

James Bond – Medium-dry vodka martini (shaken, not stirred)

Dracula – Blood

Jeffrey Beaumont in *Blue Velvet* (1986) – Heineken

Withnail – Anything as long as it's alcoholic!

Leon in *Leon* (1994) – Milk

The Dude in *The Big Lebowski* (1998) – White Russian

Lil in *Coyote Ugly* (2000) – Whisky ('Jim, Jack, Johnny Red, Johnny Black, and Jose; all my favourite men')

— CRITICAL OPINION —

There's a famous theatrical anecdote about the English playwright Simon Gray. In the interval of his latest play, he popped into the bar next to the theatre for a quick drink. A fellow audience member, evidently with the same idea, appeared beside him with a friendly smile. 'Saw the same guy's last,' he said. 'That was crap too.' Gray shook his head in sympathy, replying, 'State of Broadway.' His companion continued, 'Somebody ought to give him the bum's rush. Got enough crap of our own. Don't need his.' Gray nodded, 'Yeah.'

— THEATRICAL WALK-OUTS —

Who says 'The show must go on'? Some performers are so temperamental or so disheartened by their material or reviews that they simply walk out mid-run. The last decade has seen several high-profile cases in London's West End.

In 1994 celebrated English actor Nicol Williamson was due to open in a new one-man show about film star John Barrymore, called *Jack: A Night Out On The Town With John Barrymore*, at the Criterion Theatre. And open he did – but the evening closed prematurely when Williamson declared that he was bored after ten minutes and left the theatre.

A Simon Gray play, *Cell Mates*, at the Albery Theatre in 1995 brought a much-anticipated stage turn by Stephen Fry. The reviews weren't ecstatic, but neither were they disastrous. What did proved disastrous for the show was what happened after the papers delivered their verdict. Fry took to his heels, abandoning London and the show. His co-star Rik Mayall and replacement Simon Ward were not big enough draws for a production sold on Fry's name. The moneymen lost a reported £300,000. Fry surfaced some time later in Bruges.

In 2003, comedian Michael Barrymore – once the darling of the British public but less popular after an investigation into a man's death in his swimming pool and reported addiction problems – made his comeback at Wyndham's Theatre. The reviews were negative, and the opening night audience less than enthusiastic, with audible heckling and a lady whose handbag Barrymore emptied onto the stage giving him none-too-amused glares. Barrymore looked shaken, and evidently was so by the whole venture. After four nights he quit, talking of moving to New Zealand.

— HUSBANDS AND WIVES ON SCREEN —

Some husband-and-wife teams who play lovers in front of the cameras as well as behind them.

Couple	In...
Lauren Bacall and Humphrey Bogart	Various, including *The Big Sleep* (1946) *Key Largo* (1948)
Elizabeth Taylor and Richard Burton	*Cleopatra* (1963) *Who's Afraid Of Virginia Woolf* (1966) *The Taming Of The Shrew* (1967)
Ali MacGraw and Steve McQueen	*The Getaway* (1972)
Mia Farrow and Woody Allen	Various, including *Zelig* (1983) *Broadway Danny Rose* (1984)
Nicole Kidman and Tom Cruise	*Far And Away* (1992) *Eyes Wide Shut* (1999)
Kim Basinger and Alec Baldwin	*The Getaway* (1994)

— MATT AND NATH'S RECORD-BUSTIN' WEEK —

In January 2004 it was announced that a new Broadway record had been set for a single week's box-office takings. Over the New Year's Eve week, Matthew Broderick and Nathan Lane's return to the roles they created in the Mel Brooks musical *The Producers* (based on the 1968 film starring Gene Wilder and Zero Mostel) prompted a rush for tickets – and a staggering gross of $1,600,243!

— PAUL NEWMAN'S PUBLIC APOLOGY —

One of the all-time great film actors, Paul Newman, was so ashamed of his performance in *The Silver Chalice* (1954) that he took out a large advert in *Variety*, the movie industry magazine, apologising for it!

— FALSTAFF'S SACK EXPLAINED —

Sir John Falstaff, Shakespeare's great comic knight, is frequently heard calling for his beloved drink of sack – 'let a cup of sack be my poison' (*Henry IV, Part One*). But what is this mysterious beverage?

Apparently, it is a version of the medieval drink, mead, which was most probably brought to England by the Druids and is believed to be the oldest-known alcoholic drink. It's honey-based, with 12 to 16 per cent alcohol volume. Originally thought to be the drink of the gods, it was considered an aphrodisiac and drunk by medieval couples for the month after their weddings to help fertility (hence the term, 'honeymoon').

Sack is made by fermenting eight or more pounds of honey to a gallon of water, and is very sweet. It was thought to have antiseptic qualities, and indeed the sugar would have helped reduce infections and honey contains natural antibiotics. However, the reason Falstaff guzzled it with such fervour is because it was known as the drink of a warrior – the Vikings used to drink mead before battle because it gave an energy rush, a dulled sense of pain and a loss of inhibition. And for Sir John, it would have helped him believe himself to be the great knight he posed as.

— SWEARY SEX PISTOLS —

One of the biggest-ever controversies on British TV occurred when the notoriously foul-mouthed pop group The Sex Pistols let fly during the TV chat show, *Today* in December 1976. Host Bill Grundy became embroiled in an argument with the group after they began swearing freely on his show. According to the *Sun* newspaper, not only was Thames flooded with complaints, one viewer – a 47-year-old lorry driver from Hertfordshire named James Holmes – was so disgusted that he kicked in the screen of his new TV set!

— CIRCUS ARTS —

Here is a list of the central circus arts, established since the first modern circus was staged on 9 January 1768 by Philip Astley in London.

- Acrobatics, including contortion and hand-to-hand balancing
- Aerial acts, including tightrope walking, trapeze, Spanish web and Corde lisse (*French term, literally meaning 'smooth cord', denotes an act where acrobats perform on a free-hanging rope*)
- Animal training, including equestrian feats
- Clown
- Fire-eating
- Fire-breathing
- Hoola hoop
- Human cannonball (*where a person is propelled into the air by compressed air or a strong spring – such people have been known to reach speeds of around 60 miles per hour*)
- German wheel
- Juggling, including contact juggling, devil sticks and Diabolo (Chinese yoyo)
- Knife-throwing
- Magic
- Mime
- Plate-spinning
- Side show
- Sword-swallowing
- Stilts
- Unicycle
- Poi (*derived from the New Zealand tradition where the Maoris mash the kalo plant to make a food called poi – by twirling bags of kali attached to strings – in the circus poi swinging means the practice of twirling devices from the hands, for instance fiery wicks or brightly coloured bags*)
- Ventriloquism

— DVD REGIONS —

Digital Video Disc (DVD) releases are separated into regions, which (unless you have a multi-region DVD player) means that the content manufacturers can stagger international releases. So for instance a DVD Region 1-locked movie release will play only on Region 1 machines. The DVD regions are as follows.

DVD Region 1 – USA and Canada
DVD Region 2 – Europe and Japan
DVD Region 3 – The Orient (except Japan)
DVD Region 4 – Australia and New Zealand
DVD Region 5 – Asia and Africa

— BLUESCREEN —

Developed by Petro Vlahos, with important progress made by Zbig Rybczynski, blue-screen allows actors or presenters to appear to be surrounded by a different background to what is actually around him or her. One of the first and most common uses is in TV weather forecasts, where the presenter seems to be pointing to a map – however he is actually standing in front of an evenly lit, pure blue screen. The blue is filtered away, by taking out everything under and/or over a set level of brightness, and another image inserted.

Blue is usually chosen because the human skin has very little blue in it, so is easy to differentiate. However, green is also popular, orange has been used as has – often television for digital compositing – grey, which is easy for a computer to recognise. Red is occasionally used for special purposes.

On television Blue Screen is more commonly known as Chroma-Key, though there's also a similar – more sophisticated – TV process called Ultimatte, which allows composites to include transparent objects, smoke and shadows.

— AROUND THE WORLD IN FILM FESTIVALS —

Don't try to plot a round-the-globe trip with this selection (it's not meant for easy touring) but it is a brief illustration of the huge number of film festivals around the world. Dates can often change from year to year.

- Women In Cinema Seattle Film Festival (FF), US, January
- Wild And Scenic Environmental FF, Nevada City, US, January
- 3 Continents Human Rights Festival (documentaries relating to human rights), Johannesburg, South Africa, September
- Goteborg FF, Sweden, January
- Festival Du Cinema De Paris (shorts), France, January
- London FF, UK, October
- Fest, Belgrade, Yugoslavia, January
- Bio Reykjavik's 'Bedda' Underground Film Awards, Iceland, Jan.
- Tehran Short FF, Iran, October
- Kidfilm, Texas, US, January
- Bangkok International FF, Thailand, January
- Tokyo International FF, Japan, November
- Freedom FF (films from Eastern and Central Europe relating to the theme of freedom and impact of Stalinism), LA, US, January
- Docpoint (documentaries), Helsinki, Finland, January
- Taipei Golden Horse FF, Taiwan, November
- Nodance (for alternative film-making and debut film-makers), Hermosa Beach, US, January
- Rotterdam FF, The Netherlands, January
- Mostra Curta Cinema/Rio De Janeiro International Short FF, Brazil, November
- New York Jewish FF, US, January
- Berlin FF, Germany, May
- Victoria Independent Film & Video FF, Canada, January
- Cannes FF, France, May
- Brussels Gay & Lesbian FF, Belgium, January
- Golden Rose Of Montreux, Switzerland, May
- Slamdunk FF, Venice, US, January
- Gay And Lesbian FF, London, March
- Slamdance FF, LA, US, January
- Moscow International Film Festival, Russia, July
- Sundance FF, Salt Lake City, US, January
- Venice FF, Italy, August
- Frankfurt International FF, Germany, January
- Zimbabwe International FF, Harare, Zimbabwe, August

— TONIGHT, ON *TONIGHT*... —

America's NBC network premiered its successful *The Tonight Show* in 1953. Between then and 2004, with the 50th anniversary looming, the show has had four hosts.

Steve Allen was *The Tonight Show*'s first face, presenting it live for the first time in June 1953. To begin with, the show went out only on New York's WNBT, but such was Allen's success that it went national on NBC in September 1954. He chatted amiably with guests, made jokes and played piano. But by 1956 Allen had another prime-time show and hosted *The Tonight Show* Wednesdays to Fridays. Guest hosts such as Joey Bishop and Joan Rivers fronted the other two weeknights.

In summer 1957 Allen left *The Tonight Show* and was succeeded by Jack Parr, who positioned himself as a talk-show host who asked intelligent questions. He was also, however, sensitive. A network censor cut one of his jokes in February 1960 and he walked off the set in the middle of the show in protest. When he came back some weeks later, his first sentence was, 'As I was saying...!' After five years, Parr finally left in 1962.

Following Parr, Johnny Carson brought along a sidekick, Ed McMahon, for some knockabout verbal comedy. Carson started his shows with a comic monologue, a feature that is now a staple of talk shows. Guest hosts were used again when Carson began to take long holidays – in fact these became a running joke on the show. But Carson was immensely popular and became one of America's best-loved entertainers. His last show after almost three decades, on 22 May 1992, saw Carson serenaded by Bette Midler.

When Carson began taking his long holidays, NBC finally settled things with a regular guest host in 1986: the stand-up comedian Jay Leno. After Carson left, there was a standoff between Leno and his rival for the job, another NBC show host, David Letterman. The nod went to Leno but, not to be beaten, Letterman defected to rival network CBS and set up his *Late Night* programme as a direct competitor to Leno. Leno lengthened the opening monologue and brought in a high-profile bandleader, the jazz star Branford Marsalis (later replaced by Kevin Eubanks). In 2001 Leno signed a contract to stay with the show until 2005.

— THE *STAR WARS* FAMILY TREE —

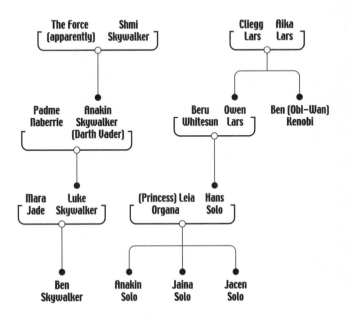

— THE WORLD'S PRICIEST PIECE OF FILM —

How much can a piece of film be worth? Depending on what's on it, a heck of a lot. The most expensive reel of film ever is the famous footage, shot by Abraham Zapruder, of President Kennedy's assassination on 22 November 1963. Zapruder, who was a bystander to the killing, happened to capture the shooting on his camera. According to the *Guinness Book Of World Records*, an arbitration panel ordered the US government to pay $615,384 per second of film to Zapruder's heirs for giving the film to the National Archives. The complete film, which lasts for 26 seconds, is valued at $16 million.

— COUCH POTATOES —

Who says that TV is good for you? According to *Time Magazine* (issue 19 January 2004), Wisconsin resident Timothy Dumouchel threatened to sue a cable company because they left him with free cable TV for four years after he requested that it be cancelled. Dumouchel alleged, 'I believe that the reason I smoke and drink and my wife is overweight is because we watched TV every day for the last four years.'

— CROSS-DRESSERS IN THE MOVIES —

Some of the best-loved/most famous cross-dressers on the silver screen.

Character	Actor	Movie
Josephine	Tony Curtis	*Some Like It Hot* (1959)
Daphne	Jack Lemmon	*Some Like It Hot* (1959)
Norman Bates	Anthony Perkins	*Psycho* (1960)
Dr Frank-N-Furter	Tim Curry	*The Rocky Horror Picture Show* (1975)
Zaza Napoli	Michel Serrault	*La Cage Aux Folles* (1978)
Dorothy Michaels	Dustin Hoffman	*Tootsie* (1982)
Count Victor Grezhinski	Julie Andrews	*Victor/Victoria* (1982)
Anshel	Barbra Streisand	*Yentl* (1983)
Dil	Jaye Davidson	*The Crying Game* (1992)
Euphegenia Doubtfire	Robin Williams	*Mrs Doubtfire* (1993)
Ed Wood	Johnny Depp	*Ed Wood* (1994)
Felicia*	Guy Pearce	*The Adventures Of Priscilla, Queen Of The Desert* (1994)
Vida Boheme	Patrick Swayze	*To Wong Foo, Thanks For Everything! Julie Newmar* (1995)
Mrs Coleman/ Starina	Nathan Lane	*The Birdcage* (1996)
Thomas Kent	Gwyneth Paltrow	*Shakespeare In Love* (1998)
Brandon Teena	Hilary Swank	*Boys Don't Cry* (1999)

* *Bernadette, played by Terence Stamp, is a transsexual rather than a cross-dresser*

— DEATH IS NO BAR TO TV FAME —

In December 2003 one of weirdest-ever pieces of television was filmed at England's Hampton Court Palace. When an alarm bell went off to alert palace staff that a door had been opened near an unused exhibition hall, they ran to check. However, the door was closed. So they checked the Closed Circuit Television (CCTV) footage from the nearby camera. What they saw chilled them to the bone. A ghostly grey figure wearing a sweeping cloak was seen opening the door, leaving, and closing it behind him.

That area of the palace is believed by many to be haunted by a ghost nicknamed 'Skeletor'. Security guards had heard the door slamming mysteriously twice before. If it is a camera-friendly ghost, 'Skeletor' could be any of several ghouls rumoured to hang around Hampton Court – including both Jane Seymour and Catherine Howard, Henry VIII's 3rd and 5th wives, as well as the ghost of Prince Edward's nurse.

— THE FIRST MUSICALS —

Musical theatre evolved out of operetta – a form of opera that often interspersed music with spoken passages. It's an American invention and the first musical is usually thought to be *The Black Crook* (1866), a melodrama with songs which ran for a whopping five hours, but was still a huge hit. The late 1800s and early 1900s saw the art form evolve as high-kicking musical comedies – often revues. Sigmond Romberg provided frothy charmers like *The Student Prince* and *The Desert Song*, while Rudolf Friml wowed New York and London with *Rose Marie*.

But it was Jerome Kern and Oscar Hammerstein who made the first great breakthrough with *Showboat* (1927). Here was a musical that addressed a serious subject, racism, and opened with a chorus of black workers grimly chorusing 'Niggers all work on the Mississippi'.

Lyricist Hammerstein reinvented the musical once again when he joined with composer Richard Rodgers for *Oklahoma!* (1943). The tale of love among frontier life had song and speech merged into real, perfectly paced theatre – a huge step forward, and the musical was up and running!

— THE TV CHEFS —

The chefs dominating the British airwaves in 2004:

Chef	Associated with...	TV Programmes
Ainsley Harriott	Various London hotels	*Ready Steady Cook*
Rick Stein	Rick's Seafood Restaurant (Padstow)	*Food Heroes* *Rick Stein's Taste Of The Sea*
Jamie Oliver	River Café (London) Fifteen (London)	*The Naked Chef*
Raymond Blanc	Le Manoir Aux Quat'Saisons (Oxford)	*Blanc Mange*
Madhur Jaffrey	n/a	*Saturday Kitchen*
Nigella Lawson	n/a	*Nigella Bites*
Delia Smith	The City Brasserie (at Carrow Road Stadium, home of Smith's Norwich City Football Club, Norwich)	*How To Cook*
Antony Worrall Thompson	Notting Grill (London)	*Ready Steady Cook* *Saturday Kitchen*
Nigel Slater	The Savoy (London)	*Real Food*

— 'I CAN'T TAKES NO MORE!' —

Sometimes the acting bug just bites, no matter how hard you try to avoid it. Jack Mercer was born to a pair of actors in 1910, but was determined not to follow his parents into the family business. He loved visual art, so trained to become an animator, landing a job at the Fleischer film studios, producers of the *Betty Boop* cartoons. Yet it was not as an artist that he was to become famous. One day Dave Fleischer heard Mercer singing the theme song to their cartoon series *Popeye* and suggested that he record a cartoon or two. So Jack Mercer became the voice of Popeye, voicing the spinach-guzzling sailor for 294 cartoons over 45 years from 1934. He died in 1956.

— Z IS FOR —

According to David Thomson's 2002 *Biographical Dictionary Of Film*, Garry Marshall's *Chicago* (2002) is the first feature film ever to have two leading ladies whose surnames start with the letter 'Z' – Renee Zellweger and Catherine Zeta-Jones. There aren't many other important Hollywood figures whose names do start with that letter, to tell the truth. Robert Zemeckis, Oscar-winning director of *Forrest Gump* (1997) as well as the *Back To The Future* (1988) series and *Cast Away* (2000), is certainly one. Fred Zinnemann (1907–97), director of *From Here To Eternity* (1953), *Oklahoma!* (1955) and *A Man For All Seasons* (1967), was another. Edward Zwick has directed some successful movies, including *About Last Night...* (1986), *Legends Of The Fall* (1994) and *The Siege* (1998). There's producer (of *The English Patient* (1996) among much else) Saul Zaentz, and the two legendary moguls Adolph Zukor and Darryl Zanuck. And, since we're 'Z' obsessed, it may be worth mentioning that Catherine Zeta-Jones's breakthrough movie was – wait for it – *The Mask Of Zorro*, in which Antonio Banderas carves large Z's around various film sets!

— PLEASE GIVE UP THE DAY-JOB: WHAT THE STARS DID FIRST —

What the stars did before their big break.

Sean Connery – posed nude for art classes, also polished coffins
Harrison Ford – carpenter
Wesley Snipes – parked cars at Columbia University
Burt Reynolds – American football player (drafted by Baltimore Colts)
Whoopi Goldberg – worked in a funeral home (applying make-up to corpses), also a bricklayer
Steve Buscemi – drove an ice-cream van, also a fire-fighter
Madonna – worked at Dunkin' Donuts
Charlie Chaplin – janitor
Arnold Schwarzenegger – had his own successful body-building equipment mail order company
Pierce Brosnan – a circus fire-eater
Al Pacino – cinema usher
Ellen DeGeneres – legal secretary

— NIJINSKY —

One of the most famous ballet dancers of all time, Vaslav Fomich Nijinsky, born in Kiev in 1889, was not – by common consent – pretty to look at. Jean Cocteau once described him as 'all professional deformity. His Mongol-type face was joined to his body by a very long, broad neck. The muscles of his thighs and calves stretched the stuff of his trousers and made him look as if his legs were bent backwards. His fingers were short, as if cut off at the joints.'

Nevertheless, he was an utterly magnetic figure on stage, and became the star of Russia's Maryinsky Theatre. When he met the great ballet impresario Sergei Diaghilev, he fell under his spell, professionally and personally. Becoming Diaghilev's lover, Nijinsky defected to his Paris company, the Ballet Russe. It was one of the legendary theatre partnerships, one that lasted until Nijinsky led the company on its 1913 tour of South America. Diaghilev, scared of the crossing, stayed at home, and once away from his hypnotic personality Nijinsky's eye wandered. He married fellow dancer Romola de Pulszky in Buenos Aries. When the tour returned and Diaghilev found out he was possessed by a jealous rage and fired them both.

The rage didn't last forever and Diaghilev helped get his old friend out of Hungary when he was interned there during World War I. Around 1916 Nijinsky began developing odd paranoias. He seemed to become scared of everything. He was convinced that a trapdoor was left open somewhere on stage for him to fall through. He retreated nervously from other dancers, seemingly terrified of them. Dementia praecox was diagnosed and Nijinsky danced his last role at the age of only 27. He spent the rest of his life in and out of mental hospitals and died in London in 1950. His fame, however, lives on and he remains an iconic figure in the history of dance.

— FILMS ON FILM —

Film directors sometimes like to pay homage to favourite movies by including them in their own films. Here are some classic examples.

• Woody Allen frequently puts in references to his cinematic hero, Ingmar Bergman, and in 1977's *Annie Hall*, Allen's Alvy takes Diane Keaton's Annie to see Bergman's *Face To Face* (1975).

• In *Poltergeist* (1982), the 1943 flick *A Guy Named Joe* is playing in a bedroom. *Poltergeist*'s writer/producer Steven Spielberg later remade the story of a dead pilot who comes back as a ghost, as *Always* (1989).

• While waiting up for Richard Gere in Garry Marshall's *Pretty Woman* (1990), Julia Roberts watches the 1963 Cary Grant/Audrey Hepburn classic *Charade*.

• In Martin Scorsese's *Goodfellas* (1990), Lorraine Bracco's Karen watches Alan Crosland's *The Jazz Singer* (1927) on TV.

• In Quentin Tarantino's *Pulp Fiction* (1994), Bruce Willis's Bruce the Boxer is woken up by Maria de Medeiros's Fabienne watching *Nam's Angels*, Jack Starrett's 1970 film about fights between the Viet Cong and Hell's Angels.

• In Tarantino's *Jackie Brown* (1997), Bridget Fonda's Melanie is watching the 1947 movie *Dirty Mary Crazy Larry*. That film starred Fonda's father, Peter Fonda.

— MARILYN'S FAVOURITES —

In his autobiography, Laurence Olivier complained of the extent to which Marilyn Monroe's acting coach, Lee Strasberg, controlled her. When Lee was not there, his wife deputised and exerted huge influence on the star. But even Olivier may not have realised just how devoted Marilyn was to her teacher. When she died in 1962 at 36, she left an estate valued at $1.6 million. Her will specified that 75 per cent of that should go to Lee Strasberg, with 25 per cent going to her psychoanalyst, Dr Marianne Kris. Her mother, Galdys Baker Eley, was left $5,000 a year in a trust fund.

— A ROYAL RUMBLE —

If you ever visit London's Theatre Royal, Drury Lane, one of the city's grandest venues, look upwards as you enter the circular chamber just beyond the lobby on your way to the stalls. Adding to the general red velvet opulence are two gold signs, one to the left, one to the right. One says 'King's Side', the other 'Prince's Side'. This dates back to one evening when King George III decided to take in some theatre. On his way to his seat – in that same circular chamber – he encountered his son, the Prince of Wales. The two did not get on at the best of times, but on this occasion the king was so infuriated at the sight of his heir that he jumped him and wrestled him to the floor. After tussling with him for some time, the king got back to his feet and furiously declared that the theatre should henceforth have two royal boxes – one for the king and one, on the opposite side, for the prince, and similarly they would each stick to their own sides of the theatre to minimise the chances of bumping into one another there again! Therefore, Drury Lane is the only theatre in London with two royal boxes, each with its own royal toilet.

Indeed, Drury Lane was not the luckiest theatre for George III. One evening in May 1800 a man fired two shots at him as he sat in his royal box. It is said that, despite the near miss, the king was so unconcerned that he continued to watch the play and even fell asleep during the interval!

— BLAIR WITCHCRAFT: HOW TO CONJURE A MAGICAL PROFIT —

The biggest-ever cinematic investment-to-profit ratio was delivered by 1999's frightener, *The Blair Witch Project*. Largely through canny Internet marketing, what was a microscopically modest budget of $22,000 resulted in a film that grossed around $240.5 million worldwide. Or, to put it another way, they made their budget back 10,931 times over!

— BETTING ON THE BOX —

They may have been set up as a sports betting company, but the clamour for odds on the big *Dallas* TV mystery of 1980, 'Who shot JR Ewing?', persuaded William Hill to open books on screen gambles. There have now been hundreds of TV and movies-related bets.

• According to Hill, they've opened books on Will Smith to become President of the USA – and the same for Arnold Schwarzenegger, even though (as a non-American by birth) the rules would have to change for him to even run! Sometimes, though, the risky bet pays off. In 2003 William Hill offered odds of 20/1 for Jennifer Lopez and Ben Affleck not to get married – this was a few days before the planned ceremony, everything seemed set for the wedding to go ahead. The few who took the high odds were of course most satisfied when the wedding was called off at the last minute.

• Reality TV shows have brought in welcome new revenue for the company, with total bets on who will win each series of British TV's *Pop Idol* frequently reaching six-figure sums. In 2003 James from North Yorkshire has even put £10 on *Pop Idol* winner Will Smith to be the British Prime Minister at some point in the future. William Hill have given him odds of 1,000/1.

• A book was opened in 2003 on who will be cast as the new TV *Doctor Who*. At the time of posting, the company put comedian Alan Davies top with odds of 8/1, with Richard E. Grant (14/1), Sean Pertwee (16/1) and Patrick Stewart (20/1) just behind him. Michael Caine lagged far behind at 66/1, with Don Cheadle bringing up the 100/1 rear!

• Meanwhile, anyone who guessed correctly that the BBC's 2003 *The Big Read* series would have ended with Tolkien's *The Lord Of The Rings* being voted the UK's favourite book would have got evens when the book opened. On the other hand, Philip Pullman fans would be bitterly disappointed that the author's *His Dark Materials* came so close at third place. It had long odds, and had it won gamblers could have picked up winnings at a smooth 50/1!

— *COUNTDOWN'S* DICTIONARY OF THE STARS —

Countdown was the first programme ever broadcast by British TV's Channel 4 on 2 November 1982, and in its third decade is still going strong. It was based on the French series *Des Chiffres et Des Lettres*. One of the enduring charms of the series is the rotation of celebrity guests who help look through the dictionary. There have been hundreds, and not always people you'd put in a room together, but here's an intriguing selection.

Pam Ayres
Joan Bakewell
Clare Balding
Thelma Barlow
Don Black
Jo Brand
Barry Cryer
Richard Digance
Vanessa Feltz
Clement Freud
Stephen Fry
Lesley Garrett
Richard Griffiths
Christine Hamilton
Russell Harty
Roy Hudd
Gloria Hunniford
David Jacobs
Helen Lederer
Laurence Llewelyn-Bowen
Sue MacGregor
Magnus Magnusson
Hayley Mills
Mo Mowlam
Barry Norman
Michael Parkinson
Eve Pollard
Esther Rantzen
Tim Rice
Anne Robinson
Arthur Smith
Barbara Taylor Bradford

Carol Thatcher
Ann Widdecombe
Toyah Willcox
Kenneth Williams
Richard Wilson
Ernie Wise
Terry Wogan
Gabby Yorath

— THE NAKED TRUTH ABOUT ROBERT OPAL —

The 1974 Oscar ceremony was raunchy enough already –
porn star Linda Lovelace arrived in a carriage drawn by
two white horses, actress Edy Williams wore a leopard-
skin bikini underneath a fur coat. But things got a whole
lot naughtier when co-host David Niven prepared to
announce the next presenter, Elizabeth Taylor. A naked
man suddenly ran behind him smiling for all he was
worth and making a peace sign. Niven wittily quipped,
'Isn't it fascinating to think that the only laugh that man
will probably ever get is for stripping and showing his
shortcomings?' and conductor Henry Mancini and the
orchestra launched into a spirited rendition of *Sunny Side
Up*. The world was amused and shocked, and the moment
passed into Oscar legend. But what happened next for the
streaker, the 33-year-old Robert Opal?

Security marched him backstage, where he revealed that
he had sneaked in as a fake member of the press. The
event gave him enough notoriety to launch a short career
as a stand-up comedian. He became a popular guest
speaker at Hollywood parties, and even hired himself out
as a streaker (for dancer Rudolf Nureyev and composer
Marvin Hamlisch). But the fame soon faded, and the late
1970s saw him running a sex shop in San Francisco. His
story did not end happily. On 8 July 1979 a robbery at his
shop turned bloody and Opal was fatally shot.

— BASIL BRUSH – ICON AND STAR —

British TV's best-loved fox, the lovable and upper-crust Basil Brush, was originally created in 1964 by Peter Firmin and Ivan Owen (who supplied Mr Brush's voice). He was intended to be the co-star on a children's TV puppet show, with a puppet called Spike McPike leading the cast.

But it was Basil who soon became the star of *The Three Scampis* and, five years later, he landed his very own TV show on BBC One. It was such a success that it was broadcast in 14 countries, attracting audiences of up to 13 million. After an argument over scheduling in 1981, Basil was dropped. But you can't keep a good fox down for long, and Basil made his comeback to star in the popular *Crackerjack* show with Stu Francis.

When Ivan Owen died in 2000 at the age of 77, his most famous creation had just bounced back into fashion once more, with a new series and a lifetime achievement prize from the *Loaded* magazine awards (which made him officially 'cool' for the new generations). In 2003 Basil recorded a CD – *Boom Boom/Christmas Slide* – and entered the race to be Christmas number one.

In a newspaper interview Mr Brush declared his acting heroes to be 'Johnny Gielgud, Larry Olivier, Ralphy Richardson and not forgetting Brian the Snail' and his favourite TV channel to be the Fox Network.

— INDIANA JONES – A DOG'S LIFE —

Indiana Jones may possess one of the most dashing names in cinema, but – as is revealed in *Indiana Jones And The Last Crusade* (1989) – his real name is Henry Jones Jr. The adventurous archaeologist prefers the name Indiana because it was the name of his beloved family dog.

In fact, the movie is correct. The name did come from a dog called Indiana, belonging to producer George Lucas. Lucas then wanted to add the most boring surname possible, so he called his hero Indiana Smith – which was changed to Jones just before shooting began.

— THE STEAMY SIDE OF THE SCREEN – PURVEYING PORN —

Thanks to the advent of video and DVD machines, of multi-channel television, and not to mention the computer screens of the Internet, the pornography film industry is exploding. An American federal study in 1970 put the total retail value of the entire hard-core pornography industry in the US at between $5 million and $10 million. By 2000, according to a report in *The New York Times*, there were nearly 10,000 adult movies made every year in the Los Angeles area alone. Industry magazine *Adult Video News* put the number of hard-core video rentals for 1999 at 711 million. The rental business in America was at that time worth around $4 billion a year.

It was the appearance of the VCR in people's living-rooms that prompted the steady rise (so to speak) of the porn movie industry. By 1985 about three-quarters of all households in the US had a VCR – and the single film *Deep Throat* (1972), starring Linda Lovelace, earned more than $100 million in sales.

Now, major companies like AT&T and General Motors produce or distribute pornographic films. One company that distributes pornographic movies to hotels, On Command, was valued at over $400 million in 2000.

— CLOWN RECORD —

The official record for the largest gathering of clowns ever was set in 1991 in the UK's Bognor Regis, when 850 clowns met for their annual convention.

— UNDERSTUDY – A JOB FOR LIFE! —

Mrs Nancy Seabrooke won the record for the longest-serving understudy when in 1979 she retired from the cast of the Agatha Christie play *The Mousetrap* in London. She had understudied the part of Mrs Boyle for around 6,240 performances, over a period of 15 years. She got to perform the part 72 times.

— THREE FILMS ABOUT BUSES —

Summer Holiday (1963) – Cliff Richard's finest hour featured the pop star and friends trekking across Europe on a London Transport AEC Regent III RT.

Speed (1994) – Keanu Reeves and Sandra Bullock stuck on a bus that will be blown up if its speed drops below 50 miles per hour. Several different buses were used during filming, including the GM New Look fleet number 5303 (with a driving mechanism fitted on the roof, so that the real driver could operate from there, while interior shots were being filmed), a TDH 5301 (a bus with a top speed of eight miles per hour, used for the undercarriage scenes) and two GM New Look 4519s (used for the big jump scene).

The Adventures Of Priscilla, Queen Of The Desert (1994) – Priscilla is the name of the bus aboard which two drag queens and a transsexual journey across the desert in Australia to reach a performing job.

— THE LEICESTER SQUARE WALK OF FAME —

London's own, rather smaller, answer to the Hollywood Walk Of Fame can be found in Leicester Square, bordering the grassy square itself. Not always hugely publicised, the square is nevertheless circled by some rather impressive handprints and company logos. Here's the list, together with locations, in full.

East Terrace (North to South)
Warner Brothers
Clint Eastwood
Sigourney Weaver
Richard Attenborough
Richard E. Grant
Helena Bonham-Carter
Walt Disney
Pierce Brosnan
Arnold Schwarzenegger
Jeremy Irons
Maggie Smith

Ben Kingsley
Michael Caine
John Gielgud
Rank
Joan Collins
Nigel Hawthorne
Sadie Frost
Jude Law
Robert Carlyle

West Terrace (North to South)
MGM
Bruce Willis
Ralph Fiennes
Ian McKellen
20th Century Fox
Kate Beckinsale
Sylvester Stallone
Billy Crystal
Paramount

North Terrace (West to East)
Paramount
Patrick Swayze
Tom Cruise
Kate Winslet
Michael Winner
Kim Novak
Universal
Paul Hogan

South Terrace (West to East)
Charlton Heston
John Mills
British Film Year 1985 plaque
Omar Sharif
Alan Bates
Anna Neagle

Handprints obtained, but not yet installed in the square (as of January 2004), include Sean Connery and Stephen Fry.

— THE MONEY REVOLUTION: SPORTS ON TV —

The first televised sporting event occurred when the BBC broadcast a Bunny Austin tennis match on 21 June 1937. Only around 2,000 homes had television sets, and it went by almost unnoticed by the majority of watchers. Few suspected what a source of TV revenue sport would become, or how central to the schedules.

In 1948 the TV broadcast rights for the Summer Olympics in London were sold for £1,500. By stark contrast, the rights for the Sydney Olympics in 2000 brought in over $1.3 billion. The 2008 Olympics in Beijing have been sold for around $894 million for US TV and around $443 million for European TV. But even this is small potatoes next to the 2002 deal between American television and the National Football League – worth a pretty-good-by-any-reckoning $17.6 billion.

And the huge audiences that high-profile sporting events attract can lead to enormous sums paid by advertisers. To take a 30-second ad slot in the 2002 US Super Bowl final, advertisers were looking at a hefty payment of $2.2 million.

— SHAKESPEARE AND THE HIGH C'S —

Many of the major Shakespeare plays have been given the tonsil-bearing operatic treatment. Sometimes they've been successful, sometimes not...

In Shakespeare's home country, Henry Purcell composed a 1695 *Tempest*, based on the Shakespeare comedy and full of songs and dances. His *The Faerie Queen* of three years earlier had also leaned towards dance; a version of *A Midsummer Night's Dream*, it departed from the play with set pieces including a Chinese masque! Centuries later Benjamin Britten tried again, with a 1960 *Dream* that has held its place in the repertoire rather better than the less-literal Purcell. Britten's senior contemporary Ralph Vaughan Williams tackled *The Merry Wives Of Windsor* with his 1929 opera *Sir John In Love*. In 2004 Thomas Ades premiered his opera of *The Tempest* at London's Royal Opera House (a play reportedly mauled by David Garrick and JC Smith in the 1700s).

Generally, though, the English seem to have been somewhat overawed by Shakespeare, with fewer successful operas than some other countries.

Notably Italy. Giuseppe Verdi, a Shakespeare fanatic, composed three of the most popular operas in the repertoire – *Macbeth*, *Otello* (*Othello* without the h, following Rossini's opera in 1816) and *Falstaff* (from *The Merry Wives Of Windsor*). Another *Macbeth* came in 1919 from Swiss-born Ernest Bloch, rarely heard today, and another German, Otto Nicolai, had his own bash at *The Merry Wives Of Windsor*, *Die Lustigen Weiber Von Windsor* (1849). So did an earlier Italian, Antonio Salieri, with *Falstaff* (1799). The Shakespeare that Verdi always wanted to tackle was *King Lear*, but its magnitude defeated even him, and he constantly found excuses to put it off. The irascible old king had no opera, therefore, until Germany's Aribert Reimann wrote the explosive *Lear* (1978). 2001 saw a second version premiere in Helsinki, from the Finnish composer Aulis Sallinen.

The French have produced several Shakespearean operas. Both Hector Berlioz and Charles Gounod composed *Romeo et Juliette*s (there are at least 24 operas of that play, also including Vincenzo Bellini's 1830 *I Capuleti E I Montecchi*), both still frequently performed. Berlioz also tackled *Much Ado About Nothing* with *Beatrice et Benedict*. As for the moody Dane, Francesco Gasparini's *Ambleto* was a 1712 flop, and the play had to wait for 19th century Frenchman Ambroise Thomas's *Hamlet* for a hit.

Samuel Barber's specially commissioned opera, *Antony And Cleopatra*, opened the Metropolitan Opera's new Lincoln Center home in New York in 1966.

There have been other, more obscure or forgotten efforts; such as German singspiel *Falstaff*s by Peter Ritter (1794) and Carl Ditter von Dittersdorf (1796), an English version by Gustav Holst (*At The Boar's Head*), Stephen Storace and Lorenzo da Ponte's 1786 version of *The Comedy Of Errors*, *Gli Equivoci*, and Richard Wagner's little-known *Das Liebesverbot* (*Measure For Measure*). Yet there are still no high-profile operas of *The Merchant Of Venice*, *Twelfth Night*, or *Richard III*.

— INDIAN AFFAIRS: THE BIRTH OF BOLLYWOOD —

On 7 July 1896 the Lumiere Brothers showed six silent short films at Bombay's Watson Hotel. It was the seed that would lead to the growth of the world's biggest film industry – Bollywood (the word comes from joining the name Bombay, the city now called Mumbai, with Hollywood).

The first Indian filmmaker was Harishandra Bhatvadekar, who displayed two shorts using Edison's projecting kinetoscope in 1899. In May 1913 came the first Indian feature film (though there had been an earlier, half-British feature), Dada Saheb Phalke's *Raja Harishchandra*, shown at the Coronation Cinema in Bombay.

The 1920s saw the shaping of a bustling Indian film industry, with companies springing up and flourishing. And when sound arrived, unlike in the West, it was an immediate sensation, totally replacing the silent films – aptly for an industry that came to specialise in big, colourful film musicals. The first Indian talkie was Ardershir Irani's *Alam Ara* (1931), shown at Bombay's Majestic Cinema. The same year, talkies were seen in Bengal and South India.

The turbulence of the next decades was good for the industry. The 1930s saw films about social injustice, and the Second World War as well as Indian Independence brought hugely popular 1940s movies such as Mehboob's *Roti*, Uday Shanker's *Kalpana* and SS Vasan's *Chandrelekha*.

The First Film Festival of India was staged in 1952, and the industry was on the international map. Later that decade came the first Indian movie to catch the attention of the rest of the world – Satyajit Ray's *Pather Panchali* (1955). It won an array of international awards, including a major prize at the Cannes Festival.

Romantic and action films were predominant. But a new wave came with Malayalam cinema, which produced movies such as Mrinal Sen's *Bhuvan Shome*. If classic Indian cinema was showing dream worlds, escapism, the new movement concentrated on social implications and art-house aspirations. So came the new group of directors – Sen, Ritwik Ghatak and Satyajit Ray. Ray's stories dealt with rural and urban humanist themes. Ghatak galvanised the Indian cinema with his tales of the refugees from East Bengal.

Many of the new wave directors came from the south – Bharathan, Jayakantan, TS Ranga, Bhagyaraj, won awards and kudos. Shaji K Karun's *Piravi* (1988) was shown at nearly 40 film festivals.

While in the late 1980s and 1990s musical love stories make a big comeback with hits like *Mr India* (1987) and *Main Pyaar Kiya* (1989), new talents continue to emerge to take Indian cinema in new directions. Meera Nair won the Golden Camera award at Cannes for *Salaam Bombay* (1989), while her second film – the hard-centred *Monsoon Wedding* (2001) – was almost a Mike Leigh-style look at love and marriage. It won a Golden Lion at the Venice Film Festival, as well as BAFTA and Golden Globe nominations.

The Indian film industry is enormous, having produced around 27,000 feature films and become the world's largest. Bollywood, centred around Mumbai, yields over 300 films each year. In 2002 Ashutosh Gowariker's *Lagaan: Once Upon A Time In India* became the first Indian film to receive an Oscar nomination, for Best Foreign Language Film. However, shadows loom over Bollywood – in 2001 India's Central Bureau Of Investigation seized every print of *Chori Chori Chupke Chupke* after learning that members of the Mumbai underworld funded the movie.

— BRUCE WILLIS: FILMING IN HARLEM —

Filming in New York's Harlem district can be a dangerous business. A key scene in *Die Hard With A Vengeance* (1995) required Bruce Willis, as policeman John McLane, to parade around the predominantly African-American district wearing a sandwich board that read 'I hate niggers' (the character is forced to do this by the villain). However, even with security precautions it was deemed too dangerous to have Willis actually do this, so instead the board he actually wore read 'I hate everyone', and the wording was digitally changed afterwards.

— STEPPING OUT WITH NORMA DESMOND —

Sunset Boulevard by Andrew Lloyd Webber and Don Black provided British stage star Elaine Paige with her big Broadway break in 1996. However, she was much shorter than the first Norma Desmond in that production. On opening night, therefore, when the stage directions called for her to regally descend the vast staircase that dominated the stage the audience were treated to a view of her face alternately disappearing and reappearing behind the banister.

To address the fault, the set designer subsequently added around a foot and half to each step. Just as well, as Norma spent a lot of her time on that staircase; according to Paige, she trod 867 steps per performance!

— *PHONE BOOTH* – RING BACK? —

According to an article in *The New Yorker* magazine, the movie *Phone Booth* (2002) started making the Hollywood rounds as a script by Larry Cohen in 1998. The story was about a man who picks up a public telephone to be told that if he hangs up he will be shot and 20th Century Fox bought the rights. After some months during which it was considered by the likes of Mel Gibson, Dustin Hoffman, Robin Williams and Al Pacino, Cohen released his new script called *Cellular*. The premise there was of a man who answers his mobile phone and is told by a woman on the other end of the line that she will be killed if he hangs up. Cue a furious argument between Cohen and Fox; the writer maintained that the stories and scripts were totally different; Fox thought it was basically the same idea. Finally Fox was promised that *Phone Booth* could be released before *Cellular*.

Phone Booth was released in 2002, directed by Joel Schumacher and starring Colin Farrell. *Cellular* is, at the time of writing, due for release in 2004, to star Kim Basinger.

— RESTAURANTS ON FILM —

Want to dine where your favourite movie characters ate? Here's some restaurants, around London and New York, used in some great movies*.

London

Bertorelli's, Charlotte Street – *Sliding Doors* (1998), where Gwyneth Paltrow worked as a waitress.
Café Rouge, Wellington Street – *Four Weddings And A Funeral* (1994), the café where Hugh Grant and Andie MacDowell confess how many people they've slept with.
The Globe Pub, Borough High Street – *Bridget Jones's Diary* (2001), one of Renee Zellweger's favourite hangouts.
Nobu, at the Metropolitan Hotel – *Notting Hill* (1999), where Hugh Grant and Julia Roberts had dinner.

New York

Guido's, 511 Ninth Ave – *Leon* (1994), the Italian restaurant hiding at the back of the Supreme Macaroni Company is where Danny Aiello took care of business.
Kat'z Deli, 205 E Houston Street – *When Harry Met Sally* (1989), yes, this is where Meg Ryan staged her fake orgasm, watched by Billy Crystal and director Rob Reiner's mum.
Carnegie Deli, 854 Seventh Ave – *Broadway Danny Rose* (1984), where a group of ageing comedians fondly swap stories about Woody Allen's Danny Rose.
The Moondance Diner, 80 6th Ave – *Spider-Man* (2002), where Mary Jane (Kirsten Dunst) is working when she bumps into Peter Parker (Tobey Maguire) after graduation.

* Of course, restaurants are subject to closure or moving, so phone before you turn up!

— FRIENDS FACTS #4 —

• The art on the walls of Central Perk coffee shop is changed every three episodes.

• The first line spoken in the very first episode of *Friends* was 'There's nothing to tell.'

• Courteney Cox, who plays Monica in the series, was the first person ever to say the word 'period' on American television, in a Tampax commercial.

— SCIENTOLOGY – THE MOVIE STARS' RELIGION —

The controversial Church of Scientology, started in Los Angeles in 1954 by the sci-fi writer L Ron Hubbard, has attracted some very high-profile film stars. Including Ginger Rogers, Tom Cruise, John Travolta, Kelly Preston, Nicole Kidman (who may be disaffected since her split with Tom Cruise), Jenna Elfman, Kirstie Alley and Priscilla Presley. Travolta even took a pay-cut on the movie *Battlefield Earth*, based on a Hubbard story, so that more money could go to the church.

However, although stars such as Cruise and Travolta often talk about their close affinity to the church, not many people actually know very much about it. Rather more was discovered in 1995 when *The Washington Post* newspaper obtained and published some of Hubbard's secret writings – which reportedly are only shown to members who have reached the church's highest levels of awareness (apparently by paying thousands of dollars). *The Washington Post* reported that the 'scriptures' dictate the following history.

Some 75 million years ago Xenu, the wicked leader of the Galactic federation, was faced with overpopulation and so froze many people in alcohol and glycol and transported them via a spaceship to Teegeeak. The planet of Teegeeak is now known as Earth. Those people were chained to a volcano and blown up with hydrogen bombs. Human misery today is caused by their souls.

There are those who think that Scientology has its sinister side. The Internet is full of accusations and conspiracy theories – such as that Scientology arranged Michael Jackson's marriage to Scientologist Lisa Marie Presley so that he could be indoctrinated and used to recruit young fans.

— STROLL AROUND THE MOVIES: CAMDEN —

If you want to stroll around an area rich in film history, you could do a lot worse than London's atmospheric borough of Camden and its surrounds. A pleasant drive can show you some memorable film locations. Here are some suggestions.

Start around the King's Cross area. Check out St Pancras Chambers for locations in *Batman* (1989). Nearby is King's Cross Station, a prominent venue for Michael Caine in *Alfie* (1966).

Next, drive up to Camden Town Hall for a setting used in the Anthony Hopkins-starrer *Shadowlands* (1993). Camden was, of course, much used by the drinking, out-of-work actors in *Withnail And I* (1987).

Keep going up towards Hampstead. In 1999 the stately Kenwood House was used for *Notting Hill* (where Julia Roberts was making a film within the film). Hampstead Heath itself was much used in *Monty Python And The Holy Grail* (1975). And Parliament Hill on that heath was used in *The Omen* (1976).

— MAKING A KILLING ON TV —

The days when TV was the poor relation of cinema are long gone. These days, actors can make vast amounts from television performances. The highest-ever paid TV stars include Kelsey Grammer, paid a far-from-meagre $1.6 million per episode (in the 2002/2003 series) of *Cheers* spin-off *Frasier*. NBC's *Friends* aren't far behind, with each of the six main cast members on $1 million per-episode from 2002. And you don't have to be post-pubescent to be rich in TV world; teenage twins Mary-Kate and Ashley Olsen (born June 1986), stars of *Full House* and Fox's *So Little Time*, reportedly earn a combined salary of around $1 billion (from TV appearances and related merchandise). Mind you, they started early, landing their big break in *Full House* at the age of nine months and becoming the youngest self-made millionaires in American history (by the age of 10).

— HOW FRED ASTAIRE NEARLY NEVER MADE IT —

When Frederic Austerlitz Jr, aka Fred Astaire – soon to become the most famous dancer Hollywood has ever known – went for his first screen test the report was not encouraging. 'Can't act. Can't sing. Balding. Can dance a little.'

Nevertheless, Astaire was hired by RKO, who teamed him with his most famous leading lady, Virginia Katherine McMath, or Ginger Rogers. Their cinematic debut as a partnership, in *Flying Down To Rio* (1933), set the screen alight, and they starred together in another eight films.

The Gay Divorcee (1934)
Top Hat (1935)
Roberta (1935)
Swing Time (1936)
Follow The Fleet (1936)
Shall We Dance? (1937)
Carefree (1938)
The Story Of Vernon and Irene Castle (1939)

— A PLAY WITH AN ALL-MALE CAST —

RC Sherriff's *Journey's End*, set in a French trench during World War I, premiered in a public reading in 1928, starring Laurence Olivier. It became an international smash. Hollywood took notice and Sherriff was called to write the screenplays for *Goodbye Mr Chips* (1939) and *The Dam Busters* (1954). *Journey's End* was directed by the then unknown director James Whale, who also went to Hollywood and made *Frankenstein* (1931) and *The Invisible Man* (1933).

— MOVIEOKE —

Following the international craze that is karaoke, in 2004 New York film buffs' club the Den Of Cin came up with a cinematic equivalent. Movieoke, as it has been dubbed, involves projecting a scene from a film into a big screen, while the participants see a monitor with the lines as subtitles. They act out the lines as the original plays behind them!

— SIMON COWELL PUT-DOWNS —

A selection of devastating judgements from *Pop Idol* and *American Idol* say-it-like-it-is judge Simon Cowell...

'My advice would be if you want to pursue a career in the music business, don't.'

'That was terrible, I mean just awful' – when a fellow judge suggested that the contestant take singing lessons, Cowell countered, 'You have to have a talent in order to progress it. I don't believe Cassandra has a singing talent. She's completely wasting her money. Sorry.'

'If you had sung like that two thousand years ago, people would have stoned you.'

'Did you really believe you could become the American Idol? Well, then, you're deaf.'

'If your lifeguard duties were as good as your singing, a lot of people would be drowning.'

'You have just invented a new form of torture.'

'That was extraordinary. Unfortunately, it was extraordinarily bad.'

'You sang like a ventriloquist's dummy.'

— A PLAY WITH AN ALL-FEMALE CAST —

The Women by Clare Boothe Luce, was staged on Broadway in 2002 with a cast of 24. Jennifer Tilly starred, while the first Broadway production in 1936 included Doris Day in its line-up. The play is set among the gossipy women's social circles of 1930s Manhattan; but the gossip turns nasty when an infidelity is revealed. The movie adaptation of 1939 featured more than 130 characters, all played by women. That's not all – every animal used in the film was also female!

— BRITISH TV COMEDIES AMERICANISED —

British TV has a long, proud tradition of having its best TV comedies plucked by American networks, and reworked with a new cast – often bearing little resemblance to the original. Here are some prominent examples.

British Series | **US Equivalent**

Steptoe And Son (1962) | *Sanford And Son* (1972)
Recast among a Los Angeles community of African-Americans. Redd Foxx starred and enjoyed a five-year run.

That Was The Week That Was (1962) | *That Was The Week That Was*
Quite successful, original British presenter David Frost transferred in 1963 to the US version, alongside Alan Alda, Buck Henry, Henry Morgan and guest stars including Woody Allen.

Till Death Us Do Part (1966) | *All In The Family* (1971)
Warren Mitchell's cantankerous Alf Garnett became Carol O'Connor's Archie Bunker. An enormous hit.

On The Buses (1969) | *Lotsa Luck* (1973)
A star vehicle for Dom DeLuise, that only ran for one season.

Man About The House (1973) | *Three's Company* (1977)
One of the biggest UK to US comedy successes. John Ritter played a man who shares his flat with two beauties. Ran until 1984 and yielded two spin-off series, *Three's A Crowd* and *The Ropers*.

Porridge (1974) | *On The Rocks* (1975)
Ronnie Barker's prison inmate may be fondly remembered in the UK. Few Americans remember Jose Perez as the Latin American equivalent, Hector Fuentes, in the remake.

Fawlty Towers (1975) | *Amanda's* (1983)
John Cleese's Basil Fawlty suddenly became a woman, in the form of Bea '*Golden Girls*' Arthur. It was such a flop that the last four episodes were never broadcast.

Fawlty Towers (1975) | *Payne* (1999)
In the second (actually third if you count the lone ABC 1978 pilot *Snavely* starring Harvey Korman) remake attempt, John Larroquette took the

Cleese role, as Royal Payne, the proprietor of the Whispering Pines Inn, on the Californian coast. JoBeth Williams played his wife Constance, with Rick Batalla as the bellhop Mo and Julie Benz as the chambermaid Breeze O'Rourke.

The Fall And Rise Of	*Reggie* (1983)
Reginald Perrin (1976)	

Richard Mulligan followed where Leonard Rossiter so memorably led, but the remake didn't last long.

Agony (1979)	*The Lucy Arnaz Show* (1984)

Maureen Lipman's hit series was remade for Lucille Ball's daughter, but wasn't a long-runner.

Dear John (1986)	*Dear John* (1988)

Judd '*Taxi*' Hirsch starred. The show ran for four seasons, which was longer than the UK version!

Whose Line Is It Anyway? (1988)	*Whose Line Is It Anyway?*

A 1998 hit, following the format of the UK original, often with the same cast. Drew Carey hosts on ABC.

Birds Of A Feather (1989)	*Stand By Your Man* (1992)

Starred Rosie O'Donnell and didn't see out one season.

One Foot In The Grave (1990)	*Cosby* (1996)

Richard Wilson's Victor Meldrew became Hilton Lucas, played by Bill Cosby. It ran for four years, but not particularly similar to the original.

Men Behaving Badly (1992)	*Men Behaving Badly* (1992)

Instead of the English no-hopers played by Martin Clunes and Neil Morrissey, NBC had Gary and Tony living in a cool apartment in Indianapolis. Starred Rob Schneider and ran for two seasons.

Cold Feet (1997)	*Cold Feet* (1999)

Only ran for four episodes.

Coupling (2000)	*Coupling* (2003)

A failure, cancelled after four episodes.

— JUST HOW LONG IS *GROUNDHOG DAY*? —

In Harold Ramis's 1993 comedy *Groundhog Day* Bill Murray plays Phil Connors, a mean-spirited TV weatherman. He becomes trapped in a town he hates, Punxsutawney, when he inexplicably lives the same day (2 February) over and over again – Groundhog Day. Eventually he learns humility and many other skills along the way, before he finally is allowed to see February 3rd.

But how long does he actually spend in that one day? The film actually shows him live through 2 February 34 times, but in fact there must have been a much longer repeat. *Groundhog* students, consider the following events.

• Connors becomes an expert in piano, which even for a gifted student must take at the very least one year of constant practice.

• He becomes an adept ice-sculptor, which must take at least a year.

• He becomes a medical doctor, which in the US takes at least six years (he says that doctor is an honorary title, but this seems to be him just being modest.

• We must presume that there is a gap of at least, say, two months between his first days of discovery and the subsequent depression, which leads him to try to commit suicide. (It's implied that there is, since we see him lazing about the guesthouse, and he knows every answer to *Jeopardy* on the television.)

• Before he gets depressed there is a reckless stage, during which we see him date two women, but presumably he went through many more! Let's call it two months.

• In addition to all this, once he'd found hope, he learned exactly what was going on at all times to everyone in the town. No mean feat, this has to be at least two years.

• Finally, he talks of learning to throw cards into a hat through practising for four or five hours a day for six months.

So I suggest that the least-possible amount of time Phil spends living 2 February in Punxsutawney is between 10 and 11 years!

— MUSTN'T OFFEND THE LOCALS! —

Often, major movies undergo slight – sometimes not so slight – adjustments for local audiences' sensibilities. Here are some examples.

The 1973 martial-arts classic *Enter The Dragon* has been subjected to various cuts in the UK. A 1979 version of the film was trimmed by the British censors to delete a fight that involves nunchakas, leaving the scene following, where Bruce Lee sits with the weapons suddenly dangling around his neck, unexplained.

For the German TV version of *Die Hard* (1988), the German terrorists Hans and Karl have been renamed, as the distinctly American-sounding Jack and Charlie!

Steven Spielberg's Holocaust masterpiece *Schindler's List* (1993) was seen in most countries with the song *Yerushalayim Shel Zahav* ('Jerusalem Of Gold') at the end. However, this made Israeli audiences laugh, because there it is a famous pop song dating from 1967. So Spielberg substituted a song written by the World War II Jewish partisan fighter (who was assassinated by the Nazis) Hannah Senesh, called *Eli Eli*.

The 2001 Ben Affleck-starrer *Pearl Harbor* had certain changes for Japanese versions. For instance a scene where Japanese women are seen in kimonos while Doolittle raids Tokyo was cut, and whereas Alec Baldwin as Doolittle originally said, 'Kill as many of those bastards as possible,' Japanese audiences heard him say, 'I myself would choose a tasty target.'

— HOW TO WIN AN OSCAR IN EIGHT MINUTES —

Having missed out on the Best Actress Oscar in 1998 for her role as Queen Victoria in *Mrs Brown*, Judi Dench landed the Best Supporting Actress Oscar for another Queen, Elizabeth I, in *Shakespeare In Love*. Many industry-watchers thought that the Academy were trying to make amends for the earlier omission – especially as Dench won for a film in which she spent precisely eight minutes on screen!

— VAGINA TALK —

Since Eve Ensler's one-woman play about the female genitalia was premiered in New York in 1996, scores of actresses have performed it. The role-call of the genitally obsessed includes these actresses:

Eve Ensler
Cate Blanchett
Kate Winslet
Jerry Hall
Sophie Dahl
Meera Syal
Maureen Lipman
Jenny Éclair
Miriam Margolyes
Edie Falco
Mariella Frostrup
Danii Minogue
Sian Phillips
Ruthie Henshall
Caprice
Lisa Stansfield
Melanie B
Honor Blackman
Samantha Bond
Loretta Swit
Anita Dobson
Rosie Perez
Julie Kavner
Audra McDonald
Hayley Mills
Brooke Shields
Erica Jong
Anabella Sciorra
Robin Givens
Amy Irving
Rita Moreno
Claire Danes
Maria Tomei
Calista Flockhart
Teri Hatcher
Ricki Lake

Julia Stiles
Teri Garr
Gina Gershon
Alanis Morissette

— WHATEVER HAPPENED TO SHIRLEY TEMPLE? —

Shirley Temple was cinema's first and probably most successful child star, getting her big break at the age of three. The curly-haired (reportedly her hair, always done by her mother Gertrude, always had precisely 52 golden curls), dimple-cheeked cutie sang, danced and acted her way to the top – between 1936 and 1938 she was the number one box-office star in the world! Two drinks and a colour ('temple blue') were named after her, and babies – including Shirley MacLaine – were named after her. Her films became huge hits, including *The Littlest Rebel* (1935), *Captain January* and *Poor Little Rich Girl* (1936), *Heidi* (1937), *The Little Princess* (1939) and *Young People* (1940).

However, as happens with so many child stars, once Temple grew up she lost much of her cinematic appeal. In 1949 she renounced film acting. What happened next confirmed the fairy-tale image of the little girl who could do no wrong. Temple turned her attention to politics after marrying Charles Black in 1950 and becoming Shirley Temple Black.

She found success in her new career. If there were no Oscars, there were ambassadorships to Ghana (1974) and Czechoslovakia (1989). She became a US delegate to the United Nations, and in 1979 was the first woman to serve as US Chief of Protocol. She has served on the boards of the United States Commission for UNESCO, the United Nations Association, the National Committee on US-China Relations, the American-China Society and the US Citizens' Space Task Force. In 1983 she helped to found the American Academy of Diplomacy and co-founded the International Federation of Multiple Sclerosis societies.

A grandmother now, Temple Black lives in California with her husband. Her hobbies include golf, gardening, cooking and fishing. But not, as far as can be discovered, tap-dancing or acting!

— EXPLETIVES CORNER —

Offensive as it may be to some, there are some moments when bad language passes into movie legend.

• Clark Gable's Rhett Butler telling Scarlett that, 'Frankly my dear, I don't give a damn,' at the end of *Gone With The Wind* (1939).

• There's the famous moment in Martin Scorsese's *Raging Bull* (1980) when Robert De Niro's Jake LaMotta asks his brother (played by Joe Pesci), 'Did you f*** my wife?' What makes it even more effective is Joe Pesci's shocked expression; to achieve this, De Niro actually said to him, 'Did you f*** your mother?' The line was dubbed in afterwards.

• For sheer cursing bravado you've got to hand it to Al Pacino's raging Tony Montana in *Scarface* (1983) – 'You wanna f*** with me? Okay…Say hello to my little friend!'

• Steve Martin is at his aggrieved best in *Planes, Trains & Automobiles* (1987) as Neal Page complaining to a car rental agent.
   Agent: 'I don't really care for the way you're speaking to me.'
   Neal Page: 'And I really don't care for the way your company left me in the middle of f***ing nowhere with f***ing keys to a f***ing car that isn't f***ing there. And I really didn't care to f***ing walk down a f***ing highway and across a f***ing runway to get back here to have you smile at my f***ing face. I want a f***ing car right f***ing now!'
   Agent: 'May I see your rental agreement?'
   Neal: 'I threw it away.'
   Agent: 'Oh boy.'
   Neal: 'What?'
   Agent: 'You're f***ed.'

• And every young teenager in 1988 was quoting Bruce Willis in *Die Hard* – 'Yippee-ki-yay, motherf***er!'

• Pick your expletive from wonderful David Mamet movie *Glengarry Glen* Ross (1992). Perhaps the finest is Alec Baldwin's ruthless master-salesman's reply to Ed Harris's 'What's your name?' Baldwin turns on him – 'F*** you! That's my name! You know why, mister? Cause you drove a Hyundai to get here tonight. I drove an $80,000 BMW. That's my name.'

• The opening sequence of *Four Weddings And A Funeral* (1994), where Hugh Grant – late for a wedding – peppers the screen with panicked murmers of 'f***itty f***'.

• Then of course there's Yolanda's (Amanda Plummer) screamed opening to *Pulp Fiction* (1994) – 'Any of you f***in' pr*cks move and I'll execute every mother-f***in' last one of you!'

— CHILD STARS WHO LOST THEIR MONEY —

In 1999 the Associated Press ran a story about American former child stars who had lost the fortunes they had made during their years of fame. Paul Petersen starred in *The Donna Reed Show* (1958) until he was 21. He had accumulated a great deal of wealth, but spent it – on things like 20 cars, 5 homes and 30 TVs.

Similarly, *Lassie*'s John Provost – who started his career at the age of three and hit it big when he played Timmy in the long-runner – spent his own nest egg. And *The Courtship Of Eddie's Father* (1969) star Brandon Cruz lost most of his money in bad real-estate deals. He also did his share of big spending, having bought 12 surfboards, 6 wetsuits and airplane tickets in 1 day when he decided to go on a trip surfing around the world.

The reason for the AP story was perhaps the ultimate irony. The financial services company SunAmerica Inc. was paying each of them to appear on talk shows and tell their stories. What is the moral of the story, from the company's point of view? Even wildly successful child TV stars need sound financial planning!

— SCREEN STARS' CHILDREN WITH UNUSUAL NAMES —

Famous parent(s)	Child(ren)
Emilio Estevez	Paloma
Ving Rhames	Rainbow, Freedom
Gary Oldman	Gulliver
Jason Lee	Pilot Inspektor
Eddie Murphy	Zola Ivy
Tea Leoni/David Duchovny	Kyd Miller
Robin Wright-Penn/Sean Penn	Hopper

— WHO KILLED BRUCE LEE? —

Bruce Lee was an enigma during his lifetime. Born at the Chinese hour of the dragon (between 6am and 8am), in the year of the dragon (1940), the Hong Kong dance champion gave lessons on-board ship to fund his passage to America, where he helped define the martial-arts movie genre. But it was his death that became the mystery, the myth.

In 1973, at the too-young age of 32, Bruce Lee Jun Fan Yuen Kam was buried in Seattle's Lakeview Cemetery – wearing a costume from his most enduring film hit, *Enter The Dragon* (1973). Coincidentally, for months before the actor actually died, rumours had been flying around that he had been killed or wounded (reportedly, Lee once picked up the phone to a Hong Kong journalist asking if he was still alive).

In fact, in July 1973, Lee suffered a brain edema, and fell into a coma from which he never recovered. What caused the brain swelling has been argued and speculated about among Lee fans for decades.

Here are some of the clues. The autopsy found evidence of cannabis in Lee's stomach, which could have started a fatal chemical reaction, though the coroner rejected this idea. Queen Elizabeth Hospital's Dr RR Lycette put the tragedy down to a bad reaction to the headache pill Lee had taken that afternoon. The death was officially attributed to 'misadventure'.

But there were other theories. Some suggested the Chinese mafia were to blame because the star refused to pay protection money. Others believed that a rival martial artist pressed him with a dim mak (touch of death). Some of the more bizarre theories include a curse brought about by Lee's recent acquisition of a Hong Kong house that was supposed to be haunted, another that he died while having sex with the actress Betty Tingpei (not so bizarre actually, Lee was at Tingpei's house when he died). Still others put it down to *Oni*, to evil spirits – a theory reinforced when Lee's son Brandon was killed while filming *The Crow* (1994). Drugs, a grudge fight, or simply too much intensity while training – ideas abound.

However, the film industry was not to be outdone by the action star's death. He had filmed fight scenes for the movie *Game Of Death*, so two doubles (wearing dark sunglasses throughout his scenes) were employed to finish Lee's part and the picture was released in 1978.

— SADDAM HUSSEIN, ONE-TIME KING OF THE MUSICALS —

The biggest-ever musical production in Iraq was the Iraqi National Theatre's 2001 staging of *Zabibah And The King*, based on the book by one S Hussein. The tale of a king whose lover is raped, it's a musical metaphor for the 1991 allied invasion of Iraq (the rape takes place on 19 January – the same date the '91 Iraq conflict began). In the show, the king wins through, before dying a hero. It was at least the second musical to use Saddam as inspiration – the melodic *South Park* movie (1999) featured Saddam Hussein himself (well, a picture of him) as Satan's gay lover. So while the Iraqi dictator's capture by American forces in 2003 means it is unlikely that any more musicals will be written by him, he may well feature as a character in the shows of others. *A Torture Line*, anyone?

— STUNTS UNDERTAKEN BY THE STARS OF *JACKASS* —

Since it first appeared on MTV, *Jackass* has sought to push the boundaries of bad taste by having a group of friends do unspeakably disgusting or painful things to themselves and each other, including:

• swallowing a goldfish, then vomiting it up alive
• pole vaulting into raw sewage
• human bowling (putting on a hard hat, lying on a skateboard and being thrown into a group of metal dustbins)
• skiing down a mountain while sitting in a portaloo on skis, with trousers round ankles
• being shot out of a cannon
• tightrope-walking (for the first time) over an alligator-filled pool with raw chicken hanging out of walker's pants
• crashing golf buggies
• paper cutting between own toes
• paper-cutting own tongue
• shooting firework from posterior

— CLASSIC MOVIES REMADE —

A selection of the many remakes (the film industry is not renowned for its constant originality).

The 39 Steps (1935) – Alfred Hitchcock's espionage yarn was redone twice. Kenneth More starred in Ralph Thomas's 1959 version, Robert Powell in Don Sharp's 1978 rehash. Both have lasted in their own right.

Sabrina Fair (1954) – Writer-director Billy Wilder and stars Audrey Hepburn and Humphrey Bogart made this brothers-in-love yarn a classic, but film critics traditionally thought it was one of Wilder's minor works. Which is why Sydney Pollack's 1995 retread was eagerly anticipated, especially as it had Harrison Ford and Julia Ormond in the leads. Without it being a disaster, however, it's fair to say that it did not improve on the original!

The Seven Samurai (1954) – Akira Kurosawa's magnificent tale of samurai defending villagers was transformed by Hollywood for 1960's cowboy classic *The Magnificent Seven* (remade as a TV series in 1998).

Invasion Of The Body Snatchers (1956) – Don Siegel's sci-fi scarer starring Kevin McCarthy is actually probably less well known than its 1978 remake, starring Donald Sutherland.

Psycho (1960) – Another Hitchcock, perhaps his most famous thriller, was remade, to widespread mystification, in 1998 as a shot-by-shot retread by director Gus Van Sant. Vince Vaughn, Anne Heche and Julianne Moore starred. A flop.

Ocean's Eleven (1960) – Frank Sinatra's Danny Ocean led his Rat Pack friends on a daring Las Vegas robbery. Forty-one years later a new Danny Ocean, this time in the comely form of George Clooney, assembled a starry team including Brad Pitt, Elliott Gould and Matt Damon on another Vegas heist – this time helmed by Steven Soderbergh. And guess what? The remake was a success!

Thunderball (1965) – This remake is an interesting, maybe unique, case. Sean Connery starred in this hit James Bond adventure. Then, in 1983, when he decided to come back as Bond, it was in a *Thunderball* remake called *Never Say Never Again*. So the same star played the same part in the same story twice!

Planet Of The Apes (1968) – Charlton Heston made a cult hit of a film about apes ruling a planet. There were several sequels, and in 2001 Tim Burton made a new version of the original with Mark Wahlberg, Tim Roth and Helena Bonham Carter. It wasn't judged to be Burton's finest hour.

The Italian Job (1969) – One of the great British 1960s crime capers, the Michael Caine-starrer was redone in 2003 with Mark Wahlberg, Charlize Theron, Edward Norton and Donald Sutherland. However, much of the plot and the Italy/England locations were changed.

Get Carter (1971) – Michael Caine again, in Mike Hodges's violent, but acclaimed gangster film. There was surprise when Sylvester Stallone took the Caine role for the 2000 remake, which is not generally thought to match the original.

El Mariachi (1992) – Texan director Robert Rodriguez attracted the attention of major studios when his $7,000 budget story of a guitarist on the run from a gang showed well in cinemas, becoming an Indie classic. His next big-screen film, *Desperado* (1995) starring Antonio Banderas, was a virtual remake, as was his 2003 movie *Once Upon A Time In Mexico*!

— SAUDI ARABIA: LAND WITHOUT CINEMAS —

While many states ban certain films for religious, cultural or political reasons, in Saudi Arabia this doesn't happen in quite the same way. According to the country's London-based information office, there simply are no public cinemas in Saudi Arabia. There are no theatres either, although some shows are produced in ad hoc or festival conditions. Is the absence of any cinema industry for religious reasons – many clerics in the country see watching films as a form of idolatry – or to keep tight controls on the spreading of information and (specifically Western) ideas? Probably both.

— AR RAHMAN – 'THE MOZART OF MADRAS' —

When in 2002 composer and producer Andrew Lloyd Webber announced that his latest London stage musical, *Bombay Dreams*, would be composed by the Madras-born Bollywood music-writer AR Rahman, many Brits had never heard of him. Bollywood has traditionally been so shrouded in its own culture for so many years that its great superstars are far from household names in the West.

Rahman, born in January 1966, had by the 21st century sold CDs in comparable quantities to Madonna and Britney Spears (as early as 1995 he had sold more than 40 million albums over a three-year period). By the time *Bombay Dreams* opened in 2002, he'd scored over 40 Bollywood movies, singing in 6 of them. To Bollywood fans, Rahman is the genuine article – a megastar.

Born AS Dileep Kumar, he comes from a musical family. His father was a conductor and arranger for Malayalam films and started his son learning the piano at the age of four.

But when Dileep was nine, his father died from a mysterious illness – which some neighbours nervously attributed to black magic – and Dileep suddenly had to support the family. He found work aged 11 as a keyboard player with a popular troupe, eventually dropping out of school.

When one of Dileep's sisters fell ill in 1988, they feared the worst. When all hope seemed lost a Muslim Pir blessed her and she recovered. Amazed, the family converted to Islam and Dileep took on the name Allah Rakha Rahman, commonly abbreviated to AR.

After winning a scholarship to study music at Oxford University, Rahman learned about Western classical music, something that would influence and expand his terms of reference once he established himself as a composer. Which wasn't long in coming. In 1987 Rahman came up with a TV advertising jingle for Allwyn's watches. It was so successful that over the following five years he composed over 300 jingles, winning awards and industry respect.

Not only did his success help him to start the Panchathan Recor Inn music studio next to his house (now one of India's finest), Rahman was approached by filmmakers. When he scored K Balachander's movie *Roja* (1992) his life changed dramatically. The film was a smash and Rahman's music one of the main reasons. He became famous and gave up the ads. From there it has been a steady upwards climb, with his soundtrack for the 1995 film *Bombay* alone grabbing sales of over five million! In 1997 he became the first musician from India to be signed by Sony Music, and is the only person ever to win India's prestigious Padmashree award for services to music. He became popularly known as 'The Mozart of Madras'.

At the time of writing, *Bombay Dreams* is scheduled to open in New York, in spring 2004. The London production is still running. And Rahman is reportedly to contribute music to what is expected to be the most expensive musical ever staged in London – *The Lord Of The Rings*, set to open in 2005.

— CROUCHING TIGER, RINGING CASH TILLS —

It's always hard for non-English language films to make a dent at the lucrative American and European box offices, but some – occasionally – manage.

However, despite the critical successes of movies like *Cinema Paradiso* (1989), *Amelie* (2001) and *Monsoon Wedding* (2001), only one non-English language film has so far earned over $200,000,000. In 2000 Ang Lee's balletic martial arts fantasy *Crouching Tiger, Hidden Dragon* (or *Wo Hu Cang Long*) high-kicked to number 226 in the all-time high grossers' list, with $209,700,000.

The phrase 'crouching tiger, hidden dragon', coming from Chinese mythology, means the act of pretending to be weaker than you are. Lee's tiger certainly sprang, though, both at the box-office and at the Oscars where it bagged four prizes including Best Foreign Language Film. Such was its success that it is perhaps surprising that there has been no sequel. After all, *Crouching Tiger, Hidden Dragon* is the fourth in the five-book 'Crane/Iron' sequence by Wang Du Lu – the others being *Crane Frightens Kunlun*, *Precious Sword, Golden Hairpin*, *Sword's Force, Pearl's Shine* and *Iron Knight, Silver Vase*.

— ACTORS OSCAR-NOMINATED FOR FILMS DIRECTED BY WOODY ALLEN —

Actor	Year	Film	Oscar
Diane Keaton*	1977	*Annie Hall*	Best Actress
Woody Allen	1977	*Annie Hall*	Best Actor
Geraldine Page	1978	*Interiors*	Best Actress
Maureen Stapleton	1978	*Interiors*	Supporting Actress
Mariel Hemingway	1979	*Manhattan*	Supporting Actress
Michael Caine*	1987	*Hannah And Her Sisters*	Supporting Actor
Dianne Wiest*	1987	*Hannah And Her Sisters*	Supporting Actress
Martin Landau	1989	*Crimes And Misdemeanors*	Supporting Actor
Judy Davis	1992	*Husbands And Wives*	Supporting Actress
Dianne Wiest*	1994	*Bullets Over Broadway*	Supporting Actress
Jennifer Tilly	1994	*Bullets Over Broadway*	Supporting Actress
Chazz Palmintieri	1994	*Bullets Over Broadway*	Supporting Actor
Mira Sorvino*	1995	*Mighty Aphrodite*	Best Actress
Samantha Morton	1999	*Sweet And Lowdown*	Supporting Actress
Sean Penn	1999	*Sweet And Lowdown*	Best Actor

* *Won the Oscar*

— RAMBO HAILS OSAMA —

In 1999 the popular Pakistani husband-and-wife film stars Rambo and Sahiba decided to honour the terrorist leader Osama bin Laden the best way they knew how – they named their son after him. Rambo, whose real name is Afzal Khan, seemed oblivious to the irony that his own screen name comes from the most famous, if fictional, American soldier of all, and said at the time that, 'Both Sahiba and myself are inspired by contemporary Muslim hero Osama bin Laden, therefore, we have named our son after him.' And what if he decides to become a film actor like his Dad? Should he take the screen name of Rocky?

— PRODUCING THE PRODUCERS —

When Mel Brooks first dreamed up the story of a Broadway producer who sets out to create a sure-fire flop as an investment scam, he wanted to stage it. But the real-life Broadway producer Kermit Bloomgarten said 'no', advising the young Brooks that 'There are too many scenes. Make it into a movie.'

So a movie it became, But there was a hitch. Brooks wanted to name the whole show after the musical his lead characters produce – *Springtime For Hitler*. However, the distributors and cinema owners flatly refused. So the film became *The Producers*. Just after the publicity and posters were in place, there was a change of heart and Brooks was given permission to use *Springtime For Hitler*. It was, sadly, too late.

In 2001, *The Producers* finally found a life on the Broadway stage, as a hit musical (originally starring Matthew Broderick and Nathan Lane). It was in fact so successful that, at the time of writing, there are plans to turn the musical back into a new feature film to star Lane, Broderick and Nicole Kidman. Any chance that the first title might be reinstated? Not according to Brooks at a London launch for the show – '*The Producers* is known now. It's a brand name.'

— FILMS DIRECTED BY DAVID FINCHER —

The Beat Of The Live Drum (1985)
Madonna: The Immaculate Collection (videos for *Express Yourself, Oh Father* and *Vogue*) (1999)
Alien 3 (1992)
Aerosmith: Big Ones You Can Look At (1994)
Se7en (1995)
The Game (1997)
Fight Club (1999)
Madonna: The Video Collection (video for *Bad Girl*) (1999)
Panic Room (2002)

— A-LISTERS VOICING THE TOONS —

Since Kathleen Turner did an uncredited turn as the voice of Jessica Rabbit in *Who Framed Roger Rabbit* (1988), it has been popular for A-list Hollywood stars to supply the vocals for animated characters. So much so that plenty of cartoon flicks have casts that live-action films would envy. In the golden year of 1998, three films came out which numbered 24 major stars between them...

Film	Stars	Character
Antz (1998)	Woody Allen	Z
	Dan Ackroyd	Chip
	Anne Bancroft	Queen
	Danny Glover	Barbatus
	Gene Hackman	General Mandible
	Jennifer Lopez	Azteca
	Sylvester Stallone	Weaver
	Sharon Stone	Princess Bala
	Christopher Walken	Colonel Cutter
The Prince Of Egypt (1998)	Val Kilmer	Moses, God
	Ralph Fiennes	Rameses
	Michelle Pfeiffer	Tzipporah
	Sandra Bullock	Miriam
	Jeff Goldblum	Aaron
	Danny Glover	Jethro
	Patrick Stewart	Pharaoh Seti I
	Helen Mirren	The Queen
	Steve Martin	Hotep
	Martin Short	Huy
A Bug's Life (1998)	Kevin Spacey	Hopper
	Madeline Khan	Gypsy Moth
	Roddy McDowall	Mr Soil
	David Hyde Pierce	Slim
	Julia Louis-Dreyfus	Atta

— THE GREAT QUIZ-SHOW SCANDALS —

The greatest TV quiz-show scandal of all time started with Louis G Cowan's brainchild, *The $64,000 Question*. The top-rated CBS show debuted in June 1955 – contestants had to answer a series of 11 consecutive questions to win the $64,000 jackpot.

Great play was made of the secrecy of the questions. The first four were picked – seemingly at random (though it was later revealed they were pre-selected) by an IBM computer. Subsequent questions were kept in a New York bank vault that was guarded by two men.

The show was a smash, its audience peaking at a staggering 55 million Americans. Cowan was even made a vice-president of CBS. Other stations launched their own rival shows and there was a *$64,000 Question* spin-off called *The $64,000 Challenge*.

Then the sky fell. In May 1958 a scandal broke; another CBS quiz show, *Dotto*, was accused of being fixed. The ball started rolling and it ran over a clutch of crooked shows. A Grand Jury heard that *The $64,000 Challenge* had given answers in advance to the Rev. Charles E Jackson so that he would win. By October 1958, *The $64,000 Question* and its great rival *Twenty-One* were taken off the airwaves.

Cowan was forced to resign. Many quiz-show executives found themselves pariahs – temporarily – in TV-land. In 1960 amendments were made to the US's Communications Act, stipulating that no contestants could be given any answers or revealing information in advance (there was even a 1994 Hollywood movie made of the saga, directed by Robert Redford and starring Ralph Fiennes). Quiz shows were all but wiped out and for a while western and detective serials took their place.

Like all genres, they came back and by the turn of the millennium quiz shows were again among the biggest money-spinners and audience-grabbers on the box. Yet lessons had not been learnt totally. In 2003, Britain's *Who Wants To Be A Millionaire* (in many ways the successor to *The $64,000 Question*) was won by Major Charles Ingram. Subsequently Ingram, his wife Diana and co-contestant Tecwen Whittock were convicted of deception. They had in fact used coded signals to steer Ingram to the big win. A film version of this too is reportedly planned…

— KEEPING IT IN THE FAMILY —

Here are some parents and children in the movie biz.

Child	Finest Hour
Jamie Lee Curtis	*A Fish Called Wanda* (1988)
Parent(s)	**Finest Hour**
Tony Curtis	*Some Like It Hot* (1959)
Janet Leigh	*Psycho* (1960)

Child	Finest Hour
Carrie Fisher	*Star Wars* (1977)
Parent(s)	**Finest Hour**
Debbie Reynolds	*Singin' In The Rain* (1952)
Eddie Fisher	*Butterfield 8* (1960)

Child	Finest Hour
Mia Farrow	*Rosemary's Baby* (1968)
Parent(s)	**Finest Hour**
Maureen O'Sullivan	Jane, in the *Tarzan* series (1932–42)

Child	Finest Hour
Jane Fonda	*On Golden Pond* (1981, with her dad)
Peter Fonda	*Easy Rider* (1969)
Parent(s)	**Finest Hour**
Henry Fonda	Many, including *On Golden Pond* (1981, with his daughter)

Child	Finest Hour
Bridget Fonda	*Single White Female* (1992)
Parent(s)	**Finest Hour**
Peter Fonda	*Easy Rider* (1969)

Child	Finest Hour
John Huston	*Chinatown* (1974)
Parent(s)	**Finest Hour**
Walter Huston	*The Treasure Of The Sierra Madre* (1948, directed by John Huston)

Child	Finest Hour
Anjelica Huston	*Prizzi's Honor*
	(1985, directed by John Huston)
Parent(s)	**Finest Hour**
John Huston	*Chinatown* (1974)

Child	Finest Hour
Colin Hanks	*Orange County* (2002)
Parent(s)	**Finest Hour**
Tom Hanks	Many, including *Big* (1988)

Child	Finest Hour
John Cusack	*Grosse Point Blank* (1997)
Joan Cusack	*Addams Family Values* (1993)
Parent(s)	**Finest Hour**
Dick Cusack	*The Fugitive* (1993)

— *THE AVENGERS* – MR STEED'S PARTNERS —

In the popular British TV series, the impeccably mannered English crime-fighter John Wickham Gascone Berresford Steed (played by Patrick Macnee) had a string of attention-grabbing assistants.

Carol Wilson (appeared 1961–62), played by Ingrid Hafner.

Dr Catherine Gale (appeared 1962–64), played by Honor Blackman.

Emma Peel (appeared 1965–67), played by Diana Rigg.

Rhonda (appeared 1968–69), played by Rhonda Parker.

Purdey (appeared in *The New Avengers*, 1976), played by Joanna Lumley.

For the ill-fated 1998 movie version of *The Avengers*, Steed was played by Ralph Fiennes, Emma Peel by Uma Thurman. McNee voiced the part of Invisible Jones.

— CELEBREALITY —

On 5 January 2003, *The New York Times* coined a new word: 'celebreality'. The newspaper defined it as the turning upside-down of the reality TV genre, so that celebrities are shown on TV acting like everyday people (instead of everyday people trying to act like celebrities). Shows like *The Anna Nicole Show*, *The Osbournes*, and *I'm A Celebrity, Get Me Out Of Here!* are examples.

It also has been suggested that celebreality characters will not be top-flight stars like Julia Roberts or Russell Crowe, but those some way down the ladder – like Chris Eubank, Stephen Baldwin or Tony Blackburn.

— SEINFELD'S GIRLFRIENDS —

It's not just audiences who love Jerry Seinfeld. The comedian had a steady stream of girlfriends on his popular TV show. Here are some of the more memorable.

Sidra – Played by Terri Hatcher. Sidra is offended when she finds out that Jerry has asked Elaine to check if her breasts are real.

The virgin – The girl who refuses to sleep with Jerry and eventually loses her virginity to John F Kennedy Jr.

Ellen – Jerry's 'perfect' girlfriend is dumped because his parents like her.

Sue Ellen Mishkie – Heir to the O'Henry chocolate company, Jerry has to give evidence against her in court, but goes easy because he fancies her!

Delores – The girlfriend whose name Jerry can never remember.

The nudist – The girlfriend who never likes to wear clothes.

The tractor story girl – The girlfriend who, thinking Jerry is someone else on the phone, tells him about 'the tractor story'. Which, it transpires, is about how she caught gonorrhoea.

— AMAZING FINDS ON THE *ANTIQUES ROADSHOW* —

The long-running TV series has uncovered some incredible things over the years…

• The most valuable find was 25 Filipino watercolours, shown to the Roadshow in Brussels by a Belgian banker. The collection was valued at a minimum of £100,000, and was later auctioned for £265,000.

• Similarly a Richard Dadd painting was owned by a man who thought it was a print and was about to move it to his garden shed! It was bought by the British Museum in 1987 for £100,000.

• The best find at a car-boot Roadshow was a painting of cats by Henrietta Ronner, which had been bought for 50p. Roadshow experts valued it at a £15,000 minimum. It later sold for £22,000.

• A Skegness Roadshow event revealed a William Burges bottle that had for decades been thought lost, though pictures of it exist in the Victoria & Albert Museum. The owner had no idea what it was, and was rather surprised when it was valued between £20,000 and £30,000!

• A commode was sold for £50,000 (would be worth £80,000 today, according to Roadshow experts) after it turned out to be an English George III bombe marquetry commode dating from around 1773.

• A curiosity box that George III is said to have given to his illegitimate daughter, containing a piece of christening cake for HRH Prince Of Wales in 1842. And that wasn't all – there were also some clippings from George III's beard and moustache!

• One of the best novelties was a pocket watch made almost entirely of wood and ivory. The expert who inspected it, Simon Bull, warned that the problem with these very rare items is that they only work if kept in the oven or the fridge – because they expand and contract with moisture. Still, he valued it at between £4,000 and £5,000.

• In Leeds someone brought a permit for a cigarette lighter for Roadshow inspectors! It was given to a man working in Portugal in 1947, who had previously been ordered to get one by a plainclothes policeman.

— 'THESE GO TO ELEVEN' —

In Rob Reiner's 1984 'rockumentary' *This Is Spinal Tap*, a fly-on-the-wall look at 'Britain's loudest band', Nigel Tufnel (Christopher Guest) shows off his amplifier to Marty DiBergi (Reiner) in this classic exchange.

> Nigel: 'The numbers all go to 11. Look, right across the board, 11, 11, 11, and...'
>
> Marty: 'Oh, I see. And most amps go up to ten?'
>
> Nigel: 'Exactly.'
>
> Marty: 'Does that mean it's louder? Is it any louder?'
>
> Nigel: 'Well, it's one louder, isn't it? It's not ten. You see, most blokes, you know, will be playing at ten. You're on ten here, all the way up, all the way up, all the way up, you're on ten on your guitar. Where can you go from there? Where?'
>
> Marty: 'I don't know.'
>
> Nigel: 'Nowhere. Exactly. What we do is, if we need that extra push over the cliff, you know what we do?'
>
> Marty: 'Put it up to 11.'
>
> Nigel: 'Eleven. Exactly. One louder.'
>
> Marty: 'Why don't you just make ten louder and make ten be the top number and make that a little louder?'
>
> Nigel (pause, while he thinks about it): 'These go to 11.'

— CANDID CAMERA —

The technique of the hidden camera was commercially pioneered at around the same time in the USSR and the USA. Soviet filmmaker Dziga Vertov hid cameras for the feature-length documentary about daily life in 1920s Russia, *Kino-Eye* (1924), so that passers-by in cafes, bars, camps and kitchens had no idea they were being filmed.

In America, meanwhile, the great director Erich von Stroheim's 1924 movie *Greed* features a scene in which a female character runs out of a junk shop and screams that she has found a dead body. Passers-by look shocked and run for help. In fact, it was a real street into which the actress ran, and unsuspecting members of the public to whom she appealed. Von Stroheim had a camera hidden, ready to catch their entirely genuine reactions!

— SOME MOVIES TURNED INTO MAJOR STAGE MUSICALS —

Singin' In The Rain
The Full Monty
The Producers
Metropolis
Carrie
The Witches Of Eastwick
Tommy
Fame
Whistle Down The Wind
Sunset Boulevard

At the time of writing, there are also plans for Mel Brooks to follow his hugely successful adaptation of *The Producers* (now scheduled to be filmed once more, in its musical form) with a similar musicalisation of *Young Frankenstein* and for the producer of a TV-to-stage musical, *Jerry Springer: The Opera*, to follow that hit with a stage musical of *It's A Wonderful Life*.

Incidentally, the 1989 Richard Curtis movie *The Tall Guy* featured a hilarious parody of movie-to-stage musicals, when the lead character (played by Jeff Goldblum) starred in a London stage musical of *The Elephant Man*, simply called *Elephant*! It included the treasurable lyric: 'Somewhere up in heaven there's an angel with big ears'. The sequence was filmed on the stage of the Lyric Theatre in London's Shaftesbury Ave.

— *TITANIC*: DOWN WENT THE SHIP, UP CAME THE PRICES —

After James Cameron's movie *Titanic* became the all-time highest-grosser and cruised home with 11 Oscars, the price of even the most obscure memorabilia from the real *Titanic* shot up. Often, according to experts, by as much as six times the pre-movie price!

At a British auction held in January 1999 (in the town of Devizes in Wiltshire), a coffee-table leg that had been made out of driftwood from the ship sold for £800. Two coat hangers went for £150. A letter written by one of the disaster's survivors fetched £8,000.

— SHOWBIZ FOLK'S FAMOUS LAST WORDS —

Tallulah Bankhead: 'codeine…bourbon.'

Phineas Barnum: 'How were the circus receipts in Madison Square Gardens?'

Ludwig van Beethoven: 'Friends applaud, the comedy is over.'

Humphrey Bogart: 'I should never have switched from Scotch to Martinis.'

Lenny Bruce: 'Do you know where I can get any sh*t?'

Charles Chaplin (replying to a priest's prayer, 'May the Lord have mercy on your soul'): 'Why not? After all, it belongs to him.'

Anton Chekhov: 'It's been a long time since I've had champagne.'

Noel Coward: 'Goodnight my darlings, I'll see you tomorrow.'

Joan Crawford: 'Damn it, don't you dare ask God to help me.'

Bing Crosby: 'That was a great game of golf, fellers.'

WC Fields: 'God damn the whole friggin' world and everyone in it but you, Carlotta.'

Henrik Ibsen (responding to a nurse's claim that he was feeling better): 'On the contrary.'

Al Jolson: 'This is it! I'm going. I'm going.'

Eugene O'Neill: 'Born in a hotel room and God damn it, died in a hotel room.'

Rudolph Valentino: 'Don't worry chief, it will be alright.'

Oscar Wilde: 'Either that wallpaper goes or I do.'

Florenz Ziegfeld: 'Curtain! Fast music! Ready for the last finale! Great! The show looks good. The show looks good.'

— THE *CARRY ON* STAGE SHOWS —

If the *Carry On* franchise was a movie phenomenon, there were significant stage spin-offs.

The first *Carry On* stage show – featuring sketches in the *Carry On* style – was called *Carry On London*. It opened in September 1973 at the Birmingham Hippodrome and was a roaring success, transferring to London's Victoria Palace and staying there until March 1975. It starred Sid James, Barbara Windsor, Kenneth Connor, Peter Butterworth, Bernard Bresslaw and Jack Douglas.

The 'sequel' came in June 1976, when *Carry On Laughing* opened at Scarborough's Royal Opera House. Team regulars Jack Douglas, Kenneth Connor and Peter Butterworth starred.

It was 16 years before the third and, to date, final *Carry On* stage outing. In fact, *Wot A Carry On In Blackpool* (1992), which played Blackpool's North Pier, only featured two of the regulars – Barbara Windsor and Bernard Bresslaw. But the show's spirit of seaside naughtiness was exactly in the *Carry On* tradition!

— THE *CARRY ON* FILMS —

Film	Starred...
Carry On Sergeant (1958)	William Hartnell, Bob Monkhouse, Shirley Eaton, Eric Barker, Dora Bryan, Bill Owen, Kenneth Connor, Charles Hawtrey, Kenneth Williams
Carry On Nurse (1959)	Shirley Eaton, Kenneth Connor, Charles Hawtrey, Hattie Jacques, Leslie Philips, Joan Sims, Kenneth Williams
Carry On Teacher (1959)	Ted Ray, Kenneth Connor, Charles Hawtrey, Leslie Philips, Joan Sims, Kenneth Williams, Hattie Jacques
Carry On Constable (1959)	Sid James, Eric Barker, Kenneth Connor, Charles Hawtrey, Kenneth Williams, Leslie Philips, Joan Sims, Hattie Jacques, Shirley Eaton
Carry On Regardless (1961)	Sid James, Kenneth Connor, Charles Hawtrey, Joan Sims, Kenneth Williams, Bill Owen, Hattie Jacques
Carry On Cruising (1962)	Sid James, Kenneth Williams, Kenneth Connor
Carry On Cabby (1963)	Sid James, Hattie Jacques, Kenneth Connor, Charles Hawtrey, Bill Owen, Jim Dale
Carry On Jack (1963)	Kenneth Williams, Bernard Cribbins, Juliet Mills, Charles Hawtrey, Donald Houston, Jim Dale
Carry On Spying (1964)	Kenneth Williams, Bernard Cribbins, Barbara Windsor, Charles Hawtrey, Eric Barker, Jim Dale
Carry On Cleo (1964)	Kenneth Williams, Sid James, Kenneth Connor, Charles Hawtrey, Joan Sims, Jim Dale, Amanda Barrie
Carry On Cowboy (1965)	Sid James, Kenneth Williams, Jim Dale, Charles Hawtrey, Joan Sims, Angela Douglas, Peter Butterworth
Carry On Screaming! (1966)	Harry H Corbett, Kenneth Williams, Jim Dale, Fenella Fielding, Joan Sims, Charles Hawtrey, Peter Butterworth, Bernard Bresslaw, Angela Douglas

Carry On Don't Lose Your Head (1966)	Sid James, Kenneth Williams, Jim Dale, Charles Hawtrey, Peter Butterworth
Carry On Follow That Camel (1967)	Phil Silvers, Kenneth Williams, Jim Dale, Charles Hawtrey, Peter Butterworth, Joan Sims, Bernard Bresslaw
Carry On Doctor(1967)	Frankie Howerd, Sid James, Kenneth Williams, Jim Dale, Charles Hawtrey, Hattie Jacques, Barbara Windsor, Joan Sims, Bernard Bresslaw, Peter Butterworth, Anita Harris
Carry On Up The Khyber (1968)	Sid James, Kenneth Williams, Charles Hawtrey, Roy Castle, Joan Sims, Bernard Bresslaw, Terry Scott, Angela Douglas, Julian Holloway, Peter Butterworth
Carry On Camping (1969)	Sid James, Kenneth Williams, Charles Hawtrey, Joan Sims, Terry Scott, Hattie Jacques, Bernard Bresslaw
Carry On Again Doctor (1969)	Sid James, Kenneth Williams, Charles Hawtrey, Jim Dale, Barbara Windsor, Hattie Jacques, Patsy Rowlands
Carry On Up The Jungle (1970)	Frankie Howerd, Sid James, Joan Sims, Kenneth Connor, Charles Hawtrey, Terry Scott, Bernard Bresslaw
Carry On Loving (1970)	Sid James, Kenneth Williams, Charles Hawtrey, Joan Sims, Hattie Jacques, Terry Scott, Bernard Bresslaw, Richard O'Callaghan, Jacki Piper, Patsy Rowlands, Bill Maynard
Carry On Henry (1971)	Sid James, Kenneth Williams, Joan Sims, Terry Scott, Barbara Windsor, Peter Gilmore, Kenneth Connor, Patsy Rowlands, Bill Maynard
Carry On At Your Convenience (1971)	Sid James, Kenneth Williams, Charles Hawtrey, Hattie Jacques, Joan Sims, Bernard Bresslaw, Patsy Rowlands
Carry On Matron (1972)	Sid James, Kenneth Williams, Charles Hawtrey, Hattie Jacques, Joan Sims, Bernard Bresslaw, Terry Scott, Barbara Windsor, Kenneth Connor, Kenneth Cope, Bill Maynard, Patsy Rowlands

Carry On Abroad (1971)	Sid James, Kenneth Williams, Charles Hawtrey, Joan Sims, Bernard Bresslaw, Barbara Windsor, Kenneth Connor, June Whitfield, Peter Butterworth, Hattie Jacques, Jimmy Logan
Carry On Girls (1973)	Sid James, Barbara Windsor, Kenneth Connor, Joan Sims, Bernard Bresslaw, June Whitfield, Jack Douglas, Peter Butterworth, Patsy Rowlands
Carry On Dick (1974)	Sid James, Barbara Windsor, Kenneth Williams, Hattie Jacques, Bernard Bresslaw, Joan Sims, Kenneth Connor, Peter Butterworth, Jack Douglas, Patsy Rowlands, Bill Maynard
Carry On Behind (1975)	Elke Sommer, Kenneth Williams, Bernard Bresslaw, Kenneth Connor, Jack Douglas, Joan Sims, Peter Butterworth, Windsor Davies, Liz Fraser, Patsy Rowlands
Carry On England (1976)	Kenneth Connor, Windsor Davies, Judy Geeson, Patrick Mower, Jack Douglas, Joan Sims, Melvyn Hayes, Peter Butterworth, Dianne Langton
That's Carry On (1978)	Kenneth Williams, Barbara Windsor
Carry On Emmanuelle (1978)	Kenneth Williams, Suzanne Danielle Kenneth Connor, Jack Douglas, Joan Sims, Peter Butterworth, Beryl Reid
Carry On Columbus (1992)	Jim Dale, Bernard Cribbins, Leslie Philips, June Whitfield, Sara Crowe, Alexei Sayle, Richard Wilson, Maureen Lipman, Julian Clary, Keith Allen, Jack Douglas, Rik Mayall, Nigel Planer, Jon Pertwee, Peter Gilmore, Tony Slattery, Martin Clunes

NB: At the time of writing, a new entry in the series, *Carry On London*, is about to begin pre-production. No casting is confirmed yet, but the film is scheduled to begin shooting in May 2004.

— SOME *CARRY ON* FILMS THAT NEVER GOT PAST THE DRAWING BOARD —

Popular rumours of *Carry On* movies that never got made...

What A Carry On... – About an amateur dramatics society.

Carry On Smoking – Sid James was to play a fireman training new recruits.

Carry On Flying – About RAF recruits, got to pre-production.

Carry On Spaceman

Carry On Again Nurse – Announced as film number 31, never happened.

Carry On Dallas – A spoof on the TV soap opera *Dallas*.

Carry On Down Under – Planned for 1988, about sewage farmers in Australia – was to have been a spoof of the TV series *Neighbours*. Used practically the same script as the abandoned *Carry On Dallas*.

Carry On Nursing – Was to have been filmed in 1988. Had *Carry On Columbus* been a success, *Nursing* would have followed around 1993.

— LEO THE LION —

Of all the pre-studio logos, the best known is probably MGM's roaring lion. Though the image first appeared in 1916 as a logo for the Goldwyn Pictures Corporation, it first found its way onto film for the 1928 silent feature *White Shadows Of The South Seas*. As it was a silent movie, Leo's roar was heard over a phonograph record! The roaring lion is called Leo, and the ornate golden ring around his head bears the company's motto – *Ars Gratia Artis*, which means 'Art For Art's Sake'. Many lions have played Leo over the decades, including Slats, Jackie and Tanner.

— WHO'S WHO IN THE INVENTION OF TELEVISION —

Joseph Henry and **Michael Faraday** – electromagnetism pioneers, pave the way for communication through electricity in 1831.

Abbe Giovanni Caselli – the first person to send an image through wires, with his pantelegraph, in 1862.

George Carey – the civil servant from Boston who designed a 'selenium camera' that would transmit moving images by electricity, in 1876.

Eugen Goldstein – the first person to invent the phrase 'cathode rays', his description of the light that results when an electric current is pushed through a vacuum tube; also in 1876.

Alexander Graham Bell – having invented the photophone to move sound with electricity, in 1880 Bell talks about extending the photophone to carry images.

Paul Nipkow – the German engineer invents his 'electric telescope', which sends images over wires with 18 lines of resolution, using technology based on rotating discs.

Constantin Perskyi – the first person to use the word 'television' in discussions about the emerging technology at the 1900 Paris World's Fair.

Boris Rosing – putting together the Nipkow system with a cathode ray tube, Rosing builds the first-ever working mechanical television in 1906.

Vladimir Zworykin – the Russian inventor develops and patents a TV camera tube in 1923, which he calls the iconscope, or 'electric eye', and later the kinescope. It is the iconscope that becomes the model for future TV research. Later Zworykin admitted to being so disgusted at what was broadcast on TV that he wouldn't let his own children watch it!

John Logie Baird – the great Scottish rival of American Charles Jenkins, Baird is the first person in the world to send moving silhouettes using a system advanced from Nipkow's. Another forerunner of the era is **Vladimir Zworykin** who, among other achievements, patents the colour television. But in 1926 Baird forges ahead with a system working with 30 lines of resolution at 5 frames per second. After Utah-born engineer **Philo Farnsworth** gets the patent on his 'Image Dissector', the first totally electronic television system, and in 1928 **Charles Jenkins** becomes the first person to receive a television licence, from the Federal Radio Commission in America, Baird builds the first-ever television studio in 1929.

Peter Goldmark – generally credited as the first man to bring into use a colour broadcasting system, which he did in 1949 by spinning a red, blue and green wheel in front of a cathode ray tube. The first colour broadcasts of hospital operations caused several people watching to faint!

Robert Adler – invents in 1956 what becomes to many people the most important peripheral TV development: the remote control!

— *SATURDAY NIGHT LIVE* ALUMNI —

An American institution, the TV comedy show *Saturday Night Live* is a famous breeding-ground for funnyman (and funnywoman!) film stars. Here are some of the alumni who made it big:

Dan Ackroyd
James Belushi
John Belushi
Albert Brooks
Dana Carvey
Chevy Chase
Billy Crystal
Joan Cusack
Robert Downey Jr
Janeane Garofalo
Christopher Guest
Julia Louis-Dreyfus
Eddie Murphy
Bill Murray
Mike Myers
Randy Quaid
Chris Rock
Adam Sandler
Harry Shearer
Martin Short
Ben Stiller

— BROADWAY MAPPED —

The Great White Way, and the major theatres around it...

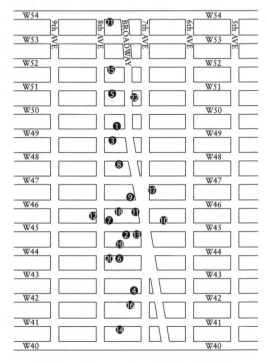

1	Ambassador	12	Martin Beck
2	Booth	13	Minskoff
3	Eugene O'Neill	14	Nederlander
4	Ford Center For The Performing Arts	15	Neil Simon
		16	New Amsterdam
5	Gershwin	17	Palace
6	Helen Hayes	18	Richard Rodgers
7	Imperial	19	Shubert
8	Longacre	20	St. James
9	Lunt-Fontanne	21	Studio 54
10	Lyceum	22	Winter Garden
11	Marquis		

— SHAKESPEARE RETREADS —

The Boys From Syracuse – Lorenz Hart (lyrics), Richard Rodgers (music) and George Abbot (book) turned to *The Comedy Of Errors* for their now-famous musical.

Kiss Me Kate – Cole Porter brushed up his Shakespeare with his great 1948 musical based on and around *The Taming Of The Shrew*.

West Side Story – Leonard Bernstein's 1957 reworking of *Romeo And Juliet* amongst the gangs of New York.

Rosencrantz And Guildenstern Are Dead – Tom Stoppard made his name with his 1967 *Hamlet*, as seen by two peripheral characters.

Umabatha – The Zulu Macbeth – 'The Scottish Play' as reinvented by Zulus, a worldwide hit after 1969 premiere, frequently revived.

Return To The Forbidden Planet – Bob Carlton's 1990 musical saw *The Tempest* filtered through rock 'n' roll classics and a story set in space!

The Donkey Show – *A Midsummer Night's Dream* reinvented as transvestite 70s-style disco love-in, an off-Broadway cult success in 1999.

Shakespeare's R&J – *Romeo and Juliet* as performed by a group of male American students, rapturously received in New York and London.

— *CHICAGO* TRANSLATED —

The 2002 movie *Chicago* features a number called 'The Cell Block Tango', in which Catherine Zeta-Jones as Velma Kelly leads 'the six merry murderesses of the Cook County Jail' in a steamy recounting of their crimes. One of the women insists that she is not guilty in Hungarian, left untranslated. For the overly curious, here's what she says:

'What am I doing here? They say my famous lover held down my husband while I cut off his head. But this isn't true! I am innocent! I don't know why Uncle Sam thinks I did it. I tried to explain at the police station but they didn't understand me.'

— IN BRIEF: THE 'HOLLYWOOD' STUDIOS —

Your guide to the major Hollywood studios' famous California shooting lots. In fact, many are actually located outside of Hollywood, in popular though nearby parts of California such as Burbank!

The Original Metro Goldwyn Mayer (MGM) Studios: Although 10202 W Washington Blvd was a movie studio before MGM bought it in 1924, they turned it into perhaps the most famous and iconic movie studio in history. This is where Mickey Rooney was Andy Hardy, where Judy Garland trod the Yellow Brick Road (which is still there), where the Marx Brothers ran riot and Tarzan swung through the trees. Located in Culver City, MGM is there no more; Sony now runs the site. Films shot there include: *The Wizard Of Oz*, *Gone With The Wind*, *Ben-Hur* (1959), *Doctor Zhivago* (1965), *Show Boat* (1951), *Singin' In The Rain* (1952), *Gigi* (1958), and (under Sony) *Spider-Man* (2002) and *Men In Black II* (2002).

Walt Disney Studios: In 1937, flushed with the success of his animated movie *Snow White And The Seven Dwarfs* (1937), Walt Disney bought 51 acres in Burbank (at 500 S Buena Vista Street) and turned it into a world-class animation studio. Although its reputation has been founded on such animated classics as *Bambi* (1942), *Peter Pan* (1953), *The Jungle Book* (1967) and *The Lion King* (1994), the studio has also turned out some great live-action pictures, from *Mary Poppins* (1964) to *Honey, I Shrunk The Kids* (1989), *The Sixth Sense* (1999) and *Pirates Of The Caribbean* (2003). Oh, and visitors to the studio are often taken aback by a large building adorned by seven 160-foot-tall stone dwarfs!

Warner Bros Studios: Jack, Sam, Harry and Albert Warner had enough money after hitting it big with Al Jolson and *The Jazz Singer* (1927) to set up shop at 4000 Warner Blvd, Burbank, in 1928. This is where Humphrey Bogart filmed *Casablanca* (1942), where Marlon Brando smouldered in *A Streetcar Named Desire* (1951) and where Richard Burton and Elizabeth Taylor bickered in *Who's Afraid Of Virginia Woolf?* (1966). Warner carved their reputation with black-and-white dramas, but later moved into frothy all-colour extravaganzas such as *My Fair Lady* (1964) and *Superman* (1978). And, more recently, the moneymaking machine that is the *Harry Potter* series! It's also much in demand for TV shows, including *Everybody Loves Raymond* and *The Drew Carey Show*.

Dreamworks: movers and shakers Steven Spielberg, Jeffrey Katzenberg and David Geffen founded the baby of the bunch, Dreamworks SKG, in

1994. They haven't physically set up their own lot yet, but with financial success having arrived with *Saving Private Ryan* (1998), *Gladiator* (1999), *Minority Report* (2002) and the like, it may not be far away. In fact, the group spent much of the late 1990s trying to acquire and build a stunning community-style studio in LA's Playa Vista area, near Marina Del Rey. It was to have incorporated the world's largest sound stage (42,500 feet), with the entire lot incorporating 1,087 acres. In 1999, the group announced that the project would not go ahead, for financial reasons (though they also had faced strong environmental protests). So, for now, they remain tenants of Universal.

Universal Studios: Yes, we all know what great rides Universal Studios offers. But did you know that the 100 Universal City Pl site is the largest film and TV studio in the world? Originally built on a chicken farm in 1915, the studio found early success with monster movies like *Frankenstein* (1931) and the same year's *The Wolf Man* – with top fright stars Boris Karloff, Bela Lugosi and Lon Chaney Jr on its books. More money came from the likes of Alfred Hitchcock's *The Birds* (1963) and the *Airport* series (from 1970). And, in 1969, Universal brought in a young director who would become the biggest money-maker the movies had ever seen – Steven Spielberg, who generated hit after hit from the TV movie *Duel* (1971) and *Jaws* (1975) all the way to *Schindler's List* (1993), after which he founded his own studio (see above). More recently, the studio has been the venue for the filming of *Meet The Parents* (2000), *Bruce Almighty* (2003) and *The Hulk* (2003).

20th Century Fox Studios: This famous movie company, behind such mega-hits as the *Star Wars* series, *The Sound Of Music* (1965), *Die Hard* (1988) and the highest-grosser of all time, *Titanic* (1997), almost destroyed itself with the huge crash that was the Elizabeth Taylor–Richard Burton starrer *Cleopatra* (1963). They lost so much money that much of their Century City backlot had to be sold off. Today, film and TV work still goes on at what remains of the 20th Century Fox Studios (at 10201 Pico Blvd) – *The X-Files* and *NYPD Blue* were filmed here. But it's also fun to spot Fox film landmarks around Century City – such as Fox Tower on Avenue Of The Stars, which was the building taken over by terrorists in 1988's *Die Hard*.

Paramount Studios: Paramount's beginnings were humble, operating from a horse barn, but in 1926 they moved to 5555 Melrose Ave, in Hollywood itself. The company did so well that they had to expand and bought the next-door neighbour, RKO Studios. Orson Welles filmed *Citizen Kane*

(1941) here, Hitchcock shot *Rear Window* (1954) and *Psycho* (1960), and the Marx Brothers recorded *Duck Soup* (1933). In fact, classic after classic was churned out at this address featuring the movie business's most illustrious names – Fred Astaire, Cary Grant, Katharine Hepburn, Bing Crosby, Elvis Presley. Later Harrison Ford starred in the *Indiana Jones* trilogy, Eddie Murphy was a *Beverly Hills Cop* and Jim Carrey headlined *The Truman Show* (1998). The actor Charles Buchinski was so inspired by the sprawling studio that he named himself after its iron Bronson Gate, becoming Charles Bronson!

Paramount Ranch: If it sounds like a home for famous Westerns, that's what Paramount Ranch, a, 27,000-acre offshoot of Paramount Studios, is in the wilderness-like Agoura Hills. This is where Gary Cooper, John Wayne, Henry Fonda, Kirk Douglas, Randolph Scott and many more sharpened their shooting in films like *Gunsmoke* (1931), *Paleface* (1948) and *Gunfight At The OK Corral* (1957) and TV series such as *Charlie's Angels* and *The Dukes Of Hazzard*. The ranch is still busy and recent years have seen filming on projects like 1999s *The Flintstones: Viva Rock Vegas* and *Sabrina, The Teenage Witch*.

Sunset-Gower Studios: More famously, 1438 N Gower Street, Hollywood, used to be Columbia Pictures Studios. Harry and Jack Cohn's mighty company was begun in 1920 and stayed in residence here for five decades. This was the site for Frank Capra's *Mr Smith Goes To Washington* (1934), *On The Waterfront* (1954) and *Dr Strangelove* (1964). Columbia tended to use other studios' stars, as when they borrowed Clark Gable, who was out of favour at MGM, and put him in *It Happened One Night* (making him a star in the process). After Columbia left the venue in 1972, Sony eventually bought the studios. But Sunset-Gower Studios, as it's now called, remains one of California's most in-demand lots to paying tenants, mostly TV programmes.

— AY? —

In 1816, the French author JR Ronden attempted to stage a play that did not use the letter 'a'. It premiered in Paris, where the audience was so offended by the idea that they rioted and the play was not allowed to finish.

— TITLE TURNAROUNDS —

It is common practice for the names of movies to be changed in different territories, but sometimes the new titles are, well, somewhat surprising.

Original Title	Changed to...
Great Expectations (1946)	*Bleeding Tears Of Lonely Star* (China)
Oliver Twist (1948)	*Lost Child In Foggy City* (China)
Guys And Dolls (1955)	*Heavy Youths And Light Girls* (Germany)
Grease (1978)	*Vaselina/Vaseline* (Venezuela)

— WHAT IS IT ABOUT THOSE GOLDEN GLOBES TOILETS? —

What's the worst place to be when you receive a major award? Obviously, apart from some dank prison in a tin-pot dictatorship, that is. Well, it happened in 1998 to *Chicago Hope* actress Christine Lahti. When Michael J Fox and Laura San Giacomo announced that Lahti had won the Golden Globe for Best Actress In A Series Drama, the lucky winner was in the toilet. As the presenters frantically stalled for time, with Fox stammering, 'Christine is, er, indisposed at the moment, I believe,' and San Giacomo asking whether this was 'history in the making', Robin Williams began some inspired ad libbing. Finally Lahti appeared, to be given a towel by Williams on which to wipe her hands. Apologising to her mother, Lahti giggled, 'I was just flushing the toilet and someone said you won and I thought they were joking, and I thought, "What a terrible joke!"'

Well, it had to happen to someone and at least others could learn from that mistake. Only they never learn. Lo and behold, at the 2001 Golden Globes, Renee Zellweger won for *Nurse Betty* and, er, she was in the bathroom. Presenter Hugh Grant was the one stalling this time, and he joked that she was so drunk she was in fact under the table. When she did finally reappear to walk through the hall and onto the stage, TV viewers were treated to a camera shot of Christine Lahti. The phrase 'They'll never live it down' springs to mind.

— 'MAKE MINE A MITCHELL!' —

Some opera singers, especially sopranos, weave such spells with their on-stage performances that devoted chefs have named dishes after them. Most famous, the Australian singing legend Dame Nellie Melba inspired both Melba Toast and Peach Melba. Italian diva Luisa Tetrazzini was immortalised by the Chicken Tetrazzini. Both of those august ladies were munching their namesakes in the early 20th century. More recently, American soprano Renee Fleming has had a dessert named after her, by the leading New York chef Daniel Boulud. The concoction of amaretto cookies, chocolate, hazelnuts and clementines has been dubbed 'La Diva Renee'.

Oh, and about those famous Melba foods. Dame Nellie's real name was Helen Porter Mitchell. So if you want to seem in the know, ask for a Peach Mitchell. Then again, you could end up getting strange looks.

— THE MOVIES OF MORECAMBE AND WISE —

Best-known as TV comedians, legendary English act Eric Morecambe and Ernie Wise tried to replicate their small-screen success to the cinema several times, never quite succeeding.

Movie	Date	Plot
The Intelligence Men	1965	A café owner (Morecambe) is recruited by MI5 agent Wise to protect a Russian ballerina.
That Riviera Touch	1966	Eric and Ern play traffic wardens who get caught up with smugglers while on holiday in the south of France.
The Magnificent Two	1967	This time the duo are travelling salesmen in a South American country where Eric is mistaken for its assassinated president.
Night Train To Murder	1983	Eric's niece Kathy becomes a rich heiress, and finds her life in danger. The bumbling duo are on hand to help – or hinder.

— A *CLUELESS* GLOSSARY —

Amy Heckerling's 1995 high-school romance movie was not only a hit, it introduced the movie-going public to an entire pantheon of trendy words and phrases, many of which passed into common use among teens. But in case you haven't seen the film, or need a quick crammer, here's a short but essential glossary of *Clueless*-speak.

> a Baldwin – a sexy guy
> a Betty – a sexy girl
> a heifer – a fat person
> ensembly challenged – a person with bad dress sense
> hymenally challenged – a virgin
> jeeping – having sex in a jeep
> laced – high (in the narcotic sense)
> surfing the crimson wave – a woman having her period

As for the many phrases offered for homosexuality, it's best to quote the student character Murray (Donald Faison): 'Your man is a cake boy...He's a disco-dancing, Oscar Wilde-reading, Streisand ticket-holding friend of Dorothy.'

— THE BIG THREE —

Only three films have ever bagged all five top Oscars: Best Picture, Best Director, Best Actress, Best Actor and Best Screenplay.

It Happened One Night (1934), directed by Frank Capra, written by Robert Riskin and starring Clark Gable and Claudette Colbert.

One Flew Over The Cookoo's Nest (1975), directed by Milos Forman, written by Lawrence Hauben and Bo Goldman, and starring Jack Nicholson and Louise Fletcher.

The Silence Of The Lambs (1991), directed by Jonathan Demme, written by Ted Tally, and starring Anthony Hopkins and Jodie Foster.

— THE WORST MUSICALS EVER —

Bad musicals are a spectator sport among theatre-goers, the theatrical equivalent of gladiatorial massacres (which were, let's not forget, theatre). Some are so outlandish and disastrous that they have passed into infamy.

Which Witch – Nowegians Ingrid Bjornov and Benedicte Adrian were most famous for getting 'nul points' in the 1984 Eurovision Song Contest before this musical, about a woman accused of witchcraft in the Middle Ages. The Norwegians loved it, London (where it opened in 1992) couldn't believe what it was seeing – *Variety* critic Matt Wolf remembers a scene featuring genitals hanging from trees! It closed swiftly, but not before provoking a minor diplomatic incident between Britain and a much-affronted Norway.

Carrie – So maligned was this 1988 Royal Shakespeare Company effort at musicalising Stephen King's famous horror story, which played in Stratford and New York, there was even a book written about flop musicals called *Not Since Carrie*. One of the many stand-out sequences had college boys killing a pig, to obtain blood to dump over Carrie, including the unforgettable line, "It's a simple little gig/You help me kill a pig"!

The Fields Of Ambrosia – This romp about a travelling state executioner and his electric chair (the fields of Ambrosia "where everyone knows ya", symbolised heaven) was such a flop in London, where it opened at the Aldwych Theatre in January 1996, that the producer offered audiences their money back if they didn't like the show by the interval!

— THE ORIGINAL *FAME* SCHOOL —

The movie, TV series and stage show of *Fame* were set at New York's High School of Performing Arts, a real school whose full name is the Fiorello H La Guardia High School Of Music and Art and Performing Arts (previously the performing arts and the music and art schools were separate). The movie was filmed at the school premises on 121 West 46 Street in 1980. In 1984 it moved to a nine-storey building (with 1,100-seat concert hall and 500-seat theatre) a stone's throw away from Lincoln Center. It was the first government-funded arts school in the US and Jim Moody – who played Mr Farrell in the movie – is in fact a drama teacher there.

Competition to get into the *Fame* school remains fierce, with around 15,000 applicants every year. Of these, somewhere between 650 and 800 students will be given their big chance to sweat!

— BAD JUDGEMENT CALLS —

Some actors have passed on great roles to take less-than-great ones instead. Ah well, as the screenwriter William Goldman wrote, 'Nobody knows anything.'

Actor	Offered
John Travolta	Bill in *Days Of Heaven* (1978)
Opted for	**Role went to**
Moment By Moment (1978)	Richard Gere
Actor	Offered
John Travolta	Julian Kaye in *American Gigolo* (1980)
Opted for	**Role went to**
Urban Cowboy (1980)	Richard Gere
Actor	Offered
John Travolta	Zack in *Officer And A Gentleman* (1982)
Opted for	**Role went to**
Staying Alive (1983)	Richard Gere
Actor	Offered (reportedly)
John Travolta	Billy Flynn in *Chicago* (2002)
Opted for	**Role went to**
Basic (2003)	Richard Gere
Actor	Offered
Richard Gere	John McClane in *Die Hard* (1988)
Opted for	**Role went to**
Miles From Home (1988)	Bruce Willis
Actor	Offered
Michael Madsen	Vincent Vega in *Pulp Fiction* (1994)
Opted for	**Role went to**
Wyatt Earp (1994)	John Travolta
Actor	Offered
Michelle Pfeiffer	Clarice, *Silence Of The Lambs* (1991)
Opted for	**Role went to**
Frankie And Johnny (1991)	Jodie Foster
Actor	Offered
Debra Winger	Alex Forrest in *Fatal Attraction* (1987)
Opted for	**Role went to**
Black Widow (1987)	Glenn Close

— THE GOLDEN AGE OF TV ADVERTISING —

The golden age of television advertising – at least in a nostalgia sense – were the 1950s and '60s, when commercial products sponsored American TV series. This meant that the stars of the show were often obliged to appear in quaint ads, usually at the end of or during their shows, to promote the brands.

One of the most fondly remembered is *Hennesy* (1959–62), the Jackie Cooper and Roscoe Carnes naval comedy. Following each episode the stars would appear to promote Kent cigarettes with their Micronite filters. Kellogg's sponsored the Hanna-Barbera cartoon characters in the early 1960s and Yogi Bear and his fellow toons would tell viewers how Kellogg's Corn Flakes were 'the best to you each morning'. Kellogg's were in fact very active in TV endorsements and had scored an early hit with *Superman* (1951–7). George Reeves as Clark Kent would show up to reassure his furious and hungry newspaper editor that Jimmy Olsen was on the way with Kellogg's Sugar Smacks (or some similar scenario).

A personal fave – kids' show *Captain Midnight* (1954–6) appealed to his young audience to 'join the secret squadron…but you must promise to do as I do. Keep yourself healthy and mentally alert and drink Ovaltine every day. It's the official drink of the secret squadron. It gives us what we need for rocket power!'

— SOME UNUSUAL DISHES FEATURED IN FILMS —

• In *Indiana Jones And The Temple Of Doom* (1984) the intrepid adventurers are served the Maharajah's finest monkeys' brains, beetles and eyeball soup.

• The poor diners in Peter Greenaway's cult classic *The Cook, The Thief, His Wife And Her Lover* (1989) had to eat some pretty revolting things. Not least, dog excrement (though in fact, the director reportedly used chocolate mousse) and paper.

• The 'drum' dish in *Big Night* (1996) was a meal fit for Louis Prima!

• In *Titus* (1999), a big-screen version of Shakespeare's play *Titus Andronicus*, Anthony Hopkins in the title role feeds an unwitting Jessica Lange the bodies of her two murdered sons, baked into pies. And who said gory drama began with Tarantino?

• *Fatal Attraction* (1987) features a certain notorious bunny-boiling scene. No one eats it, but I think it counts!

— BREAKING RECORDS: JANET JACKSON'S FLASHDANCE —

When singer Janet Jackson exposed a breast on stage at the 2004 US Super Bowl (fellow warbler Justin Timberlake pulled at her costume, ripping some of it away, an occurrence they put down to 'wardrobe malfunction') it seems she broke records. Internet records. Search engine Lycos reported that the day after the show searches relating to the incident broke the record for the one-day search record. It beat the previous record, held for the 11 September 2001 attacks on New York's World Trade Center, and had around 80 times as many requests as the usual number-one showbiz search, Britney Spears.

At rival internet site Yahoo!, the story was much the same. They reported that searches for Jackson and the breast-baring episode accounted for an incredible 20 per cent of all searches. Well, when Janet Jackson's top falls off, what else matters?

Amusingly, some web artists put a Jackson satire on the Internet – with Miss Piggy in a similar pose to Jackson, one breast exposed.

— DR LECTER, I PRESUME? —

Anthony Hopkins certainly enjoyed his notoriety when he played psychotic killer Hannibal Lecter in *The Silence Of The Lambs* (1991). He told interviewers that after the movie was released, he would sneak into cinemas, wait until the scary bits, then tap some terrified lady on the shoulder and, in his Lecter drawl, ask, 'Are you enjoying the film?' It never failed to get a reaction!

— PIONEER DRAMA TEACHERS —

These days, with drama such a popular choice in the university curriculum and plays a regular feature on English teachers' syllabuses, it doesn't occur to us that the scholarly study of plays was once as bizarre as, say, Madonna studies seems to some people now (there are indeed courses available to study the work of the pop diva). Yet it took two teaching pioneers to introduce plays and the production of plays as a serious university subject in America. One was George Pierce Baker (1866–1935), the other Frederick Henry Koch (1877–1944).

In 1905 Baker became the first-ever professor of dramatic literature at Harvard, his alma mater (though he was thought somewhat too avant-garde for Harvard and later moved to Yale). In 1905 he started a course in playwriting and soon developed a mission: He wanted to find a generation of American playwrights. He started the '47 Workshop where his students could have their plays produced – and during his time he taught soon-to-be bright lights of the stage including Eugene O'Neill and George Abbott.

Koch, who was also one of the first to teach about the production and writing of plays, had no such grand design. Still, he founded the Carolina Playmakers – a drama group comprising students from the University Of Carolina. They toured between Georgia and Washington and their short plays usually focused on the history and culture of the southern American states. If Koch didn't discover a clutch of playwrights for Broadway (though some students like Paul Green did well), he inspired amateur companies across the country and gave impetus to the writing of plays about the American south. Later he founded a playwrights' school in Banff, Canada.

And thanks to both of these gentlemen, drama eventually became a staple subject of schools and universities around America.

— IT'S CALLED WHAT?! —

Four of the longest film titles ever:

• *Un Fatto Di Sangue Nel Commune Di Siculiana Fra Due Uomini Per Causa Di Una Vedova Si Sospettano Moventi Politici. Amore-Morte-Shimmy. Lugano Belle. Tarantelle. Tarallucci E Vino* (1979)   Made in Italy, by Lina Wertmuller. For English audiences, the title was translated into a snappier one word, *Revenge*.

• *The Persecution And Assassination Of Jean-Paul Marat As Performed By The Inmates Of The Asylum Of Charenton Under The Direction Of The Marquis De Sade* (1967) A classic from English theatre and film director Peter Brook, frequently and understandably abbreviated to the title *Marat/Sade*. The movie cast features Brit thesps Patrick Magee, Ian Richardson and Glenda Jackson.

• *Cafeteria, or How Are You Going To Keep Her Down On The Farm After She's Seen Paris Twice* (1973) Made in the US. One of the shortest films ever made has one of the longest titles. The tagline was 'The short and sweet story of a girl and her 26 cows'. It lasts for one minute.

• *Schwarzhuhnbraunhuhnschwarzhuhnweisshuhnrothuhnweiss Oder Put-Putt* (1967) Werner Nekes's West German flick defies pronunciation.

— PICTURES IN THE SKY —

For those who like flying, half the fun is seeing what film the flight crew will announce. For those who don't, the movie is often an essential distraction. But movies have been a central part of long-distance air travel for nearly 80 years. The first film to be shown on an aeroplane was *The Lost World*, which Imperial Airways screened on 6 April 1925, on a converted Handley-Page bomber. The flight went from London to Paris.

— SOME ESSENTIAL VIETNAM FILMS —

Title	Director	Stars
The Deer Hunter (1978)	Michael Cimino	Robert De Niro John Cazale Christopher Walken Meryl Streep
Apocalypse Now (1979)	Francis Coppola	Martin Sheen Robert Duvall Marlon Brando
Platoon (1986)	Oliver Stone	Willem Dafoe Tom Berenger Charlie Sheen
Full Metal Jacket (1987)	Stanley Kubrick	Matthew Modine R Lee Emery
Hamburger Hill (1987)	John Irvin	Anthony Barrile Michael Boatman Don Cheadle Michael Dolan Dylan McDermott
Good Morning, Vietnam (1987)	Barry Levinson	Robin Williams Forest Whitaker Tung Thanh Tran
Born On The Fourth Of July (1989)	Oliver Stone	Tom Cruise Kyra Sedgwick Willem Dafoe

— LESLIE NIELSEN: NOT FROM THE FUNNY FARM! —

Leslie Nielsen may be one of the funniest men on film, but his family have traditionally held rather more serious jobs. His father was a member of the Royal Canadian mounted police, while his brother Eric served as Deputy Prime Minister of Canada! By the way, Leslie Nielsen was not always such a comedy specialist as he is these days – he once even screen-tested for the part of the villain Messala in *Ben-Hur* (1959)!

— WHAT HAPPENED TO ADRIAN CRONAUER? —

The madcap radio DJ in Vietnam, famously played by Robin Williams in the 1987 movie *Good Morning, Vietnam*, went on to a distinguished career. He spent some time jumping jobs – managing a radio station, working as programme director for a TV station, running his own advertising agency, recording voice-overs for TV and radio commercials, working as anchorman for TV news. Finally, he turned to law, obtaining a Doctor of Law degree from the University of Pennsylvania. And his distinguished career in law culminated with his senior partnership in Washington DC law firm Burch & Cronauer. He concentrates on information and communications law, often working for media companies including radio stations (an interesting turn of events considering the outspoken nature of his wartime broadcasts – though in fact Cronauer was not nearly as irreverent as Williams). He is on the editorial advisory board of the Federal Communications Law Journal, the Bar Association of the District of Columbia and works with various other organisations as adviser and/or speaker. He is still a regular guest on radio and television talk shows.

— KIDS' FAVES ARE DRUGS FRONTS?!!! —

Many children's films and TV shows are subject to urban myths (or are they real?) accusing them of various innuendos. One of the most famous is 1960s cult animated series *The Magic Roundabout*, which supposedly contained all manner of references to drugs; lines like 'keep off the grass', and the appearance of 'magic mushrooms' were held to be giveaways, as was Dylan, the sleepy, guitar-playing hippy bunny. Oh, and Dougal the dog loved sugar lumps (which, some fans claim, could have been soaked in LSD).

Another favourite for the subtext-theorists is Disney's *Snow White And The Seven Dwarfs* (1937). Apparently, the seven dwarfs take you through the seven stages of drug addiction – you're Happy, Dopey, Sneezy, Bashful, Grumpy, Sleepy and finally you need a Doc. Hmmm...

— METHOD ACTING OR MASOCHISM? —

The father of method acting was the Russian stage guru Konstantin Sergeivich Stanislavsky (1863–1938), who claimed that true acting called for an actor to internalise his role – to feel the emotions – in order to give the illusion of reality. Although there were sceptics in his own time, not least the playwright Anton Chekhov who felt that Stanislavsky's ultra-serious approach trampled on the comedy in his plays, the Stanislavsky cause was taken up with a vengeance in America.

There, acting teachers such as Lee Strasberg, Elia Kazan and Stella Adler evolved the Russian's ideas into what became known as 'method acting'. It taught precise ways in which a part could and should be deeply felt. In 1947 Kazan founded the now-famous Actors' Studio acting school in New York to teach method acting.

At the time, there was much controversy about method acting. British actors by and large scorned it when it reached England in the mid-1950s. Some opponents even suggested that it could damage actors who didn't know how to use the techniques properly. But many British actors just felt that making yourself undergo the agonies of your character was taking things rather too far.

The clash is amusingly caught in a story the great English actor Laurence Olivier used to tell about filming the movie *Marathon Man* (1976) with co-star Dustin Hoffman. In the film, Hoffman's character goes several nights without sleep, punctuated by torture and plenty of running. Hoffman, a keen method actor, went without sleep to prepare for the scenes. Olivier asked him why he looked in such a terrible state and Hoffman told him. The astonished Olivier gently said, 'Why don't you try acting? It's much easier.'

— BEHIND THE SCENES OF *I'M A CELEBRITY, GET ME OUT OF HERE!* —

The camp where assorted 'celebrities' are marooned is in Southern Queensland, Australia, at the foot of a dormant volcano. But the TV operation needed to record the series is vast and complex.

The camp itself has 5 manually operated cameras and 5 remote-controlled cameras, plus 20 hidden microphones. Over 4,000 tapes record footage. In the busy production office 45 computers are in use 24 hours a day.

A studio control room and 15 edit suites are crammed into 30 Portakabins. In all, these contain around £3 million worth of technical equipment. To get crewmembers to different locations around the 180-acre site, five jeeps are used. And 15 mini-buses are needed to take the crew between the site and their hotel accommodation.

The series is currently shot for Britain, the US and Germany (where it's called *Ich Bin Ein Star Holt Mich Hier Raus* – and where there was controversy after a German newspaper revealed that the stars' camp was covered by a large tarpaulin). Contestants have included:

UK: Peter Andre, Tony Blackburn, Jennie Bond, Rhona Cameron, Christine Hamilton, John Fashanu, Uri Geller, Jordan, John Lydon, Mike Read, Wayne Sleep, Phil Tufnell, Tara Palmer-Tomkinson, Anthony Worrall Thompson;

US: Maria Conchita Alonso, Tyson Beckford, Julie Brown, Bruce Jenner, Cris Judd, Robin Leach, John Melendez, Melissa Rivers, Nikki Schieler Ziering, Alana Stewart;

Germany: Mariella Ahrens, Caroline Beil, Werner Bohm, Konig Costa Cordalis, Daniel Kublbock, Antonia Langsdorf, Dustin Semmelrogge, Susan Stahnke, Carlo Thranhardt.

— SHOW-FOLK ON DESERT ISLAND DISCS —

The popular BBC radio show, running since 1942, where stars nominate the eight recordings they would like if stranded on a desert island, has thrown up some fascinating selections over the years. Here's what some stage and screen stars chose (with favourite recordings in bold), as well as their preferred book (the Bible and Shakespeare are included) and luxury:

Gillian Anderson
(book: Eckhart Tolle's *The Power Of Now*, luxury: recordings of her child and lover reading their poems)

Rolling Stones: 'You Can't Always Get What You Want'
Joan Armatrading: 'Save Me'
Radiohead: 'Exit Music (for a film)'
Nina Simone: 'Strange Fruit'
Schubert: 'Death And The Maiden'
Jane Siberry: 'Love Is Everything'
Roberta Flack: 'Hey That's No Way To Say Goodbye'
Jeff Buckley: 'Hallelujah'

George Clooney
(book: Tolstoy's *War And Peace*, luxury: an anchored yacht)

Hank Williams: 'I'm So Lonesome I Could Cry'
Pink Floyd: 'Brick In The Wall'
Dinah Washington: 'Destination Moon'
Frank Sinatra: 'Nice And Easy'
Bobby Darin: 'Artificial Flowers'
Bill Withers: 'Who Is He (And What Is He To You)?'
Van Morrison: 'Moondance'
William Shatner: 'Lucy In The Sky With Diamonds'

John Malkovich
(book: William Faulkner's *The Sound And The Fury*, luxury: a cappuccino maker)

Van Morrison: 'When The Leaves Come Falling Down'
Brook Benton: 'Rainy Day In Georgia'
Frank Sinatra: 'Once Upon A Time'
Tom Waits: 'Kentucky Avenue'
Albert Iglesias: Accordion theme, *The Dancer Upstairs* (2002)
Dr Dre: 'Still DRE'
Bruce Springsteen: 'Highway 29'
Nina Simone: 'Who Knows Where The Times Goes'

Ian McKellen
(book: a dictionary of flora and fauna, luxury: a grand piano)

        Vladimir Horowitz: 'The Stars And Stripes Forever' (Sousa)
        Samuel Barber: 'Adagio For Strings'
        Beethoven: 'String Quartet No. 13'
        Ethel Merman: 'Rose's Turn' from *Gypsy* (Styne/Sondheim)
        Lena Horne: 'Stormy Weather'
        Nina Simone: 'Mississippi Goddam'
        Harrison Birtwhistle: 'Harrison's Clocks'
        Abba: 'Dancing Queen'

Kristin Scott Thomas
(book: Jane Austen's *Sense And Sensibility*, luxury: a pair of mules by Christian Louboutin)

        Miles Davis: 'So What'
        The Clash: 'Train In Vain'
        Elisabeth Schwarzkopf: 'Morgen', *Four Last Songs* (Strauss)
        Zelenka: 'Gloria'
        Prince: 'Girls And Boys'
        Royal Welsh Fusiliers: 'Cwm Rhondda' (traditional)
        John Martin: 'Spencer The Rover' (traditional)
        Brahms: 'Adagio', *Trio No. 1 in B major for piano, violin, cello*

— *SLEUTH* – A GREAT ENSEMBLE FILM —

Anthony Shaffer's 1972 film *Sleuth*, starring Michael Caine, Laurence Olivier, Alec Cawthorne, John Matthews, Eve Channing and Teddy Martin, is one of only two films where the entire cast has been Oscar-nominated. How come? Stop reading if you haven't seen the film. Okay, the reason is because there are only two actors actually in the film – Caine and Olivier – the others, though listed, are in fact made up. Both actors were nominated for Best Actor. Neither won.

The other movie to have its entire cast nominated is 1975's *Give 'Em Hell, Harry!* It was a one-man show about Harry Truman, with the only actor – James Whitmore – also being nominated for Best Actor and also losing out.

— THE AMAZING FEATS OF FRANK ABAGNALE JR —

The subject of Steven Spielberg's 2002 film *Catch Me If You Can*, starring Leonardo DiCaprio, is a real-life figure and his story is truly filmic, truly amazing.

Born 27 April 1948, in the Bronx, New York, Frank Abagnale Jr was badly affected by his parents' divorce. While living with his father, he indulged in petty thievery with a local gang, but rejected them as too unsophisticated. The first sign of his quick but mischievous mind came when his father gave him a car and a gas station card. Frank ran a scam that led to a gas bill of thousands of dollars. Soon after, his father's business ran into difficulties – some say made worse by his son's gas card racket – and young Frank later showed remorse for having fooled his dad.

In 1964, aged 16, Frank Jr left home with a chequebook and a bank account containing $200. Securing a job in a stationery store in New York, Frank altered the birth date on his driver's licence to make him seem ten years older, so that he could earn more money. At around six feet tall and with some grey in the hair he had people convinced!

Tired of having little money, Frank left his job and began writing bad cheques to support himself. Watching airline pilots outside a hotel one day, the thought struck him that he – and his bad cheques – would be more credible posing as a pilot. So he telephoned the Pan American Airlines head office, saying he was a pilot whose hotel had lost his uniform. He was sent to collect a uniform that very day, charging it to an employee number he made up.

Next, he visited the company who made Pan Am ID cards, claiming to be a potential corporate buyer, and was given a completed (aside from the logo, which he subsequently obtained from a model Pan Am plane) Pan Am card as a sample. Teaching himself about the airline biz from libraries, supplemented by interviews with Pan Am staff (he pretended to be a student), he learned about deadheading – the practice of hitching a lift on a plane to do a job in a far-off destination, while the airline picked up the tab.

He got his US Federal Aviation Administration (FAA) license from a mail-order company that mounted licences in silver plaques. Of course he told them he was a pilot, named Frank Williams. He received the plaque, had a printer take it down in size, print it on special paper and laminate it. Frank now used his new identity – and impressive appearance – to open bank accounts around the city. He also attracted plenty of women, including stewardesses who gave him more information about the airline business. When he became knowledgeable enough, Frank felt he could try deadheading a flight to Miami. It worked, his identity was accepted and for years he deadheaded around the world – with Pan Am paying for flights and accommodation.

He became an expert in cashing bad cheques. Opening many accounts in many names, often with cash, he would use cheques with different serial numbers – having realised that they'd then be sent to different checking offices and so take longer to trace. That way he could hit the same bank with several cheques at a time.

On one plane trip to Dade County he was almost caught. Police arrested him on suspicion of being an impostor. He was saved when his fellow airline staff vouched for his identity! After that fright, Frank settled for a while in Atlanta, where he posed as a doctor (again studying his assumed profession from books), and was eventually given a supervising job on night shift. It shouldn't have called for any actual surgery, but one night he was summoned to help a child with a leg injury. He bluffed his way out, letting his junior doctors impress him by carrying out the procedure themselves, but realised that he could no longer pretend where lives could be at stake.

He went to Louisiana and dated a stewardess. Airily he informed her that, not only was he a pilot, he was also a non-practising lawyer. At a party, they actually met a lawyer who suggested that Frank get a job at the attorney general's offices. All he had to do was present his university papers to the examiner and take the Louisiana bar exam.

He couldn't resist. Forging Harvard Law School transcripts, Frank spent several weeks in study and took the exam. He failed. He tried again, with the same result. But on the third attempt, he passed! The attorney general's office made him a legal assistant with a $13,000 salary. However, when colleagues began asking too many questions, he left and went back to the skies, this time adding a TWA identity to his Pan-Am persona.

In Utah Frank became a sociology teacher at Brigham Young University for a while, and was much liked by students and dean alike. In California he met a girl he fell for and told her the truth. She, somewhat unromantically, told the police and the FBI. He evaded capture, fleeing to France. At Boston airport he was arrested, but let out on bail just before the FBI got there. Rather than flee, according to his autobiography, Frank boldly rented a security guard's uniform and stood at the airport, collecting security deposits in a large bag. Trying to escape with the loot, he found the bag to be too heavy. Luckily, though, two unwitting state troopers gave him a hand – and he made off with over $60,000!

Aged 20, having passed around $2.5 million in bad cheques, Frank was caught in France by Joseph Shea – an FBI agent who had been on his trail for years. He escaped, was caught again, and was sentenced to 12 years in prison, but released after 5. He went to work for the FBI and became one of the world's major authorities on fraud!

— AUSTIN POWERS' CHAT-UP LINES —

Yeah baby, lines from the super-spy himself!

'Nice legs. What time do they open?'

'Can I buy you a drink or do you just want the money?'

'I wish you were a door so I could bang you all day long.'

'You, me, whipped cream and handcuffs. Any questions?'

'Do you sleep on your stomach? Can I?'

'Do you believe in love at first sight or should I walk by again?'

'You've got 206 bones in your body. Want one more?'

'You may not be the best-looking girl here, but beauty is only a light switch away.'

'I know milk does a body good, but damn, how much have you been drinking?'

'I'd walk a million miles for one of your smiles and even further for that thing you do with your tongue.'

— A TRIPLE-BILL OF SUBVERSIVE CHRISTMAS FILMS —

If you want to spend Christmas watching films that are rather less sugary than the cakes everyone's eating, try these for a bittersweet triple-bill!

It's A Wonderful Life (1946) – Ironically, this Frank Capra classic is now wheeled out on TV every year as a Yuletide yarn. But when the story of a suicidal businessman who is shown his worth by an angel was first released, it was highly controversial. In an official memo the FBI even called it 'subversive' and said that the character of a mean businessman was 'a rather obvious attempt to denounce bankers...a common trick used by communists'.

Gremlins (1984) – The residents of sleepy American town Kingston Falls are prevented from having their usual pleasant Christmas when some nasty furry creatures hatch into killer gremlins! Just the thing to frighten off Santa!

The Nightmare Before Christmas (1993) – In fact, if you really want to give Santa a fright, then Tim Burton is the man to do it! His animated black comedy sees Santa kidnapped by skeletal Jack Skellington. Though the film is kind-hearted and very funny, I personally treasure the memory of little nippers being led out of the cinema in tears during this one!

— BIOPICS: WHO PLAYED WHO? —

It must be daunting playing a screen or stage star known to millions. But many have tried.

Movie	Subject	Played By
The Great Caruso (1951)	Enrico Caruso	Mario Lanza
Mommie Dearest (1981)	Joan Crawford	Faye Dunaway
The Audrey Hepburn Story (2000)	Audrey Hepburn	Jennifer Love Hewitt
The Jolson Story (1946)	Al Jolson	Larry Parks
James Dean: Race With Destiny (1997)	James Dean	Casper Van Dien
Life With Judy Garland: Me And My Shadows (2001)	Judy Garland	Judy Davis
Chaplin (1992)	Charlie Chaplin Douglas Fairbanks	Robert Downey Jr Kevin Kline
Man On The Moon (1999)	Andy Kaufman	Jim Carrey
Sinatra (1992)	Frank Sinatra	Philip Casnoff
Lenny (1974)	Lenny Bruce	Dustin Hoffman
This Year's Blonde (1980)	Marilyn Monroe	Constance Forslund
Confessions Of A Dangerous Mind (2002)	Chuck Barris	Sam Rockwell

— THE IMPORTANCE OF BEING EARNEST: A GAY PLAY? —

The 1980s saw a growing body of opinion which said that Oscar Wilde's comedy *The Importance Of Being Earnest* was in fact all about homosexuality. The play, about two friends who each lead double-lives (one calls himself Jack in the country and Ernest in town, the other has a fictitious sick friend called Bunbury who provides an excuse to frolic away from the city), has been taken as a parody of the way homosexuals had to hide their true desires in Victorian society. 'Earnest', it has been suggested, was even Victorian slang for homosexuality, and 'Cecily' (the name of another character) the slang name given to a rent-boy!

However, the actor Donald Sinden weighed in with a letter to *The Times* newspaper in 2001, claiming that he knew (in the 1940s) three of the original participants from the 1895 premiere, including Lord Alfred Douglas, who was with Wilde in Worthing when he wrote the play. None of them ever mentioned a homosexual subtext. When Sinden first heard the theory in the 1980s he consulted John Gielgud, a famous Ernest and authority on the play (and himself gay), who replied, 'No! Nonsense, absolute nonsense: I would have known.'

— *BLACKADDER* FACTS —

Some trivial facts about the British TV comedy series, which starred Rowan Atkinson and was first broadcast on 1983.

• Series co-writer (with Richard Curtis) Ben Elton often did a comedy routine to warm up the studio audience before episodes were taped.

• Tony Robinson may have been a big hit as Blackadder's long-suffering servant Baldrick, but in the TV pilot, the character was played by Philip Fox. The pilot has never yet been broadcast in the UK, though it has been aired in America.

• Reportedly, Tim McInnerny was asked to play a Percy descendant in *Blackadder III* but turned it down for fear of being typecast. He returned as the preening Captain Darling in *Blackadder Goes Forth*.

• Ben Elton is a big fan of another TV comedy, *Dad's Army*, and even named a character in *Blackadder Goes Forth* Corporal Jones.

• Only Rowan Atkinson and Tony Robinson have been in every episode of *Blackadder*, though other actors have appeared in more than one series, including Stephen Fry, Hugh Laurie, Tim McInnerny, Miranda Richardson and Rik Mayall.

— WORST OF THE WORST: THE RAZZIES —

Not all awards ceremonies are eagerly awaited by the recipients. Every year the Golden Raspberry Award Foundation holds the Razzies – the film awards for the worst of the worst. And, since the first Razzies were awarded on Oscar night in 1981, the stars have trembled!

Year	Worst Picture	Worst Actor	Worst Actress
2003	*Gigli*	Ben Affleck (*Daredevil, Gigli* and *Paycheck*)	Jennifer Lopez (*Gigli*)
2002	*Swept Away*	Roberto Benigni (*Pinocchio*)	Madonna* (*Swept Away*) Britney Spears (*Crossroads*)
2001	*Freddy Got Fingered*	Tom Green (*Freddy Got Fingered*)	Mariah Carey (*Glitter*)
2000	*Battlefield Earth***	John Travolta *Battlefield Earth*	Madonna (*Next Best Thing*)
1999	*Wild Wild West*	Adam Sandler *Big Daddy*	Heather Donahue (*Blair Witch Project*)
1998	*An Alan Smithee Film: Burn, Hollywood, Burn!*	Bruce Willis (*Armageddon, Mercury Rising* and *The Siege*)	The Spice Girls (*Spice World*)
1997	*The Postman*	Kevin Costner (*The Postman*)	Demi Moore (*G.I. Jane*)
1996	*Striptease*	Tom Arnold (*Big Bully, Car Pool* and *The Stupids*) Pauly Shore (*Bio-Dome*)	Demi Moore (*Striptease*)
1995	*Showgirls***	Pauly Shore (*Jury Duty*)	Elizabeth Berkley (*Showgirls*)
1994	*Color Of Night*	Kevin Costner (*Wyatt Earp*)	Sharon Stone (*Intersection* and *The Specialist*)
1993	*Indecent Proposal*	Burt Reynolds (*Cop-And-A-Half*)	Madonna (*Body Of Evidence*)

1992	*Shining Through*	Sylvester Stallone† (*Stop! Or My Mom Will Shoot!*)	Melanie Griffith (*Shining Through* and *A Stranger Among Us*)
1991	*Hudson Hawk*	Kevin Costner (*Robin Hood*)	Sean Young (*A Kiss Before Dying*)
1990	*The Adventures Of Ford Fairlane* and *Ghosts Can't Do It*	Andrew Dice Clay (*Adventures Of Ford Fairlane*)	Bo Derek (*Ghosts Can't Do It*)
1989	*Star Trek V*	William Shatner (*Star Trek V*)	Heather Locklear (*Return Of The Swamp Thing*)
1988	*Cocktail*	Sylvester Stallone *Rambo III*	Liza Minnelli (*Arthur 2* and *Rent-A-Cop*)
1987	*Leonard: Part 6*	Bill Cosby (*Leonard: Part 6*)	Madonna (*Who's That Girl*)
1986	*Howard The Duck* and *Under The Cherry Moon*	Prince (*Under The Cherry Moon*)	Madonna (*Shanghai Surprise*)
1985	*Rambo: First Blood Part II*	Sylvester Stallone (*Rambo* and *Rocky IV*)*Savage Island*	Linda Blair (*Night Patrol, Savage Island* and *Savage Streets*)
1984	*Bolero*	Sylvester Stallone (*Rhinestone*)	Bo Derek (*Bolero*)
1983	*The Lonely Lady*	Christopher Atkins (*Night In Heaven*)	Pia Zadora (*The Lonely Lady*)
1982	*Inchon!*	Laurence Olivier (*Inchon!*)	Pia Zadora (*Butterfly*)
1981	*Mommie Dearest*	Klinton Spillsbury (*Legend Of The Lone Ranger*)	Bo Derek (*Tarzan The Ape Man*) Faye Dunaway (*Mommie Dearest*)
1980	*Can't Stop The Music*	Neil Diamond (*The Jazz Singer*)	Brooke Shields (*The Blue Lagoon*)

* Most 'honoured' actress (9 awards and 15 nominations)
** Tied for most 'honoured' film (seven awards each)
† Most 'honoured' actor (10 awards and 30 nominations)

— THAT WAS ALAN PARTRIDGE —

Steve Coogan's comedy icon Alan Partridge, the sports reporter-turned-clown prince of chat, got his start with sports shorts for the BBC Radio 4 news programme *On The Hour*. Here's one of his enjoyable early broadcasts transcribed.

'The World Snooker Championships in Reading were thrown into chaos this afternoon when, midway through the Steve Davis/Jimmy White quarter-final, a young child stood up in the audience, stood up and shouted, "Hold on, all this game is, is two blokes hitting some balls around a table for a couple of hours. Where's the entertainment value in that?" The rest of the audience realised how foolish they had been for so many years and the disillusioned players were unable to continue.

'Later on, the British Open Golf Championship was thrown into chaos when, as Nick Faldo prepared to putt on the 17th green, a young child stood forward from the group of spectators, stood forward and shouted, "What a swiz! This is just a load of old blokes in sweaters knocking a ball about with a stick!" Faldo was sighted later in the bar mumbling, "What's the point of it all?" into an empty glass.'

— SONDHEIM THE GAMESMASTER —

Anyone who knows the musicals of American composer and lyricist Stephen Sondheim (including *A Little Night Music*, *A Funny Thing Happened On The Way To The Forum* and *Sweeney Todd*) will be familiar with his trademark brilliance with detail. In words and music there is a fastidious playfulness that teases the listener. So it may come as no great surprise to discover that his great passion away from the stage is for inventing games.

Tales of Sondheim's games are legion, and dinner-party guests are invited to pit their wits against each other with the composer's latest mind-maze (in fact, the games-obsessed character Andrew Wyke in Anthony Shaffer's play *Sleuth* is based on Sondheim). For instance, he and the actor Anthony Perkins once devised a game that sent four limousines searching for clues at locations all around New York. Another game involved group therapy sessions that were designed to aggravate tensions instead of easing them. Then there was the Monopoly-style board game where competitors had to be the first to successfully mount a Broadway show.

It got harder, according to his biographer Meryle Secrest. Jigsaws were made from abstract paintings, there were three-dimensional noughts and crosses, four-handed chess and a game whereby objects were brilliantly hidden although in plain view. Shaffer liked that one so much that he used it for the climax to *Sleuth*.

— UNLIKELY HAPPY ENDINGS —

When the film *Pearl Harbor* (2001) rolled into production there were jokes that the mainstream movie couldn't possibly show the bombing of the harbour – it would be too downbeat for Hollywood. Surely, movie fans reasoned, Ben Affleck would get there just in time with some new super-gun to see off the marauding Japs? It was not, thankfully, to be. But there are notable instances where famous endings have been changed to keep audiences happy.

One of the funniest must be the script-doctoring of Shakespeare's *King Lear* by poet laureate Nahum Tate. Figuring that he could do better than the Bard, Tate rewrote the great tragedy in a 1681 version where Lear lives, his daughter Cordelia recovers and everyone is cheerful at the close. And it was very popular, earning frequent revivals for around 150 years!

Fast forward some 300 years and the rewriters are still at it. When Disney decided to make an animated film of Hans Christian Andersen's classic fairy-tale *The Little Mermaid* (1989) they threw out the original ending. Andersen had the mermaid longing to be human so that she will have a soul. As a mermaid, her death will simply mean she turns into meaningless foam. Disney found this too obscure, so their mermaid longs for the all-American values of home and hearth. In Andersen, the mermaid dies though she gets her wish for a soul. In the movie, she loves and lives with her guy. Which, some Andersen fans may feel, completely misses the point!

— UNMASKING THE LONE RANGER —

The actor Clayton Moore most famously played one of the most famous screen heroes of all time, the Lone Ranger. He wore the iconic black mask and cowboy hat first between 1949 and 1952 and then, after a break because of an argument over how much he should be paid, until 1957. He was the Ranger for 169 television episodes and two feature films, and battling the bad guys for the cameras became his lifetime's work.

His greatest fight, however, came in 1975, with a force far more terrifying than the cowboys and Injuns. Clayton had continued to make appearances, and film advertisements, in the Lone Ranger's outfit. But when the mighty Wrather Corporation, which owned the series rights, decided to make a cinema film with a new Ranger, they ordered Clayton to take off the mask once and for all. Clayton refused, and Wrather got a court order to make him comply.

They won the battle, but Clayton won the war. Fans signed petitions to let Moore have his costume back, Wrather's new film – *The Legend Of The Lone Ranger* (1981) starring Klinton Spilsbury – was a flop, and he was again allowed to put on the mask. In fact, he had never given up. Barred from wearing a mask, he opted for wrap-around sunglasses instead! In 1985 Clayton was quoted as saying, 'I will continue wearing the hat and black mask until I ride up into the big ranch in the sky.' That journey was undertaken on 28 December 1999, and at his memorial service, the Wrather Corporation arranged for the saddle he had ridden on in his Lone Ranger years to be put on display.

— INDEX —

A, play without letter 192
Abagnale, Frank Jr 208–10
Abbott, George 189, 200
About Last Night... 135
Academy Awards 51
Ackroyd, Dan 172, 187
actors/actresses
  awards for worst 214–15
  children of 174
  cross-dressers in films 132
  famous last words 180–1
  playing bit-parts 110
  playing cameo roles 43
  playing the Devil 29
  playing God 29
  playing Jesus 9
  playing US Presidents 23
  in politics 92–3
  as pop stars 114
  previous jobs 135
  refuse great roles 197
  songs mentioning 120
  voices in cartoons 172
Ades, Thomas 146
Adler, Jacob 85
Adler, Robert 187
Adler, Stella 204
Adrian, Benedicte 196
The Adventures Of Ford Fairlane 215
advertising 146, 198
Aerosmith 24

An Affair To Remember 52
Affleck, Ben 139, 159, 214, 217
Agassi, Andre 84
Agony 157
Aiello, Danny 110, 151
air quality, in Victorian theatres 73
aircraft, films shown on 201
Airplane 49
The Al Jolson Story 212
Alcatraz, films about 63
Alda, Alan 156
Alfie 153
All The President's Men 67
Allen, Keith 184
Allen, Steve 130
Allen, Woody 7, 18, 34, 46, 58, 89, 125, 137, 151, 156, 170, 172
Alley, Kirstie 152
almost-cast in famous roles 8
Altman, Mike 72
Altman, Robert 43, 72, 82
Always 137
'Always Look On The Bright Side Of Life' 16–17
Alyn, Kirk 7
Amelie 169
American Idol 155
American Pie 65
Andersen, Hans Christian 217
Anderson, Gillian 24, 206
Andrews, Julie 22, 132

Angry Red Planet 90
The Anna Nicole Show 176
Annie Hall 137, 170
Ansky, Shloime 85
anti-semitism 56
Antiques Roadshow 177
Antony And Cleopatra 45, 147
Antz 172
Apocalypse Now 202
apple pie, recipe for 65
Arabesque 86
Arbuckle, Fatty 113
Ardiles, Osvaldo 49
Arlecchino 32
Armstrong, Vic 86–7
Arnaz, Desi 113
Arnaz, Lucy 157
Arnold, Tom 214
Arquette, Patricia 89
Arrabal, Fernando 86
Artef Theatre, New York 85
Arthur, Bea 156
Astaire, Fred 154, 192
Astin, Sean 78
Astley, Philip 127
Aston, Frank 110–11
Aston Martin 58–9
At The Boar's Head 147
Atkins, Christopher 215
Atkinson, Rowan 213
Attack Of The Clones 105
Attack Of The Mushroom People 90
Attenborough, Richard 9, 12, 144
The Audrey Hepburn Story 212
Austin, Bunny 146

Austin Powers films
 210–11
Autry, Gene 94
The Avengers 175

Babe 106
Bacall, Lauren 125
Back Roads 88
Back To The Future
 22, 135
Bacon, Kevin 63
Bagpuss 81
Bailey, James 122
Baird, John Logie
 186–7
Baker, Colin 57
Baker, George Pierce
 200
Baker, Tom 57
Bakshi, Anand 34
Balachander, K 168
Baldwin, Alec 125,
 159, 162
Baldwin, Stephen 176
Ball, Lucille 113
Ballet Russe 136
Bananas 7
Bancroft, Anne 88, 172
Banderas, Antonio
 135, 167
Bankhead, Tallulah 54,
 180
Barber, Samuel 147
Barker, Eric 182
Barker, Ronnie 156
The Barking Dog 49
Barkley, Charles 49
Barnes, Clive 17
Barnum, Phineas
 Taylor 122
Barrett, Brent 94
Barrie, Amanda 182
Barris, Chuck 212
Barrymore, John 20,
 124
Barrymore, Michael
 124–5
Bart, Lionel 48
Basic Instinct 82

Basil Brush 142
Basinger, Kim 89, 125,
 150
Batalla, Rick 157
Bates, Alan 145
Batman 54, 153
Battlefield Earth 152,
 214
Battlestar Galactica 76
Baxter, Warner 11
Baylis, Lilian 75
Bean, Sean 78
Beatrice et Benedict
 147
Beckett, Samuel 79, 86
Beckinsale, Kate 145
Becky (band) 114
Beecham, Sir Thomas
 66
Beethoven, Ludwig van
 180
Bell, Alexander
 Graham 186
Bell, Dr Joseph 20
Bella, Bruno 111
Bellini, Vincenzo 147
Bellucci, Monica 88
Belushi, James and
 John 187
Ben-Hur 15, 202
Benigni, Roberto 214
Benny, Jack 56
Benz, Julie 157
Bergen, Edgar 119
Berghaus, Ruth 81
Bergman, Ingmar 137
Bergman, Ingrid 64, 77
Berkley, Elizabeth 82,
 214
Berle, Milton 54, 56
Berliner Ensemble 81
Berlioz, Hector 147
Bernstein, Leonard
 100, 189
Berry, Halle 82
betting, TV and movie
 related 139
Bhagyaraj, K 149
Bharathan
 Kandaswamy 149

Bhatvadekar,
 Harishandra 148
Bhavabhuti 25
The Bicycle Thief 113
Big Night 198
The Big Read 139
Billings, George A 23
Billington, Michael 17
bin Laden, Osama 170
biopics 212
Bird, Larry 49
Birdman Of Alcatraz
 63
Birds Of A Feather
 157
Bishop, Joey 87, 130
bit-parts, superstars in
 110
Bjornov, Ingrid 196
The Black Crook 133
Black, Don 150
Blackadder 213
Blackburn, Tony 176
Blackman, Honor 175
Blade films 8, 29, 70,
 104
Blair, Linda 215
Blair, Lionel 33
Blair, Tony 25
*The Blair Witch
 Project* 138
Blanc, Raymond 134
Bloch, Ernest 147
blood, fake 115
Bloom, Orlando 78,
 105
Blue Peter, pets 53
The Blue Planet 70
Blue Screen 128
Body Of Evidence 55
Bogart, Humphrey 77,
 120, 125, 166, 180,
 190
Bogues, Tyrone 49
Bolero 215
Bollywood 34, 148–9,
 168–9
Bombay 168
Bombay Dreams
 168–9

Bon Jovi, Jon 114
Bond, James *see* James Bond
Bonham Carter, Helena 39, 144, 167
Bono, Sonny 92
Born On The Fourth Of July 202
Borzage, Frank 51
Bostwick, Barry 23
Boubil, Alain 79
Bowie, David 114
Boyd, Billy 78
The Boys From Syracuse 189
Boytchev, Hristo 95
Bracco, Lorraine 137
Bradley, Shawn 49
Branagh, Kenneth 44
Brando, Marlon 8, 52, 190
The Brave-Hearted Will Take The Bride 34
The Breakfast Club 22
Breath 79
Brecht, Bertolt 81
Breffort, Alexandre 88
Bresslaw, Bernard 181, 182, 183, 184
Brett, Jeremy 20
Brickbats 17
Brides Of Dracula 28
Bridget Jones's Diary 151
Britten, Benjamin 146
Broadway
    birth of 15, 41, 43
    box-office record 125
    map of theatres 188
Broadway Danny Rose 34, 151
Broder Singers 85
Broderick, Matthew 125, 171
Brolin, James 23
Bronson, Charles 38, 192

Brook, Peter 201
Brooks, Albert 187
Brooks, Mel 24, 46, 125, 171
Brosnan, Pierce 8, 110, 135, 144
Bruce, Lenny 180, 212
Bryan, Dora 182
Bryner, Yul 38
Buchholz, Horst 38
Buffy The Vampire Slayer 76
A Bug's Life 172
Bulgarian theatre 95
Bullets Over Broadway 34, 170
Bullitt 58
Bullock, Sandra 144, 172
Buono, Victor 54
Burges, William 177
Burns, George 29, 56
Burton, Richard 64, 125, 190, 191
Burton, Tim 167, 211
Buscemi, Steve 135
buses, films about 144
butlers, as murderers 92
Butterworth, Peter 181, 182, 183, 184

Caan, James 8
Caesar, Sid 46
Cage, Nicholas 31, 89
Caine, Michael 12, 20, 139, 145, 153, 167, 170, 207
Camden, film locations in 153
cameo roles 43
cameras, hidden 178
Cameron, James 179
candid camera 178
Can't Stop The Music 215
Cantona, Eric 49
Capra, Frank 192, 195, 211

Captain Midnight 198
Captain (stock character) 33
Car Cemetery 86
Carey, Drew 157, 190
Carey, George 186
Carey, Mariah 55, 214
Carlton, Bob 189
Carlyle, Robert , 145
Carmen 66
Carnes, Roscoe 198
Carrey, Jim 192
Carrie (musical) 196
Carrie (film) 179
Carry On films and stage shows 181–5
cars, in films 58
Carson, Johnny 130
Carter, Jimmy 67
cartoons, star vocals in 172
Carvey, Dana 187
Casablanca 67, 77
Caselli, Abbe Giovanni 186
Cast Away 135
Castle, Roy 183
Catch Me If You Can 208
Cates, Phoebe 82
Cats 31
Caviezel, James 9
Cawthorne, Alec 207
CCTV 133
celebreality 176
Celentano, Rosalinda 29
Cell Mates 124
Cellular 150
Chaney, Lon 191
Channing, Eve 207
Chaplin, Charlie 51, 135, 180, 212
Chapman, Graham 29
Charade 137
Chase, Chevy 187
chat-up lines, Austin Powers' 210–11
Cheadle, Don 139
Cheers 153

chefs, television 134
Chekhov, Anton 180, 204
Cher 55
Chicago 8, 135, 189
Chicago Hope 193
children
 of movie parents 163, 174
 as stars 161, 163
Chitty Chitty Bang Bang 58
Chopra, Aditya 34
Chori Chori Chupke Chupke 149
Christ, Jesus, actors who played 9
Christie, Agatha 12
Christmas films 211
Chroma-Key *see* Blue Screen
chunori 67
Churchill, Sir Winston 67
Cicciolina 92–3
cinema, first public 52
Cinema Pardiso 169
Cinematographe Lumiere, Paris 52
circuses 122–3, 127
Cirque De Soleil 122–3
Clary, Julian 184
classification system, film 113
Clay, Andrew Dice 215
Cleese, John 47, 73, 156
clichés 89
Clinton, Bill 67
Clooney, George 166, 206
Close Encounters Of The Third Kind 93
Close, Glenn 197
clowns, record gathering of 143
Clueless 195
Clunes, Martin 157, 184
Coburn, James 38

Cocktail 215
Cocteau, Jean 136
Cohen, Larry 150
Cohn, Harry and Jack 192
Colbert, Claudette 195
Cold Feet 157
Coleman, Gary 93
Colley, Kenneth 9
Collins, Joan 54, 145
The Colonel Bird 95
Color Of Night 214
colours, as gangster names 80
Columbia Pictures Studios 192
Columbino 33
Colyer, Bud 7
comedies, US versions of British TV 156–7
The Comedy Of Errors 147, 189
Commedia Dell'Arte 32–3
Confessions Of A Dangerous Mind 212
Connery, Sean 56, 63, 135, 145, 166–7
Connor, Kenneth 181, 182, 183, 184
Coogan, Steve 216
The Cook, The Thief, His Wife And Her Lover 198
Cooney, Ray 33
Cooper, Gary 192
Cooper, Jackie 198
Cope, Kenneth 183
Coppola, Anton 31
Coppola, Bruno 31
Coppola, Carmine 30, 31
Coppola, Francis Ford 30–1
Coppola, Sofia 30
Coppola, Vincent 30
Corbett, Harry H 182
Cosby, Bill 49, 157, 215

Costner, Kevin 18, 214, 215
couch potatoes 132
Countdown 140–1
Coupling 157
court cases, movie stars in 8–9
The Courtship Of Eddie's Father 163
Covent Garden *see* Royal Opera House, Covent Garden
Cowan, Louis G 173
Coward, Noel 180
Cowell, Simon 155
Crackerjack 142
crane kick 121
Crash 59
Crawford, Joan 54, 94, 180, 212
Creepshow 91
Cribbins, Bernard 182, 184
Crimes And Misdemeanors 170
Cronauer, Adrian 203
Crosby, Bing 180, 192
Crosland, Alan 137
cross-dressers, in films 132
Crossroads 55
Crouching Tiger, Hidden Dragon 169
The Crow 164
Crowe, Russell 89
Crowe, Sara 184
Cruise, Tom 12, 125, 145, 152
Cruz, Brandon 163
Crystal, Billy 29, 145, 151, 187
Curry, Tim 132
curtains, theatre 106
Curtis, Jamie Lee 174
Curtis, Richard 179, 213
Curtis, Tony 132, 174
Cusack, Dick 175
Cusack, Joan 175, 187
Cusack, John 116, 175

Cushman, Robert 17

Dadd, Richard 177
Dafoe, Willem 9
Dale, Jim 182, 183, 184
Dallas 47, 56, 139, 185
Dallesandro, Joe 91
Dalton: Code Of Vengeance II 49
Dalton, Timothy 8
The Dam Busters 154
Damon, Matt 166
Danielle, Suzanne 184
Daredevil 70
Davidson, Jay 132
Davidson, Peter 57
Davies, Alan 139
Davis, Gail 94
Davis, Judy 170
Davis, Sammy Jr 87
Davis, Windsor 184
Day, Doris 155
Day Of The Triffids 90
De Jongh, Nicholas 117
De Niro, Robert 26, 162
dead parrot sketch (*Monty Python*) 73
Dead Poet's Society 39
Dear John 157
Deconstructing Harry 58
Deep Throat 143
The Deer Hunter 202
DeGeneres, Ellen 84, 135
DeLuise, Dom 156
Demme, Jonathan 195
Dench, Judi 159
Depp, Johnny 104, 105, 114, 132
Derek, Bo 215
Desert Island Discs 206–7
The Desert Song 133
Desire Under The Elms 86

Desperado 167
Desperately Seeking Susan 55
DeVito, Danny 25
Dexter, Brad 38
Diaghilev, Sergei 136
Diamond, Neil 215
Diana, Princess of Wales 68, 120
DiCaprio, Leonardo 208
Dickens, Charles 48
Dickstader, Lew 97
Die Another Day 59, 101
Die Hard 159, 162
Die Hard With A Vengeance 149
Dilwale Dulhania Le Jayenge 34
Directors' Guild 49
Dirty Mary Crazy Larry 137
Disney, Walt 84, 144, 190, 217
Dittersdorf, Carl Ditter von 147
Djinot, Iordan 95
Do Re Mi 111
Doctor Who 57, 139
Dogstar 114
Domingo, Placido 13
Donahue, Heather 214
The Donkey Show 189
Donna Reed Show 163
Dormrose, Bret 114
Dorr, Frederick 21
Dotto 163
The Double Garden 91
Douglas, Lord Alfred 213
Douglas, Angela 182, 183
Douglas, Jack 181, 184
Douglas, Kirk 192
Douglas, Michael 22, 23, 54
Downey, Robert Jr 9, 187

Doyle, Arthur Conan 20–1
Dracula films 28–9
Drake, Alfred 94
drama teachers 200
Dream 146
Dreamworks studios 190–1
Dreyfuss, Richard 23, 110
drinks, screen characters' favourite 123
drugs, alleged references to 203
Drumen, Vasil 95
Duchovny, David 163
Duffy, Patrick 47
Dumouchel, Timothy 132
Dunst, Kirsten 151
Duvall, Shelley 15
DVDs 104–5, 128, 143
The Dybbuk 85

Earthquake 76
EastEnders, original cast of 42
'Easter Eggs', DVD 104–5
Eastwood, Clint 63, 92, 144
Eaton, Shirley 182
Ebert, Roger 55
Eccleston, Christopher 57
Edwards, Owen Dudley 20
Eisenhower, Dwight D 67
Eldridge, Florence 89
The Elephant Man 179
Eley, Gladys Baker 137
Elfman, Jenna 152
Eliot, TS 31
Elizabeth 49
Elliman, Yvonne 88
Elton, Ben 213
Eminem 55
The Empire Strikes Back 15

Endgame 86
English National
    Opera 75
The English Patient
    135
Ennosuke, Ichikawa 67
Ensler, Eve 160
Enter The Dragon 159,
    164
Escape From Alcatraz
    63
Escape To Victory 49
Estevez, Emilio 163
Ettinger, Solomon 85
Eubank, Chris 176
Eubanks, Kevin 130
Evita 55
Ewing, Patrick 49
Eyre, Richard 50

Face To Face 137
Fairbanks, Douglas
    212
The Faerie Queen 146
Faison, Donald 195
Falstaff 147
Fame 179, 196
Fantastic Four 70
Faraday, Michael 186
Farnsworth, Philo 186
Farquhar, George 15
Farrell, Colin 150
Farrow, Mia 11, 125,
    174
*Fast Times At
    Ridgemont High* 82
Fatal Attraction 199
Fawlty Towers 47,
    156–7
*The Fellowship Of The
    Ring* 14
female-only cast 155
*Ferris Beuller's Day
    Off* 22
'A Few Of My
    Favourite Things'
    100
Field, Sally 88
Fielding, Fenella 182

Fields of Ambrosia 196
Fields, WC 181
Fiennes, Ralph 145,
    172, 173, 175
film directors
    most prolific 49
    homage to
        favourite filma
        137
film festivals 129
film stars *see*
    actors/actresses
films
    about buses 144
    adapted for local
        audiences 159
    biggest investment-
        to-profit ratio
        138
    biopics 212
    Christmas 211
    cross-dressers in
        132
    foreign language
        169
    husbands and wives
        in 125
    Indian 148–9
    involving water 18
    locations, real 22
    longest 51
    longest titles 201
    mistakes in 15
    most expensive 131
    nude scenes in 82
    pornographic 143
    remakes 166
    restaurants in 151
    shortest 201
    spanking in 94
    sports stars in 49
    super-hero 70
    tag-lines 118
    highest grossing 14
    title changes 193
    turned into musi-
        cals 179
    unlikely happy end-
        ings 217
    unlikely titles 114

    unusual dishes fea-
        tured in 198–9
    worst 214–15
Fincher, David 171
Finding Nemo 14
Finney, Albert 8
Firmin, Peter 142
Fisher, Carrie 8, 174
Fisher, Eddie 174
Fitzgerald, F Scott 11
Fleischer, Dave 134
Fleming, Ian 58
Fleming, Renee 194
Fletcher, Louise 195
flights, stage 67
Folies Bergere 41
Folksbiene Company
    85
Fonda, Bridget 137,
    174
Fonda, Henry 23, 174,
    192
Fonda, Jane 174
Fonda, Peter 137, 174
food 194, 198–9
Ford, Harrison 8, 15,
    23, 86, 135, 166,
    192
Ford, Richard 48
foreign language films
    169
Forest Gump 135
Forman, Milos 195
Forsaking All Others
    94
Foster, Jodie 195, 197
Fothergill, Alastair 70
*Four Weddings And A
    Funeral* 151, 163
Fox, Michael J 193
Foxx, Redd 156
Francis, Stu 142
Frankenstein 154
Fraser, Liz 184
Frasier 153
Frears, Stephen 116
Freddy Got Fingered
    214
Freeman, Morgan 23,
    29

The French Connection 58

Friends 57, 69, 107, 152, 153

Friml, Rudolf 133

From Dusk Till Dawn 28–9

From Here To Eternity 135

Frost, David 74, 156

Frost, Sadie 145

Fry, Stephen 124, 145, 213

Full House 153

Full Metal Jacket 202

The Full Monty 179

Fungus Of Terror 90

Gable, Clark 94, 162, 192, 195

Gallagher, Peter 43

Game Of Death 49, 164

Gandhi 67

Garbo, Greta 12

Garcia, Andy 31

Garland, Judy 190, 212

Garofalo, Janeane 187

Gasparini, Francesco 147

Gaynor, Janet 51

Geeson, Judy 184

Geffen, David 190

Gelbart, Larry 46

George III 138, 177

George IV 138

Gere, Richard 89, 137, 197

Get Carter 167

Ghatak, Ritwik 149

Ghost Rider 70

Ghostbusters 22

ghosts 68, 133

Ghosts Can't Do It 215

Gibson, Mel 24, 150

Gielgud, Sir John 64, 80, 145, 213

Gigli 214

Gilbert, WS 86

Gillray, James 48

Gilmore, Peter 183, 184

Give 'Em Hell, Harry! 207

Glengarry Glen Ross 162

Glitter 55

Glover, Danny 172

The Godfather (trilogy) 8, 30–1, 105

Godspell 17

Goldberg, Whoopi 43, 135

Goldblum, Jeff 90, 172, 179

Golden Globes 193

Golden Raspberry Award Foundation 214–15

Goldfaden, Abraham 85

Goldfinger 58, 59

Goldman, Bo 195

Goldman, Ronald 8

Goldman, William 197

Goldmark, Peter 187

Goldstein, Eugen 186

Goldwyn, Sam 56

Gone With The Wind 113, 162

Good Morning Vietnam 202, 203

Goodbye Mr Chips 154

Goodfellas 26–7, 137

Gooding, Cuba Jr 110

Goodman, John 23

Gordin, Jacob 85

Gorshin, Frank 54

Gould, Elliott 166

Goulet, Robert 94

Gounod, Charles 147

Gowariker, Ashutosh 149

Grade, Lew 18

The Graduate 12

Grammer, Kelsey 153

Grant, Cary 12, 137, 192

Grant, Hugh 151, 163, 193

Grant, Richard E 22, 57, 139, 144

Gray, Simon 124

Grayson, Kathryn 94

Grease 193

The Great Caruso 212

Great Expectations 193

The Great Gatsby 11

'The Greatest Show On Earth' 122

greed 23

Greed 178

Green, Paul 200

Green, Tom 214

Greenaway, Peter 198

Greenwood, Bruce 23

Gremlins 88, 211

Grey, Jennifer 62

Griffith, Melanie 82, 215

Grimaldi, Joseph 75

Groundhog Day 158

Grundy, Bill 126

Gude, OJ 43

Guest, Christopher 178, 187

Gunton, Bob 15

A Guy Named Joe 137

Guys And Dolls 193

Gyllenhaal, Maggie 94

Hackman, Gene 58, 172

Hadley, Jerry 11

Hafner, Ingrid 175

Hagman, Larry 56

Hamburger Hill 202

Hamill, Mark 15

Hamlet 44, 45, 46, 147, 189

Hamlisch, Marvin 141

Hammer Horror films 28

Hammerstein, Oskar 100, 102, 133

Hampton Court Palace 133
Hanks, Colin 175
Hanks, Tom 175
Hanna-Barbera 198
Hannah And Her Sisters 170
Hansen, Gale 39
happy endings, unlikely 217
Harbison, John 11
Hardy, Andy 190
Harlem, filming in 149
Harriott, Ainsley 134
Harris, Anita 183
Harry Potter films 14
Hart, Lorenz 189
Hartnell, William 57, 182
Hasselhoff, David 35
Hatcher, Terri 176
Hauben, Lawrence 195
Havel, Vaclav 92
Hawke, Ethan 39
Hawthorne, Nigel 145
Hawtrey, Charles 182, 183, 184
Hayes, Melvyn 184
Hays Code 113
Haze, Jonathan 90
Heche, Anne 166
Heckerling, Amy 195
Hemingway, Mariel 170
Heneker, David 88
Hennesy 198
Henrikson, Lance 8
Henry, Buck 156
Henry, Joseph 186
Henry IV, Part One 126
Henry V 44, 45
Hepburn, Audrey 52, 137, 166, 212
Hepburn, Katharine 87, 192
Hermann, Edward 23
Hershey, Barbara 88
Heston, Charlton 12, 15, 23, 29, 145, 167

Hewitt, Jennifer Love 29
High Fidelity 116–17
High Noon 67
Hillcrest Country Club 56
Hirsch, Judd 157
Hirschbein, Peretz 85
Hitchcock, Alfred 98–9, 115, 166, 191, 192
Hodges, Mike 167
Hoffman, Dustin 8, 12, 24, 132, 150, 204
Hogan, Hulk 49
Hogan, Paul 145
Holbrook, Hal 23
Holloway, Julian 183
Hollywood
   iconic sign 71
   morality in 113
   studios 190–2
Holmes, Oliver Wendell 20–1
Holmes, Sherlock 20–1
Holst, Gustav 147
hookers 88–9
Hopkins, Anthony 23, 153, 195, 199
Hornby, Nick 116
Hoskins, Bob 89
Houseman, Laurence 86
Houston, Donald 182
Howard The Duck 215
Howerd, Frankie 183
Hubbard, L Ron 152
Hudson Hawk 215
Hudson, Rock 12
The Hulk 70
Husbands And Wives 170
husbands and wives on screen 125, 170
Hussein, Saddam 62, 165
Huston, Anjelica 175
Huston, John 174, 175
Huston, Walter 23, 29, 174

Ibsen, Henrik 181
Idle, Eric 16
If... 94
I'm A Celebrity, Get Me Out Of Here! 176, 205
IMAX 77
The Importance Of Being Earnest 212–13
Inchon! 215
Indecent Proposal 214
Independence Day 14
Indian films and theatre 25, 148–9
Indiana Jones films 8, 86, 142, 198
The Innamorati 33
The Intelligence Men 194
Interiors 170
internet, showbiz searches 199
The Intimate Revue 75
Invasion Of The Body Snatchers 90, 166
The Invisible Man 154
Irani, Ardeshir 148
Iraq, biggest-ever musical 165
Irma La Douce 88
Iron Man 70
Irons, Jeremy 144
Irving, Henry 14
Island Of The Doomed 91
It Happened One Night 195
The Italian Job 167
It's A Wonderful Life 179, 211
The Ivy 40

Jabbar, Kareem Abdul 49
Jack: A Night Out On The Town With John Barrymore 124
Jackass 165

Jackie Brown 137
Jackman, Hugh 82
Jackson, Glenda 93, 201
Jackson, Janet 84, 199
Jackson, Michael 152
Jackson, Samuel L 110
Jacques, Hattie 182, 183, 184
Jaffrey, Madhur 134
James, Clive 17
James, Sid 181, 182, 183, 184, 185
James Bond films 8, 10–11, 56, 58–9, 86–7, 166–7
James Dean: Race With Destiny 212
Jannings, Emil 29, 51
Jaws films 15, 22, 66
Jayakantan 149
The Jazz Singer 137
Jenkins, Charles 186–7
Jerry Springer: The Opera 74, 179
Jesus Christ Superstar 88
Jesus Of Nazareth 88
Jewel Of The Nile 22
Jews
    discrimination against in film industry 56
    Yiddish theatre 85
Joe Allen 40
John, Elton 24
John Paul II, Pope 71
Johnson, Ben, grave 81
Johnson, Larry 49
Johnson, Lyndon 67
Jolson, Al 97, 181, 190, 212
Jolson, Harry 97
Jones, Tommy Lee 88
Jones, Vinnie 49
Jordan, Dora 48
Jordan, Michael 49
Jordan, Neil 89
Journey's End 154
Julius Caesar 44, 45

Jurassic Park 14, 22

kabuki 67
Kajol 34
Kalidsa 25
The Karate Kid 121
Karloff, Boris 191
Katzenberg, Jeffrey 190
Kaufman, Andy 212
Kaye, Danny 12, 56
Kazan, Elia 204
Kean, Edmund 112
Keaton, Diane 137, 170
Keaton, Michael 39
Keel, Howard 90, 94
Keitel, Harvey 28–9
Keller, Sheldon 46
Kennedy, John F 131
Kern, Jerome 133
Kerr, Deborah 52
Khan, Afzal 170
Khan, Madeline 172
Khan, Shah Rukh 34
Khushove 95
Kidder, Margot 7, 87
Kidman, Nicole 125, 152
Killer Tomatoes 91
Kilmer, Val 29, 172
King, Stephen 91, 196
The King And I 52
King Lear 147, 217
King Of Kings 88
Kingsley, Ben 145
Kino-Eye 178
Kinsey, Alfred (and his report) 37
kiss, longest screen 109
Kiss Me Kate 37, 94, 189
Kissel, Howard 110–11
Kitt, Eartha 54
KITT (Knight Industry Two Thousand) 35
Kline, Kevin 23
Klingon, phrases in 115

Knight Rider 35
Knightley, Kiera 110
Knoblock, Edward 64
Knot's Landing 47
Kobrin, Leon 85
Koch, Frederick Henry 200
Korman, Harvey 156
Kosta, Paulie 114
Kostov, Stefan L 95
Kreztmer, Herbert 79
Kris, Dr Marianne 137
Kurosawa, Akira 166
Kussman, Dylan 39

LA Confidential 89
Ladd, Alan 11
Laemmle, Carl 39
Lagaan: Once Upon A Time In India 149
Lahti, Christine 193
Laliberte, Guy 122–3
Lalit, Jatin 34
Lancaster, Burt 63
The Land Unknown 90
Landau, Martin 170
Lane, Jessie 70
Lane, Nathan 46, 125, 132, 171
Lange, Jessica 199
Langella, Frank 20
Langton, Dianne 184
Larroquette, John 156
Lasky, Jesse 41
Lassie 163
The Last Temptation Of Christ 88
Late Night 130
Laughter On The 23rd Floor 46
Laurents, Arthur 100
Laurie, Miranda 213
Law, Jude 145
Lawford, Peter 87
Lawrence, Carol 94
Lawrence Of Arabia 8, 22
Lawson, Nigella 134
Lean, David 22

Leaving Las Vegas 89
Lee, Ang 169
Lee, Brandon 164
Lee, Bruce 164
Lee, Christopher 20, 28, 86
Lee, Jason 163
Lee, Stan 70
Leech, Wendy 87
Legends Of The Fall 135
Leicester Square, Walk Of Fame 144–5
Leigh, Janet 174
Lemmon, Jack 88, 132
Lenny 212
Leno, Jay 130
Leon 151
Leonard, Robert Sean 39
Leonard: Part 6 215
Leoni, Tea 163
Letterman, David 130
Liberace 54
Libin, Solomon 85
The Licensing Act (1737) 86
The Life Of Brian 16–17
Life With Judy Garland: Me And My Shadows 212
Lifeforce 82
lion, MGM 185
Lipman, Maureen 157, 160, 184
The Little Clay Cart 25
The Little Mermaid 217
Little Shop Of Horrors 90
Lloyd Webber, Andrew 31, 63, 150, 168
Lock, Stock And Two Smoking Barrels 49
Logan, Jimmy 184
London, lost theatres 27
Lone Ranger 218
The Lonely Lady 215

The Longest Most Meaningless Movie In The World 51
Lopez, Jennifer 139, 172, 214
The Lord Of The Rings (trilogy) 14, 78–9, 169
Lord, Rebecca 114
Loren, Sophia 86, 110
The Lost Boys 28
Lost In Translation 30
The Lost World 201
Louis-Dreyfus, Julia 172, 187
Love And Death 18
Lovelace, Linda 141, 143
Love's Labour's Lost 46
Lucas, George 142
Luce, Clare Boothe 155
Lugosi, Bela 191
Lumiere, Auguste and Louis 52
Lumley, Joanna 175
LuPone, Patti 89
Lust For A Vampire 28

M*A*S*H*, theme from 72–3
Macbeth 38, 44, 147, 189
McCarthy, Kevin 166
Macchio, Ralph 121
McCoy, Sylvester 57
MacDowell, Andie 151
McDowell, Malcolm 94
McDowell, Roddy 54, 172
McGann, Paul 22, 57
MacGee, Patrick 201
McGoohan, Patrick 63
MacGraw, Ali 125
McInnerny, Tim 213
McKellen, Ian 78, 145, 207

Mackintosh, Cameron 79
MacLaine, Shirley 88, 161
McLintock 94
McMahon, Ed 130
Macnee, Patrick 175
McQueen, Steve 38, 125
Macready, William Charles 112
Madonna 8, 40, 55, 135, 214, 215
Madsen, Michael 197
The Magic Roundabout 203
Magnano, Roy 9
The Magnificent Seven 38, 166
The Magnificent Two 194
Maguire, Tobey 151
Mahabharata 25
Mailhouse, Robert 114
Main Pyaar Kiya 149
male-only cast 154
Malkovich, John 206
Maltin, Leonard 55
Mamet, David 162
Man About The House 156
A Man For All Seasons 135
Man On The Moon 212
The Man With The Golden Arm 113
The Man With The Golden Gun 58
Mancini, Henry 141
Mandel, Johnny 72
Maneater Of Hydra 91
Manhattan 170
Mann, Alan 58
Mara, Adele 94
Marat/Sade 201
Marathon Man 204
El Mariachi 167
marketing ploys 110–11

Marsalis, Branford 130
Marsh, Stan 29
Marshall, EG 23
Marshall, Garry 137
Martians 119
Martin, Dean 87
Martin, Mary 56
Martin, Steve 162, 172
Martin, Teddy 207
Marvel comics 70
Marx, Groucho 56
Marx Brothers 192
The Mask Of Zorro 135
Mason, Jackie 17, 24
Massalitinov, NO 95
Matango 90
Matrix 114
Matthews, John 207
May, Mathilda 82
Mayall, Rik 124, 184, 213
Mayer, Louis B 56
Maynard, Bill 183, 184
Measure For Measure 147
Medeiros, Maria de 137
Mehboob 148
Melba, Dame Nellie 194
Mellor, David 50
Men Behaving Badly 157
Mercer, Jack 134
The Merchant Of Venice 38, 147
Mercury Theatre Company 118–19
Meredith, Burgess 54
Merman, Ethel 54
Merrick, David 110–11
The Merry Wives Of Windsor 146, 147
method acting 204
Metro Goldwyn Mayer see *MGM*
Metropolis 179
MGM 185, 190

Mickey Mouse 84
Midler, Bette 24, 130
Midnight Cowboy 88
A Midsummer Night's Dream 44, 46, 146, 189
Midway 76
Mighty Aphrodite 89, 170
The Mikado 86
Mikhail 95
Milestone, Lewis 51
Miller, Arthur 86
Mills, John 145
Mills, Juliet 182
Minnelli, Liza 215
Mirren, Helen 12, 172
Les Miserables (stage show and film) 79, 89
Miss Julie 86
Mistakes, movie 15
Mitchell, Warren 156
Mitchum, Robert 67
Modine, Matthew 82
Moffat, Donald 23
Mommie Dearest 212, 215
Mona Lisa 89
Monaghan, Dominic 79
Monkey Magic 19
Monkhouse, Bob 182
Monnet, Marguerite 88
Monroe, Marilyn 137, 212
Monsoon Wedding 149, 169
Monty Python And The Holy Grail 94, 153
Monty Python's Flying Circus 16–17, 73
Moody, Jim 196
Moody, Ron 48
The Moon Is Blue 113
Moore, Bobby 49
Moore, Clayton 218
Moore, Demi 82, 214

Moore, Fred E 97
Moore, Julianne 82, 166
Moore, Roger 20
morality and the movies 113
Moranis, Rick 90
More, Julian 88
More, Kenneth 166
Morecambe, Eric 194
Morgan, Henry 156
Morissette, Alanis 29
Morris, Frank 63
Morrison, Patricia 94
Morrissey, Neil 157
Mortensen, Viggo 29, 78
Morton, Samantha 170
Moscow State Circus 122
Moscow State Jewish Theatre 85
Mostel, Zero 125
Mother Courage 81
Moulin Rouge 104
The Mousetrap 12–13, 143
Movieoke 154
Mower, Patrick 184
Mr India 149
Mrs Brown 159
Much Ado About Nothing 45, 147
Mulan 52
Mulligan, Richard 157
Murder In The First 63
Murphy, Eddie 163, 187, 192
Murray, Bill 158, 187
musicals
  adapted from Shakespeare plays 189
  created from movies 179
  development of 133
  worst 196
My Fair Lady 52
Myers, Mike 187

Nair, Meera 149
The Naked Gun 49, 67
names
    stars' birth 12
    unusual screen
        stars' children's
        163
Nam's Angels 137
*The Navy Vs. The
    Night Monsters*
    90–1
NBC network 130
Neagle, Anna 145
Neighbours 185
Nekes, Werner 201
Nelley, Ted 9
Never Say Never Again
    167
New Amsterdam
    Theater, NY 60
New York, and *West
    Side Story* 100
Newman, Paul 126
Newmar, Julie 54
Nichols, Mike 12
Nicholson, Jack 15,
    23, 195
Nicolai, Otto 147
Nielsen, Leslie 202
Night Train To Murder
    194
Nightingale, Benedict
    117
*The Nightmare Before
    Christmas* 211
*Nightmare On Elm
    Street: The Final
    Nightmare* 66
Nijinsky, Vaslav
    Fomich 136
Nipkow, Paul 186
Niven, David 141
Nixon, Marni 52
Nixon, Richard 67
Noakes, John 53
Norman, Harold 38
Norman, Monty 88
North, Oliver 71
Norton, Edward 167
Notting Hill 151, 153

Novak, Kim 145
NTSC videos 108
nude scenes 82, 113
Nunn, Trevor 79
Nureyev, Rudolf 141

O'Brien, Richard 21
O'Callaghan, Richard
    183
Ocean's Eleven 87,
    166
O'Connor, Carol 156
O'Donnell, Rosie 157
The Office 74, 104
Oklahoma! (film and
    musical) 133, 135
Oldman, Gary 63, 163
Oliver, Jamie 134
Oliver! 48
Oliver Twist 193
Olivier, Laurence 8, 17,
    38, 44, 137, 154,
    204, 207, 215
Olsen, Mary-Kate and
    Ashley 153
Olympic Games 146
The Omen 153
On The Buses 156
*On Her Majesty's
    Secret Service* 58
On The Hour 216
*Once Upon A Time In
    Mexico* 167
*One Flew Over The
    Cuckoo's Nest* 195
*One Foot In The
    Grave* 157
O'Neal, Ryan 8
O'Neill, Eugene 86,
    181, 200
Opal, Robert 141
opera
    dishes named after
        stars of 194
    Shakespeare plays
        as 146–7
    a slippery business
        64–5
Operation Red Dawn
    62

operetta 133
Ormond, Julia 166
Orso 41
Osborne, John 86, 117
Osbourne, Ozzy 84
The Osbournes 84,
    176
Oscars 51, 159, 170,
    179, 195
O'Sullivan, Maureen
    174
Othello 44, 45, 147
O'Toole, Peter 8, 17,
    20
Out Of Africa 22
Outbreak 69
Owen, Bill 182
Owen, Ivan 142

Pacino, Al 8, 29, 30,
    135, 150, 162
Page, Geraldine 170
Paget, Sidney 21
Paget, Walter 21
Paige, Elaine 150
PAL videos 108–9
Palin, Michael 73, 94
Palmer, Joe 97
Palmintieri, Chazz 170
Paltrow, Gwyneth 40,
    132, 151
Pantelone 33
pantomimes 59, 107
Paramount Ranch 192
Paramount Studios
    191–2
Parker, Rhonda 175
Parr, Jack 130
Parsons, Nicholas 68
Partridge, Alan 216
*The Passion Of The
    Christ* 88
Pather Panchali 148
Patouillard, Vincent 51
A Patriot For Me 86
Patton 67
Pavarotti, Luciano 13
Pearce, Guy 89, 132
Pearl Harbor 159, 217

Peck, Gregory 86
Pele 49
Penn, Sean 163, 170
Pepper, Barbara 94
Perez, Jose 156
Perkins, Anthony 132, 216
Perskyi, Constantin 186
Pertwee, Jon 57, 184
Pertwee, Sean 139
Pesci, Joe 162
Peter, John 117
Petersen, Paul 163
Pfeiffer, Michelle 25, 172, 197
Phalke, Dada Saheb 148
The Phantom Menace 14
Philips, Leslie 182, 184
Phone Booth 150
Pier Theatre, Bournemouth 33
Pierce, David Hyde 172
Pinski, David 85
Piper, Jacki 183
Pirandello, Luigi 86
Pirates Of The Caribbean: The Curse Of The Black Pearl 104, 105
Pitt, Brad 166
Planer, Nigel 184
Planes, Trains & Automobiles 162
Planet Of The Apes 167
plants, killer 90–1
Platoon 202
Play It Again Sam 7, 18
Playboy 82
The Player 43
plays
    banning of 86
    shortest 79
playwriting, courses on 200

Pleasance, Angela 89
Plummer, Amanda 163
Plummer, Christopher 20
Polish Yiddish State Theatre 85
politics, showbiz folk in 92–3
Pollack, Sydney 166
Poltergeist 137
Ponte, Lorenzo da 147
Pop Idol 139, 155
pop stars
    actors as 114
    screen flops by 55
Popeye 134
pornography 143
Porridge 156
Porter, Cole 37, 189
The Postman 214
Powell, Robert 9, 166
Predator 101
predictions, in sci-fi movies 101
Presidents (US)
    actors who have played 23
    and the movies 67
Presley, Elvis 192
Presley, Priscilla 152
Preston, Kelly 152
Pret-à-Porter 82
Pretty Woman 89, 137
Price, Vincent 54
Prima, Louis 198
Prince 55
The Prince Of Egypt 172
Principal, Victoria 47
Priscilla, Queen Of The Desert 104, 144
The Producers 171, 179
profanity 113, 126, 162–3
Provost, John 163
Pryor, Richard 7
Psycho 115, 166
Pulcinella 33
Pulp Fiction 137, 163

Pulszky, Romola de 136
Purcell, Henry 146
Puri, Amrish 34

Quaid, Randy 187
The Quiet Man 94
Quinn, Anthony 8
quiz-show scandals 173

Radio City Music Hall 100
Raging Bull 162
Rahman, AR 168–9
Rains, Claude 77
Raise The Titanic 18
Rama's Later History 25
Ramayana 25
Rambo 215
Rambo and Sahiba 170
Ramis, Harold 158
Ranga, TS 149
rat pack 87
Rathbone, Basil 20
Ray, Aldo 63
Ray, Satyajit 148–9
Ray, Ted 182
Razzies awards 214–15
Reagan, Ronald 50, 67, 92
reality TV shows 139, 176
The Recruiting Officer 15
Red Dawn 62
The Red Hot Chilli Peppers 24
Redford, Robert 8, 11, 22, 173
Redgrave family 80
Reed, Oliver 48
Reeve, Christopher 7, 86, 87
Reeves, George 7, 198
Reeves, Keanu 114, 144

Reid, Beryl 184
Reid, Wallace 113
Reimann, Aribert 147
Reiner, Carl 46
Reiner, Rob 151, 178
Reinhold, Judge 82
remakes 166
Reservoir Dogs 80
restaurants 40–1, 134, 151
Return Of The Jedi 15
The Return Of The King 14
Return To The Forbidden Planet 189
Revenge 201
The Revenge Of Dr X 91
Revenge Of The Nerds 82
reviews, bad 17
Reynolds, Burt 135, 214
Reynolds, Debbie 174
Rhames, Ving 163
Rhys-Davies, John 79
Richard, Cliff 144
Richard III 44, 45, 147
Richards, Keith 104
Richardson, Ian 201
Richardson, Miranda 213
Richardson, Ralph 29, 68
Riffel, Rena 82
Rigg, Diana 175
The Rise And Fall Of Reginald Perrin 157
Riskin, Robert 195
Ritchie, Guy 55
Ritter, John 156
Ritter, Peter 147
Rivers, Joan 130
Robards, Jason 23
Robbins, Tim 15, 43, 110
Roberts, Julia 89, 137, 151, 153

Robertson, Cliff 54
Robinson, Anne 112
Robinson, Tony 213
The Rock 63
Rock, Chris 187
Rockerfeller, John D Jr 100
Rocky 8, 49
The Rocky Horror Picture Show 21
Rodgers, Richard 100, 102, 133, 189
Rodriguez, Robert 167
Rogers, Ginger 152, 154
Rogers, Kit 70
Roja 168
Rollercoaster 76
Romanian Yiddish State Theatre 85
Romberg, Sigmund 133
Romeo And Juliet 44, 45, 46, 147, 189
Romero, Cesar 54
Ronin 59
Ronner, Henrietta 177
Rooney, Micky 190
Roosevelt, President Franklin D and Eleanor 67
Rose Marie 133
Rosencrantz And Guildenstein Are Dead 189
Rosing, Boris 186
Rossini, Gioacchino 147
Rossiter, Leonard 157
Rota, Nino 30
Roth, Tim 167
Rothafel, SL 'Roxy' 100
Rowlands, Patsy 183, 184
Royal Ballet 75
Royal Opera House, Covent Garden 60
Royal Shakespeare Theatre, Stratford-

upon-Avon 61
Ruben, Aaron 46
La Ruffiana 33
Ruggiero, Allelon 39
Rush, Geoffrey 105
Ryan, Meg 12, 151
Rybczynski, Zbig 128
Ryder, Winona 9, 12, 30

Sabrina Fair 166
sack (drink) 126
Sadler, Richard 75
Sadler's Wells, naming of 75
Sagebrush Troubador 94
Salaam Bombay 149
Sale Of The Century 68
Salinger, Pierre 54
Sallinen, Aulis 147
San Giacomo, Laura 193
Sancha, Antonia de 50
Sanders, George 54
Sandler, Adam 187, 214
Sanger, 'Lord' George 122
Sanskrit, plays in 25
Sarastro 41
The Satanic Rites Of Dracula 28
Saturday Night Live 187
Saudi Arabia, lack of cinemas and theatres 167
Savoy Grill 41
Sayle, Alexei 184
Scacchi, Greta 43
Scarface 162
Scars Of Dracula 28
Scherer, Wendel 20
Schindler's List 159
Schneider, Rob 157
Schonberg, Claude-Michel 79

Schumacher, Joel 28, 150

Schwarzenegger, Arnold 8, 93, 135, 139, 144

sci-fi predictions 100

Scientology 152

Scorsese, Martin 26, 137, 162

Scott, Anthony 51

Scott, Randolph 192

Scott, Terry 183

Scott, Tony 89

Seabrooke, Nancy 143

SECAM videos 109

Secrest, Meryle 217

Secretary 94

Seed People 91

Seeds Of Evil 91

Seinfeld, Jerry 176

Sellars, Peter 23

Selleck, Tom 8

Sen, Mrinal 148–9

Senesh, Hannah 159

Sensurround 76

Serkele 85

Serrault, Michel 132

Seven Miles From Alcatraz 63

The Seven Samurai 166

Sevilla, Carmen 88

Sex And The City 96

The Sex Pistols 126

Shadowlands 153

Shaffer, Anthony 216–17

Shakespeare In Love 159

Shakespeare, William
on film 44–6
operas based on 146–7
plays by 36–7
retreads 189
see also *individual plays by name*

Shakuntala 25

Shanker, Uday 148

Sharif, Omar 145

Sharp, Don 166

Shatner, William 215

Shaw, Robert 15

The Shawshank Redemption 15

Shearer, Harry 187

Sheen, Charlie 62

Sheen, Martin 23

Sherriff, RC 154

Shields, Brooke 160, 215

Shine 67

The Shining 15

Shining Through 215

Shire, Talia 30

Shore, Pauly 214

Short, Martin 172, 187

Short Cuts 82

Showboat 133

Showgirls 82, 241

Shue, Elizabeth 89

Siberia 85

The Siege 135

Siegel, Don 166

The Silence Of The Lambs 195, 199

The Silver Chalice 126

Silvers, Phil 183

Sim, Sheila 12

Simon, Danny 46

Simon, Neil 46, 96

Simpson, Nicole Brown 8

Simpson, OJ 8, 49

The Simpsons 24–5

Sims, Joan 182, 183, 184

Sinatra, Frank 8, 87, 166, 212

Sinclair, Donald 47

Sinden, Donald 68, 212–13

Singin' In The Rain 179

Sir John In Love 146

Sisto, Jeremy 9

Six Characters In Search Of An Author 86

$64,000 Question 173

Slater, Christian 63, 89

Slater, Nigel 134

Slattery, Tony 184

Sleuth 207, 216–17

Sliding Doors 151

Smith, Delia 134

Smith, Maggie 144

Smith, Will 139

Smithee, Allen 49

Smothers, Dick and Tom 63

Snow White And The Seven Dwarfs 67, 203

So Little Time 153

Soderbergh, Steven 166

Sommer, Elke 184

Sondheim, Stephen 216–17

songs, film stars mentioned in 120

The Sopranos 97, 105

Sorvino, Mira 11, 89, 170

The Sound Of Music 22, 52, 100

South Pacific 56

South Park 165

Space Jam 49

Spacek, Sissy 8

Spacey, Kevin 39, 172

Spader, James 59, 94

spankings, in films 94

Spears, Britney 55, 199

Speed 144

Spider-Man 70, 151

Spielberg, Stephen 93, 137, 159, 190, 191, 208

Spilsbury, Klinton 218

Spontini, Gasparo 64

sport, on TV 146

sports stars in films 49

Springer, Jerry 25, 74

The Spy Who Loved Me 58

Sri Harsha 25

Stallone, Sylvester 8, 145, 167, 172, 215

stand-up comedy 96
Stanislavsky,
    Konstantin
    Sergeivich 204
Stapleton, Maureen
    170
Star Trek movies 51,
    101, 215
Star Wars 8, 14, 86,
    131
Starrett, Jack 137
Steamboat Willie 84
Stein, Rick 134
Stephens, Toby 11, 68
Steptoe And Son 156
Stewart, Patrick 139,
    172
Stiller, Ben 187
Stoker, Bram 28
Stone, Matt 9
Stone, Sharon 82, 172,
    214
Stoppard, Tom 189
Storace, Stephen 147
Strasberg, Lee 137,
    204
streakers 141
Streep, Meryl 24
Streisand, Barbra 132
Strictly Ballroom 67
Strindberg, August 86
Striptease 82, 214
Stroud, Robert 63
The Student Prince 133
stuntmen 86–7
Styne, Jule 111
*Subways Are For
    Sleeping* 111
'Suicide Is Painless'
    72–3
Sullivan, Arthur 86
Summer Holiday 144
Summerbee, Mike 49
Sunset Boulevard 150,
    179
Sunset-Gower Studios
    192
Super Bowl 146, 199
super-hero movies 70
Superman 7, 86, 198

superstitions, thespian
    61
Sutherland, Donald 86,
    90, 166, 167
Swank, Hilary 132
Swayze, Patrick 62,
    132, 145
swearing 113, 126,
    162–3
Sweet And Lowdown
    170
Swept Away 55, 214
Swordfish 82
Sydow, Max von 9

tag-lines 118
*The Taking Of Pelham
    One Two Three* 80
The Tall Guy 179
Tally, Ted 195
*The Taming Of The
    Shrew* 44, 45, 189
Tarantino, Quentin 28,
    80, 89, 137
Tarzan And His Mate
    113
Tate, Nahum 217
Taylor, Elizabeth 24,
    64, 125, 141, 190,
    191
Taylor, William
    Desmond 113
*A Teaspoon Every
    Four Hours* 17
television
    advertising 198
    betting about 139
    couch potatoes and
        132
    famous quotes
        about 66, 74
    highest-paid stars
        153
    invention of 186–7
    most watched
        events on 68
    reality 139, 176
    sport on 146
The Tempest 146, 189

Temple, Shirley 67,
    161
tenors 13
The Terminator 8
Terror At Alcatraz 63
Terror On Alcatraz 63
Terry, Ellen 80
Tetrazzini, Luisa 194
That Riviera Touch
    194
*That Was The Week
    That Was* 156
Theatre Royal, Drury
    Lane 68, 138
Theatre Royal,
    Haymarket 68
theatres
    Bulgarian 95
    conditions in
        Victorian
        London 73
    curtains 106
    largest 100
    London's lost 27
    map of Broadway
        188
    map of West End
        83
    seating 60–1
    Yiddish 85
Theron, Charlize 167
Thespis 53
The 39 Steps 166
This Is Spinal Tap 178
This Year's Blonde 212
Thomas, Ambroise 147
Thomas, Danny 56
Thomas, Kristin Scott
    207
Thomas, Ralph 166
3 D cinema 66
The Three Scampis 142
Thunderball 58, 166–7
Thurman, Uma 89,
    175
Till Death Us Do Part
    156
Tilly, Jennifer 155, 170
Timberlake, Justin 199
Tinker, Jack 117

Titanic 14, 18, 179
titles
    changes to film 193
    unlikely film 114
Titus 199
toilets, Golden Globe
    193
Tolkin, Mel 46
Tommy 179
The Tonight Show 130
Toomey, Regis 109
Top Gun 15
Top Trumps card game
    76
Toscanini, Arturo 30
The Towering Inferno
    49
Townshend, Stuart 78
Trapp Family Music
    Camp 102–3
Travers, Peter 55
Travolta, John 152,
    197, 214
Troughton, Patrick 57
True Romance 89
TV *see* television
Twelfth Night 147
20th Century Fox
    Studios 191
Twenty-One 173
*Twilight On The Rio
    Grande* 94
The Twilight Zone 49
The Two Towers 14,
    78, 104
Tyson, Cathy 89

Ultimatte see *Blue
    Screen*
*Umbatha - The Zulu
    Macbeth* 189
*Under The Cherry
    Moon* 55, 215
understudy, longest-
    serving 143
Universal Studios 39,
    191

*The Vagina
    Monologues* 160–1
Valentino, Rudolf 120,
    181
Van Dam, Jean-Claude,
    films of 68–9
Van Dyke, Dick 39
Van Loan, Philip 9
Van Sant, Gus 166
variety terms 59
Vasan, SS 148
Vaudeville terms 59
Vaughn, Robert 38
Vaughn, Vince 166
Vazov, Ivan 95
The Venus Flytrap 91
Verdi, Giuseppe 147
Vertov, Dziga 178
La Vestale 64
Victoria Regina 86
video systems 108–9
Vietnam, films about
    202, 203
*A View From The
    Bridge* 86
Vilna Troupe 85
The Virgin Suicides
    (film) 30
Vlahos, Petro 128
The Voice of
    Hollywood see
    Nixon, Marni
Voight, Jon 23, 86, 88
Vojnikov, Dobri 95
von Stroheim, Erich
    178
von Trapp family
    102–3

Wagner, Richard 147
Wahlberg, Mark 167
walk-outs, theatrical
    124
Walken, Christopher 8,
    172
Wall Street 23
Walt Disney Studios
    190
Wang Du Lu 169

*The War Of The
    Worlds* 118–19
Ward, Burt 54
Ward, Simon 124
Warner Bros 51, 190
Warner, David 29
water, films involving
    18
Waterston, James 39
Waterston, Sam 23, 39
Waterworld 18
Wayne, John 12, 94,
    192
The Weakest Link 112
Weaver, Sigourney 22,
    144
Weigel, Helene 81
Welles, Orson 118–19,
    191
Wells, HG 118
Wertmuller, Lina 201
West, Adam 54
West End
    ghosts 69
    theatre map 83
    restaurants 40–1
West Side Story (film
    and musical) 52,
    100, 189
The West Wing 104
Westerns 192
Which Witch 196
When Harry Met Sally
    151
*Whistle Down The
    Wind* 179
whistling, in theatres
    94
*White Shadows Of The
    South Seas* 185
Whitfield, June 184
Whitmore, James 207
*Who Wants To Be A
    Millionaire* 173
*Whose Line Is It
    Anyway?* 157
Wiest, Dianne 170
Wild Wild West 214
Wilde, Oscar 181,
    212–13

Wilder, Billy 66, 166
Wilder, Gene 46, 125
William, Duke of
    Clarence (later King
    William IV) 48
William Hill 139
Williams, Edy 141
Williams, JoBeth 157
Williams, John 93
Williams, Kenneth
    182, 183, 184
Williams, Ralph
    Vaughan 146
Williams, Robin 39,
    132, 150, 193, 203
Williamson, Nicol 124
Willis, Bruce 114, 137,
    145, 149, 162, 197,
    214
Wilson, Lois 11
Wilson, Richard 157,
    184
Windsor, Barbara 181,
    182, 183, 184
Winger, Debra 197
Wings 51
Winner, Michael 145
Winslet, Kate 145, 160
The Winter's Tale 38

Wise, Ernie 194
*The Witches Of
    Eastwick* 179
Withnail And I 22, 57,
    153
Wolf, Matt 196
The Women 155
Wood, Ed 91
Wood, Elijah 79
Wood, Natalie 52
Working Girl 82
Worrall Thompson,
    Antony 134
Wright-Penn, Robin
    163
Wyman, Jane 109

X-2 70
The X-Men 70

Yates, Peter 58
Yiddish theatre 85
York, Rachel 94
Yoshino, Micky 18
Young, Sean 215
Young Frankenstein
    179
Your Show Of Shows
    46

*You're In The Army
    Now* 109
Yovkov, Yordan 95
Z, trivia about the let-
    ter 135
Zabibah And The King
    165
Zadora, Pia 215
Zaentz, Saul 135
Zane, Billy 29
Zanni 32–3
Zanuck, Darryl 135
Zapruder, Abraham
    131
Zellweger, Renee 135,
    151, 193
Zemeckis, Robert 135
Zeta-Jones, Catherine
    8, 135, 189
Ziegfield, Florenz 181
Zinnemann, Fred 135
*Le Zombi de Cap-
    Rouge* 49
Zoot Suit 76
Zucker, Adolph 135
Zwick, Edward 135
Zworykin, Vladimir
    186